Jeremy Burfoot

Jeremy was born in Whangarei, New Zealand on 7 March1959.

He attended Kapiti College near Wellington from 1972-75

After he left school he worked in a number of jobs including working in a bank and an abattoir. He joined the Royal New Zealand Air Force in 1978 as a navigator. While he was there he trained for his commercial pilot's license at the North Shore Aero Club in Auckland. In 1981 he left the Air Force and went to Papua New Guinea where he flew light commercial aircraft for 3 years.

In 1984 he joined Qantas Airways as a pilot, rising to the rank of 747 Captain in 1990. From 1991-95 he took a leave of absence and flew for Japan Airlines for 4 years based in Anchorage, Alaska and Honolulu. He is now back with Qantas based in Sydney but living in Auckland. He is married with three sons.

The Ride
Around New Zealand

JEREMY BURFOOT

BURGLAR
BROTHERS
PUBLISHING

Burglar Brothers Getaways - The Ride Around New Zealand

Burglar Brothers Publishing

Published 2006 by Burglar Brothers Publishing
www.burglarbrothers.com

Copyright © Jeremy Burfoot 2007

A catalogue record for this book is available from
the New Zealand National Library.

ISBN 9780473116651 (from Jan 2007)

ISBN 0473116650

Edited by Susan Moyle

Design by Avon Willis

Cartoons by Matthew Gray

Cover Photograph by Russel Hamlet Photography

Set in Giovanni Book 11/16.25

Printed in Singapore by Tien Wah Press (PTE) Limited

Contents

Foreword

Foreword by Dame Catherine Tizard ONZ: Former Governor General of New Zealand

Little did I know when I agreed to start a "Qantas Jet ski Round New Zealand" event what I was going to find!

I knew it was a fund-raising venture for the Cancer Society and that the idea had been sparked off by one of these guys having himself, suffered a melanoma; that as Chair of the Cancer Control Council, it was my duty to support such an endeavour, and that by agreeing to be involved, I was obliging an old friend who was doing the publicity.

Duty turned to excitement and I was rapidly captivated by the magnitude and the courage of Jeremy and Brad's adventure! Over a total of 24 days, 19 were spent riding the seas off NZ's wild coasts in all weathers. They spent 147 hours in the saddle and as Jeremy himself says, with two sore butts! They covered 5,000 km. What a feat! Well done guys.

On their arrival back in Auckland, I was thrilled to be part of the welcome home and, on the spot, awarded them membership of my own personal order of "Dedicated Nutters of NZ". These are the amazing people I have met over the years who attempt impossible tasks – like saving and moving old lighthouses, accomplishing unheard of sailing feats or restoring "hopeless" historic buildings – people with a determination to achieve their goals. People with passion and ideals.

The skin cancer message has been increasingly heard over the past decade but far too many New Zealanders are still complacent about the risks or think all sun-damage can be treated and cured. We are increasingly looking after the children, I think, but neglecting ourselves. This high-profile publicity stunt got huge nation-wide coverage and greatly heightened awareness that skin cancer is everybody's concern. This journey got the SunSmart message heard throughout the country.

Part of the profits of this book will go to the Cancer Society to help it continue its work in raising awareness and providing support services for people with cancer.

And apart from its worthy objectives, it's a jolly good read!

Dame Catherine Tizard ONZ

Cancer Society

Acknowledgements

To my wife, Manola, for letting me do it and for supporting me. To my sons, Jamie, Dean and Douglas, for inspiring me to keep going. To Brad for being silly enough to attempt it and then being the best partner a man could hope for. To Colin Bower for getting me into it in the first place and being a good mate.

To all the fine people at the Cancer Society for your support and the great work you do for the people of New Zealand. To David Libeau at Qantas for taking a chance on us. To all our sponsors for making it happen. To our ground crew, Jeff, Michael, Pete and Matt, for keeping the show going.

To everyone else who helped us along the way.

Thank you. You are all Stars.

*This book is dedicated to my father Donald Jasper Burfoot
who died of cancer at age 62.
He was the best father a boy could ever hope for.*

PACIFIC
OCEAN

NEW ZEALAND

Auckland

NORTH ISLAND

TASMAN
SEA

Wellington

SOUTH ISLAND

Christchurch

Dunedin

Qantas Jet Ski Around NZ

24 days
147 hours riding
4950 kilometres
6000 litres of fuel
Route - - - - - - →

Introduction

It's all Colin Bower's fault. He was living at 7a Clifton Rd, Browns Bay when we moved in next door and he owned a Seadoo personal watercraft. Within a couple of weeks I had been talked into buying one and we started riding together whenever we had the chance. Colin has been fairly competitive throughout his life, especially in motocross, so it was inevitable that he eventually suggested we enter an endurance jet ski race at Tauranga, a couple of hours south-east of Auckland. Being mildly competitive myself (actually I'm seriously competitive) I agreed and we headed on down to Tauranga for the weekend.

The race was 100 km long and was twice around Matakana Island. At racing speed there was no way you could do it without a refuel, so each rider would need to refuel at the end of the first lap. Colin and I decided that we would share a 20 litre drum and that whoever came in first at the end of the first lap would take half and leave the rest for the other 'loser'.

At the start of the race the gun went off and sixty-plus riders all took off together in what can only be described as total mayhem. I lost sight of Colin early on in all the confusion and because I don't have eyes in the back of my head.

At the end of lap one I came in and found the drum still full so I refueled with my half, had lunch, read War and Peace and then took off on the second lap. Colin came in shortly after I left and in his words decided that "there was no possible way in my mind that Jerry could have been ahead of me", so he took half of the fuel that was left and started out on his second lap.......and ran out of fuel 10 km short of the finish.

A couple of years later Colin moved to Te Puke, so we visited him there and I brought my Seadoo with me. We decided to go for a ride down the Kaituna River. The ride down the river was great and I was enjoying myself immensely. Eventually the river mouth came into view and it was quite a sight. There were steep, 2m waves breaking right across the mouth. I reckon one of the reasons I do well as a pilot is that I have a very good sense of impending danger. I can just smell it and my immediate reaction was to decide to beach the Seadoo just up from the mouth and survey the situation before going on. There was another good indicator of impending disaster there too. At the mouth of the bar up on the bank were about fifty fishermen. In my mind that's a classic setup. It's not so bad looking stupid if no one is watching, but with all those people watching it was a given that we would embarrass ourselves.

I beached my Seadoo and looked to see where Colin was. The silly bugger had just plowed on straight out into the surf and I watched as he tackled a steep wave and came to grief in a big way. His Seadoo came over on top of him and in a split second he was floating in the rip with his Seadoo heading for the rocks. And all this right in front of the viewing gallery!

There was nothing for it but to get on my machine and head out for a rescue. I zoomed out and got into position in front of him so that he could climb on the back. During the entire time that he was climbing on large waves were coming at us and it was all I could do to stop us from being completely wiped out. Eventually he was on and I could see a large breaking wave heading towards us, so I said "Are you right, mate?" I didn't hear his reply properly, but assumed it was yes, so I screamed out through the waves to a safe point where we could organise ourselves better. I turned around to say "Gee that was close Col", but he wasn't there. I looked way back in the rip and there he was still bobbing up and down in front of the viewing gallery. When I had taken off he had been fiddling with his gloves and wasn't holding on and, of course, had fallen straight off the back again.

Can you imagine the stories the fishermen would have been telling in the pub that night? I'm guessing the words 'idiots', 'hilarious' and 'worth the price of admission' would have featured prominently. Anyway, I mounted a second rescue and got him safely out past the waves. Amazingly, his Seadoo had missed the rocks. It had floated out through the waves via the rip, and started first pop.

So Colin is the one that got me started on Seadoos, but now allow me to introduce Brad Burton(Burglar), my partner on the around New Zealand ride. Brad is an amazing guy. I first met him when I started racing go-karts in 1996 in Australia at the age of thirty-seven. Brad was twenty-one and was the Goulborn Club Champ. When I came along he was good enough to take me under his wing and teach me everything he knew about karting. The most amazing thing, and a true measure of the guy, was that even when I started to beat him he kept teaching me. He was, and still is, an amazing young man with a wicked sense of humour, a can-do attitude and a sharp mind. He is an Aussie *MacGyver*. Give him an old boot and a rusty nail and he'll build you an engine. This was to prove very useful on the ride. He is a pleasure to be around, which was also an asset when the going got tough. His style leans toward Boof-head Aussie, and this sometimes fools people into underestimating him. However, do so at your peril.

Our friendship has grown over the years. We understand each other very well. We finish each others sentences. We very rarely disagree. All these things would contribute to the successful mission ahead. One thing that annoyed me as we went around the country was how the media would mention me a lot, but not Brad. At times it was like I was the only one doing the ride and this was certainly not the case. I did a lot of the preparation and planning myself, but Brad was at least 50% responsible for the success of the ride once we got started. The media, in their defense, have said that it's because Brad doesn't speak English, and no one would understand him if he spoke Australian. I have no argument for that.

Now I know what you are wondering…how did Brad get the name Burglar? Well you have to admit it is fitting that a man descended from convicts be called Burglar, but that's not the whole story.

When we were racing karts there were about six people in the division whose names started with Bur. There was Burfoot, Burton, Bursfield and a few others. Brad and I decided it would be a fine idea one race meeting to register as Brad and Jeremy Burglar, also trading as *The Burglar Brothers*. We nearly got away with it and from then on were known as the *Burglar Brothers*. The name got more entrenched as we continued to steal all the trophies. Brad's car was known as *the getaway car* and his house as *the hideout*.

Since we stopped karting we have caught up every year for an adventure, which we always call a *Burglar Brothers' Getaway*. We have done a few of New Zealand's great walks and have kayaked the Whanganui River, but the adventure that was to prove the most important happened three years ago when Burglar hired a jet ski from a dealer in Auckland. We put it on a tandem trailer with my Seadoo and drove to Wellington, heading off with a tent, wallet and a few clothes for a week around the Marlborough Sounds and Nelson.

Our first stopover after crossing Cook Strait was the fabulous Furneaux lodge in Endeavour inlet. Furneaux is an idyllic place for both boaties, being set in a sheltered spot on the inlet, and hikers, being the first night's stopover on the beautiful Queen Charlotte Walkway.

We arrived there mid afternoon and pulled the skis up onto a floating dock, before heading towards the bar. We had just sat down at a table outside the bar when the manager turned up to ask us where we had come from and what we were doing. Without even missing a beat and in a blatant attempt to secure free beer and food we told him we were jet skiing around

New Zealand and that the film crew was following the next day.

The ploy worked a treat. It was when we were drinking our umpteenth jug, or it might have been a couple of jugs after that, that we looked at each other and said "Why don't we ride around New Zealand?" An idea was born.

When we actually planned the ride we decided to avoid Furneaux Lodge and were amused at the prospect of the manager reading about this attempt and saying, "It's been done before! I met the guys".

I still don't think the ride would have ever got off the ground though if it wasn't for my melanoma. The logistics of organising something like that are huge, and also very expensive, so you need a jolly good reason for doing it. The skin cancer awareness message was the catalyst that was needed. Sure it was a boy's adventure, but in our minds it had a purpose as well. People love a story of a challenge, but a cause gives it wings. The skin cancer awareness message meant that sponsors and media got involved and this eventually made the whole thing possible. At the same time the very things that made it possible also made it more complicated. By the time we departed we had huge media commitments and many sponsors to 'do the right thing by'. This would add to the strain of completing the ride, although I must say that the people representing our sponsors were a pleasure to deal with, and we were very grateful for that.

So, in a nutshell - We did it! There were times when we had fun. There were a lot of times when we didn't have fun. We found new levels of mental strength and physical endurance that we didn't know we had. We met a lot of absolutely fantastic people and we got the message out there. And if, in the future, we saved only one life then it was all worthwhile. Here's how it went.

Chapter 1
Melanoma

Skin cancer is preventable. Yet every year around three-hundred New Zealanders die of it. From a population of four million people, around fifty-thousand new cases of skin cancer are diagnosed in New Zealand each year.

We live in a country where getting outdoors and doing things is the norm. We also live in a country where the protective ozone layer overhead is noticeably thinner than in most other countries.

On top of the thinner ozone, temperatures here are low enough that we don't feel hot outside, so we tend to stay out there when we shouldn't. Between the hours of 11am and 4pm we should avoid being in the sun at all. If we are out there, we should be completely covered in protective gear and sunscreen should be reapplied frequently.

Particularly in the case of melanoma, the damage that causes it is done when a person is young and then shows up years later.

Unfortunately it is still perceived as cool and trendy to have a suntan. So, in spite of all the warnings, young people are still sunbathing and using sun beds to give themselves a tan.

I used to sunbath a lot as a youngster and I remember we hardly ever used sunscreen. The only time we would use sunscreen would be if our parents made us wear it. I remember getting badly burnt on numerous occasions. So it came as no surprise to me at the age of forty six that I would need to have a few minor skin cancers burnt off every now and again.

I have always liked to have a bit of a tan, but at the beginning of 2005 I didn't have time to lie around as much as normal, so I started using the sun bed once a week at my local gym. I had read the available literature on sun beds and had assured myself that they were no more dangerous than lying in the sun, and were a lot more convenient.

I am of a different opinion now, because within a couple of months a new mole had appeared in the centre of my back. In defense of the sun bed, the melanoma probably would have happened anyway, but I reckon it definitely sped up the process. My mole was about 7 mm wide and irregular in shape.

I went to my local doctor and mentioned it to him. He got that half crazed look on his face and started laughing insanely, as doctors do when they are about to attack you with a can of liquid nitrogen, and went to work on me. When he got to the new mole he said, "That one looks a bit angry doesn't it", and gave it an industrial strength blast of nitrogen. He then told me I had been very brave, gave me a lollipop and sent me home.

In most cases melanoma is more easily picked up on skin examination by your doctor, due to the presence of pigmentation. However, sometimes melanoma skin cancer cells lose their ability to produce pigment so the usual rules don't apply. These melanomas are called amelanotic and occur in about 5% of melanomas. The best thing to do if you have anything that you notice is changing on your skin is to get it checked out.

When I think about melanoma I am reminded of the film *Alien*, where the alien burrows into you without your knowledge, or permission for that matter, before taking over your body and eventually killing you in a very painful and inconvenient way. And that's what melanoma does, so you don't want it, and neither do your children. You will have to trust me on this.

A couple of weeks after seeing my doctor, I was talking to my good friend River Lamb whose father had died of melanoma a few years earlier. River's father had been a builder and had basically ignored his melanoma until it was way too late. The nature of melanomas is that they look fairly harmless on the surface until it is way too late. That's why you have to get rid of them early, when they first show and before the *Alien* thing starts. If you plan to have a melanoma, plan to get rid of it early. River suggested I go and see a doctor called Marcus Platts-Mills at the Albany Basin Accident and Medical. I made an appointment and went to see him. He looked at the mole and told me that he didn't think it was a melanoma, because of the lack of pigment. He thought it was a Basal Cell Carcinoma. Basal Cell Carcinomas are still malignant, but they have minimal metastatic potential, which means they don't tend to spread around the body. Marcus took a punch biopsy and sent it away to be examined. He phoned me a couple of days later to tell me that it was, in fact, a melanoma and that I needed to come in and have a formal excision done. *Note: It,s called formal because both surgeon and patient wear a bowtie and tux, as opposed to shorts and t-shirt for this procedure.*

Being told that you have something that is trying to kill you is very sobering news. Whenever I thought about it I felt nauseous. I went to see Marcus to get it cut out. You would think that a 7 mm melanoma would be an easy thing to cut out, but the surgeon has to ensure that he gets it all, so the cut for my melanoma was about 5 cm long, and almost as deep as the Grand Canyon.

I had it done under a local anesthetic so, although there was no pain, I could feel the cut being made. Afterwards Marcus had to seal off the surrounding blood vessels with a tool like a soldering iron. The whole room smelt like someone was barbequing. Then he finished off by stitching me up. All in all, it's a very unpleasant experience.

I couldn't exercise for two weeks after the operation, which was hard for me. I'm not the sort of person to sit around doing nothing. When I had my vasectomy done in 1997, I drove myself home and went mountain biking the next day, much to the amusement of my riding buddies who still haven't stopped talking about it.

So having stitches in was a pain and I was glad when the time came to go and get them out. I walked into Marcus' office and he said, "It's not over yet. We didn't cut out enough and we need to do it again". The *fillet* that he had cut out two weeks earlier had been sent for testing and had shown that not enough had been taken. The size of the melanoma was actually 20 mm x 12 mm, not 7 mm as it had at first appeared. This was again the result of the lack of pigment. Marcus suggested that I go and get the re-excision done by Dr Mark Gray at the Takapuna Skin Institute, as the skin institute is better set up to handle these more difficult tumours. An appointment was made and I went through the same procedure again, but with a much larger cut being required. This was not one of the high points of my life.

Now I have to go for regular checkups to keep an eye out for other developing skin cancers, and to check that the original one hasn't gone anywhere else in my body. My prognosis is good because my melanoma was caught in time, but you never can be sure.

One thing I do now to protect myself is use the services of MoleMap. MoleMap is a state of the art procedure utilising the digital imaging, archiving and diagnosis of moles and other suspicious lesions. The procedure utilises a combination of high resolution dermoscopy, imaging technology that uses high intensity light to penetrate through the surface of the skin to show the structure of moles and other lesions, and a dermatologist's expert evaluation of the images.

In addition to the increased diagnostic accuracy associated with dermoscopy, MoleMap is able to detect at an earlier stage any new, changing, and/or suspicious lesions by monitoring and comparing the images over time.

While MoleMap has the ability to identify all skin cancers, its primary focus is on the early detection of melanoma. MoleMap is not for everybody, but there are many higher risk groups among the population who would benefit from it and, with my history, it makes good sense for me to use it.

After the second operation, I sat around for another two weeks which gave me a lot of time to think. I had the month of February 2006 rostered off as leave, so I was wondering what adventure Burglar and I would undertake. It crossed my mind that riding Seadoos around New Zealand might be fun and we had talked about it before. It is timely to point out that I will refer to the machines we rode around New Zealand as Seadoos. Jet Ski is a Kawasaki brand name. Seadoo is the Bombardier Recreational Products brand name for the same thing. They are all personal water craft. We called the event *The Qantas jet ski around New Zealand,* because the general public see all personal water craft as jet skis and it would help with the general understanding of what was being attempted.

I rang Burglar and asked him if he could commit to February. He said yes, so it was then up to me to get the ball rolling. We had decided that it would be a good idea to make the whole ride useful by doing it for a charity. With my melanoma the obvious charity was the Cancer Society.

I approached John Loof, who is the head of the Auckland Cancer Society. He organised a meeting. Attending that meeting were myself, John, Phil Briars who is special events organiser for the society, Cath Saunders who does all the media organising and Wendy Fulton. As John has since mentioned to me, the Cancer Society gets a lot of well meaning people with crazy ideas. The purpose of the meeting was to determine how serious I was, and to make a judgment as to whether I was capable of pulling it all off.

I must have made a reasonable impression, because they didn't laugh at me and I wasn't thrown out face down on the road by bouncers. Cath Saunders thought that the Melanoma/Qantas Captain tie up was good for the media and everyone thought that the idea was generally a good one. We discussed possible sponsors. Getting sponsorship in New Zealand is difficult. No one except the oil companies makes that much money. The economy is just not big enough. I was to learn over the next few months that, as a rule, the companies who could afford to fork out wouldn't and those who were just scraping in a living were the most generous.

Another issue with sponsors is that they want to know what's in it for them. They all want good media coverage. But the only way you can get commitment from the media is if your event looks serious enough to justify it. In other words, sponsors need to be on board. So it's a little like the chicken and the egg. Which came first? And I found myself having to coax the whole thing along by stretching the truth a little and using a lot of words like 'probably', and terms like 'has expressed interest', or 'is involved' as to who was on board, until it became a self fulfilling thing. It was a real balancing act and it took a lot of time and hard work.

Up until now I had achieved three things in my life that took a lot of hard work. The first was becoming a New Zealand age group athletics champion as a teenager in middle distance events. This meant running up to 160 km a week for most of the year. The second was becoming a 747 Captain at age thirty, which meant years of hard study. When I was a simulator instructor as a first officer I would run late night sessions for my students and then spend hours in the simulator by myself practicing every maneuver and emergency over and over, sometimes until as late as four o'clock in the morning. The third was Duxing the Diploma in Financial Markets for Australia in 2000. This also took an extraordinary amount of hard work. My approach to all three was to be completely focused on the aim and to sacrifice, whatever it took, within reason, to achieve it. These things took a very narrow focus; almost like having blinkers on.

The task I'm currently working on is raising three boys, which is every bit as hard as the others, but takes a wider focus and flexibility, as the goal posts keep getting moved all along the way. Raising boys is nothing if not interesting. I dream about having the patience and understanding of Fred MacMurray from the television programme *My Three Sons*, and would pay big money for the services of Uncle Charlie from the same show. It is hard to keep a straight face sometimes when you are telling them off for something you used to do yourself. I had to attend a meeting at thirteen year old Jamie's school over something Jamie had done. There were two male and two female teachers at the meeting. After some time waffling back and forward over the issue I said, "Look, this is not something I might not have done myself at the same age and in the same circumstances". The two male teachers started nodding in agreement, but quickly turned serious again when they saw that the female teachers were horrified.

The funny thing about raising kids is that we do it without experience or qualifications, even though it is the most important thing we will ever do because it ensures our future. You are only qualified to do this job once you have completed it, which I suppose is the reason why grand parents are so useful in helping raise kids. The organisation of the ride was more like raising kids than the other goals I have focused on in the past, in that the focus had to stay wide and flexible as things changed along the way.

You could set yourself the goal of being a loser, then if you achieve it you would feel successful and if you don't achieve it you would feel even more successful. However, that doesn't do it for me. I set the goals extremely high for the event, as I believe you have to get way out of your comfort zone to achieve anything important.

Because I worked for Qantas I thought that would be a good place to start with for sponsorship, and it would be only fair to approach them first. To be honest I wasn't confident. Qantas is a good company to work for, but airlines generally struggle to make money, although Qantas has been more successful than most. I did know that Qantas, however, like other successful airlines, had been keeping a very tight rein on costs. Phil Briars had dealt with Qantas before and knew the marketing manager in Auckland, David Libeau. Phil said he would organise a meeting.

I attended the meeting at Qantas with Cath Saunders and Phil. To my great surprise David Libeau loved the idea. Everyone saw the Cancer Society/melanoma/Qantas/Qantas Captain tie up as being very effective. The fact that I am a Kiwi living in New Zealand, but flying Qantas' 747s internationally was seen as an additional plus. Qantas has become a major player in the New Zealand market, employing over seven-hundred people and carrying over one-mil-lion-and-six-hundred-thousand New Zealand residents in 2005, and is getting more and more involved in initiatives that benefit the community.

David's only reservation was that Qantas was, at that time, under a strict discretionary spending freeze and to get any new sponsorship opportunities approved could be extraordinarily dif-ficult. He would need to submit detailed justification to his bosses. At the same time he suggested I approach my boss, the Chief Pilot, to get him onside.

Eventually all parties agreed it would be a great idea, although in the end it was David Libeau who made it all happen. He took all of the risk of success or failure on his own shoulders. If we failed he would look bad. If we made it and Qantas received good publicity he would come out smelling like roses. In the end I believe he came out smelling like roses, but he deserved to because he supported us all the way. We were extremely grateful for his commitment.

Once Qantas was on board I set about the arduous task of attracting the other sponsors we needed. I'll talk about all of them now even though they came in one by one and some at the last minute. You need a fairly thick skin and a lot of patience doing the sponsorship thing. You get a lot of maybes that don't end up materialising and you get a lot of form responses that go something like this:

Dear Mr. Brofoot

Thank you for approaching our wonderful company for sponsorship for your exciting event.

'Company Name' is already involved in sponsorships in the community in many ways and we are already fully committed. Regrettably we cannot help you at this time.

We wish you all the best with your event.

Yours faithfully
Someone very low down the company ladder.

Roughly translated, this means, "We haven't even bothered to consider your request. We've just palmed you off with our standard form letter. Feel free to insert our response up your rectal passage".

I did have some pleasant sponsorship experiences and they ended up being the ones we went with. I approached Don Robertson and Richard Shaw at Bombardier Recreational Products to ask for two Seadoos. I have always owned Seadoos and think they are fantastic machines. There is a reason why over 50% of all PWCs sold in New Zealand are Seadoos, and that reason is that they are simply the best. Don and Richard were very enthusiastic and after talking to their head office in Australia they agreed to loan us two brand-new GTX 4Techs, a tandem trailer, spare parts, and provide access to their nationwide dealer network for repairs and scheduled maintenance. An added bonus was that the two skis were predominantly red in colour, which would suit Qantas as well.

We approached Charles Wedd from Hereiam.co.nz. His company provides GPS tracking systems for various purposes. Charles agreed to install trackers in the Seadoos and the ground vehicle so that we could be tracked at all times during the event. The upside to this was that people were able to see where we were at all times. The downside to this was that people were able to see where we were at all times. Let me explain. The upside was that Hereiam lead to a great deal of interest being added to the event, as people could track us, read our diary and make donations on the Hereiam website. An example of the downside was that we had attended a beer tasting at the Monteiths Brewery in Greymouth on a day off and had had been accused of staying there too long by various people watching on the website. We resolved in the future to park the vehicle at the nearest church and walk to the pub from there. The way the website worked was that our track was shown by a green line on the map. Any time we stopped a red dot would appear on the website showing where we stopped, and for how long.

We needed to get the vehicles and ground crew across Cook Strait both ways. My brother Tim is operations manager for the Interislander line and I have photos of him in the nude, so he readily agreed to our request.

Another Tim at Hutchwilco in Auckland decided it would be a great idea if Hutchwilco was the official event lifejacket.

The boys and girls at GME liked the idea of us wearing their emergency beacons, so they gave us one each.

Perrin Newbold of Altura Coffee in Albany gave us enough coffee to supply the troops in Iraq for a year. If you ever get a chance to visit Altura in Albany do so. The smell of the roasting machine is awesome. They sell the best coffee I have ever tasted, and I say that honestly and without the hope of future freebies when I visit. I'll be down next Wednesday at 9am, Perrin.

We tried hard to get sponsored accommodation, but failed, although some places donated the accommodation as we went around. We tried to get a campervan too, but also failed. In the end we were glad we hadn't got a campervan as it would have been too slow and would not have coped with some of the launching ramps we encountered along the way.

We worked for a long time on a vehicle to tow the trailer. We thought we had Toyota, but we didn't have them at all which is fine. The time they took to say no, however, left us in a spot as the event was rapidly approaching. In the end the cavalry came to the rescue in the form of my old mate…you guessed it, Colin 'nothing is impossible' Bower. Colin is with the Sydenham Motor Group based in Tauranga and Te Puke. It was a big call for them to provide a vehicle for us, as they would not benefit a lot from the national exposure, but provide one they did. They loaned us a brand new Kia Sorento Sport, which is four wheel drive, and is a magnificent vehicle by any standards. When you see what good value it is you can see why Kia's competitors are worried. I own a Sorento myself, and I paid for it; which is not something I do lightly.

By the way, have you ever wondered how car companies come up with car names? I wonder often. Take the Nissan Cedric, for example. How could you hope to sell a car named after an English Butler? And what about the Mitsubishi Jasper, which is named after my older brother and has given me serious 'car naming envy'. And what were they thinking when they named the Morris Minor? I would have waited for the Major to come out.

I reckon it can only be a matter of time until the Honda Baldrick comes out, or perhaps the Toyota Bruce, or the Mitsubishi Plonker. Maybe in an act of complete commercial suicide Nissan will launch the Nissan Gertrude! I guess we can't be sure what names they'll come out with next, but one thing we can be sure of is that they will be silly.

And so I find myself once again wondering about the name Sorento. My best guess is that Kia Motors in Korea has a Senior Vice President in charge of cup holders and car names called Mr. Kim. Mr. Kim has just arrived back from a holiday in Italy. He is carried up to the monthly board meeting where the Chairman says, "Welcome back Mr. Kim. How was your horiday?"

and Mr. Kim says, "Gleat. We frew to Lome in Itari and dlove to Solento and then went by boat to Capli to see the brue glotto. And I riked Solento so much that I think we should name our new vehicle after it." "Is that Solento with two 'l's or one?" says the chairman. And in the end the vehicle gets called Sorrento, but they misspell it by using only one 'r'.

Moving on....All of the telephone companies told us to bugger off because we were asking for free phone service and internet access which would have cost them nothing, but nothing is obviously too high a price. Just before the first ball was about to be bowled however, one of our ground crew, Michael Bridger, managed to contact someone high enough up in Vodafone. They came on board and we are grateful for that.

Don't ask me about the oil companies lest I start frothing at the mouth and kicking walls.

What is that? .....What about the oil companies?....Since you asked I guess it would be impolite not to tell you. My guess is that they are too busy controlling politicians worldwide and making obscene profits to give any of it away. We got a couple of the 'bugger off' form letters and a few 'we're poor' phone calls and still we had nothing.

I approached Barney Jones who is in charge of fuel and maintenance for Qantas at Auckland airport. Barney is a great guy and was pleased to help so he said he would approach the people who supply fuel to Qantas at the airport. Bear in mind that Qantas buys hundreds of millions of litres of fuel every year at Auckland Airport. I even asked Barney to pass on that even if they provided the fuel at cost, that would cost *them* nothing and would save *us* a fortune and we would be grateful. They said we could have as much aviation fuel as we wanted, but aviation fuel is as useless as a third nostril for a Seadoo. Jet fuel is kerosene and avgas is way too high in octane. They said that they should be able to help us even up until two days before the event started, but in the end it just didn't happen and we were left with a fuel bill of close to

$10,000, and the knowledge that we had helped make the bastards even richer. Ouch.

Maksgear at Tauranga became a sponsor by virtue of the fact that they installed our long range tanks. When planning the schedule for the ride I decided that it needed to be done fairly quickly otherwise interest would die down as time went by. It would be no good taking two months to do and it would hardly qualify as an achievement if we spent a couple of hours a day on the Seadoos and the rest of the time at the pub. So I set what would turn out to be a fairly arduous schedule of nineteen days riding and four days off. Some of the days were quite long. A couple were around the 360 km mark, which is a long way on a Seadoo. There was a lot of doubt from various areas that we could achieve the schedule.

Even people in the personal watercraft industry reckoned we had set the bar too high. This only made us more determined. In the end we had to adjust the schedule for the weather as we went around, using all our days off as weather days and, on two occasions, riding two days riding in one day. But we made it.

It would not have been possible without the long range tanks. From studying the map I could see that, without a support boat, in a lot of places it would be either too difficult, too time consuming, or just plain impossible to refuel. I determined that we would need long range tanks capable of almost tripling our range.

I found an engineering firm who were prepared to build the tanks and spent a lot of time discussing requirements with the builder. They needed to be light. They needed to be strong. They needed to look like they belonged on the Seadoos. They needed to be aerodynamic. They needed to have a volume of over 100 litres. We needed to be able to attach them to the Seadoos without causing permanent damage. We needed to be able to get the fuel from these tanks to the main fuel tank.

In the end the tanks fulfilled all of these requirements and I was pretty happy with them, although they had cost an arm and a leg. The tanks made the whole ride possible, but it's ironic that the whole time they did their best to cause problems for us as well. Throughout the ride rubber gaskets disintegrated and broke into small bits inside the tanks. Aluminium filings from the manufacturing and installation processes continually blocked the filters and on a couple of occasions made it all the way through the system to block the fuel pumps and injectors causing quite serious engine running problems. As well as those problems, all the baffles that had been installed inside the tanks worked their way loose and spent the rest of the ride bashing about inside the tanks and unsuccessfully, but tenaciously, trying to beat their way through the sides of the tanks.

By the beginning of January we had picked up the tanks, but they hadn't been installed. My family was getting ready to go on its annual family camp at Whananaki, north of Whangarei.

Burglar and I had decided that we would take the Seadoos on this camp and do some testing and training rides so he was coming over from Australia. My local PWC dealer had said they would install the tanks for us, but when it came time to do it they were too busy so I put out a mayday call to Matt Kneesh who owns Maksgear, the Seadoo dealership in Tauranga. I explained the situation to him and he said to bring them down the next day.

The next morning I left at sparrows and zoomed down to Tauranga leaving a trail of dust and chickens running in circles in each town I passed through. I arrived at about 9am and watched while the boys went to work. Matt, Bevan and Colin were amazing. They worked on those machines for a day and a half while I watched, got in the way, asked stupid questions and did lunch boy duties.

At the end of it all we had the tanks installed, with a fuel line going through an inline filter to an auxiliary fuel pump, which was connected by more fuel line to the top of the fuel inlet to the main fuel tank. The auxiliary fuel pump was powered from the battery through a switch that was located in a protected, but accessible, position near the front of the Seadoo. It all looked very flash. I thanked the boys for their great work and headed home, picking Burglar up from the airport on the way past. The plan was coming together.

Chapter 2
Training and Testing

When we first decided to do the ride we knew that it would be physically tough. Normally a two hour ride will leave a person a bit sore for a week and we were planning to do up to ten hours a day, for nineteen days. We determined that the two most likely things that would cause us to fail, apart from bird flu, were serious injury or mechanical failure. We were of the opinion that injury was most likely to happen at the end of the day when we were mentally and physically tired and finding it hard to concentrate. We decided that our fitness theme would be endurance and strength, in that order.

We had about four months to get seriously fit. The first thing that I had to sort out was a long term injury to my left knee. I went and saw a knee specialist in Auckland. He looked at it and suggested stretching and bike riding, which was convenient as I had planned to do a lot of bike riding for endurance training.

I started on a programme with alternating days of weight training and bike riding, with a day off after every four days. The weight training sessions lasted about ninety minutes and worked all the muscle groups. On the bike riding days I would get on my mountain bike and ride out towards Riverhead. I always made sure I went on the hilliest route and stayed out for at least two hours. I would time each route, so as to give myself something to aim to beat each time. Towards the end I was really pumping up the long

steep hills and feeling very strong. I also had some personal training sessions with Carl at the Beachside Health Club in Browns Bay.
Carl worked on exercises that would increase my core strength.
Burglar kept telling me about Pilates. I told him that I was lucky
enough to have avoided that problem. I suggested that he was very
young to have them himself and that I was sure there would be a
cure shortly, probably called *Preparation P*.

We had a few dramas along the way. About three months from
departure Burglar texted me to say that he had broken his collar
bone riding a trail bike. It was a bad break requiring a metal pin,
but he assured me it would be right for the ride. And it was.

I was doing some occasional judo training and had decided to
give it away for a while because of the chance of injury. Murphy
had one of his finest hours when about one minute before the
end of my last judo session I had one of the bigger guys fall on
my right arm and twist my wrist. This injury limited the weight
training exercises I could do and severely weakened the wrist.
It never came right and caused pain and drama for me throughout
the ride.

By the end of the four months we were both getting very fit.
In spite of my injured wrist I was lifting some pretty big weights
(I won't say how much because non-lifters wouldn't believe me
and serious weight trainers would call me a pussy). Burglar was
doing similar stuff.

When I started training I weighed 100 kg. In the four months
leading up to the ride I lost 4 kg, and on the ride I lost another 2 kg
and, as I write this two weeks after the event I still haven't found
them again, although I'm sure I'll stumble across them sometime
soon. (*Note: Just before the book went to print in December 2006, I had
found all six kilos plus an extra one that didn't belong to me.*)

We knew that we needed to do some training on the Seadoos as
well, as that would really set us up for the big ride ahead. We also
needed to test the auxiliary fuel tanks, as it was important that

they were working well. Our first big ride was shortly after the tanks had been installed. We had gone up to Whananaki with my family on our annual family camp. On the day we went out, we left fairly early and drove to Whangarei where we fueled up and discovered, to our delight, that each auxiliary tank was capable of holding up to 110 litres. This was a little more than we had hoped for and was to be quite important on the actual ride.

Our euphoria was, however, short lived - the bill for the fuel was over $500!

We launched the Seadoos at Parua Bay, near Whangarei Heads. We were interested to see how the full aux. fuel tanks would affect the way the Seadoos sat in the water and were delighted that, although the rear of the machines sat a bit lower than normal, it wasn't excessive. The next test was how they would perform in different sea conditions. Throughout the day we were pleasantly surprised as, in certain conditions, the extra weight on the back actually improved the ride by keeping the nose up a bit more than normal. In other conditions the ride deteriorated a little. Going into an oncoming swell the machines tended to bounce a little more and thump down a little harder. But, all in all we were ecstatic at the results.

We headed out through Whangarei Heads and then north up the Tutukaka Coast. This coast is truly one of the most beautiful places in the world. It would be hard to imagine how you could improve it. The weather is normally better than anywhere else in the North and the golden sand beaches are amazing. The weather was good for us that day too.

We called into Whananaki for a snack. While there we decided to see how the Seadoos handled us boarding from the rear with full aux. tanks, so we found a calm spot to do it in. The combined weight of our bodies and the fuel in the aux. tanks was about 200 kg and, to our amazement, when we climbed on them the Seadoos hardly moved. This would be very important later if we needed to board again after being thrown off in rough seas. That test completed we continued on up the coast towards Cape Brett.

At Cape Brett we approached the famous Hole in the Rock. It looked safe, so we went through the hole. It was almost flat calm so we turned around and went through again, but this time at 85 km/hr. I don't know for sure, but I reckon that's got to be a speed record for going through the hole. We played around there for a while longer and then turned on the pumps to start transferring fuel from the aux. tanks to the main. They seemed to be working okay, so we headed into the Bay of Islands and Russell.

Russell is a fantastic spot. It sits in a sheltered bay across the water from Paihia. It has a jetty and a fine-pebbled foreshore lined with trees and restaurants. There are always a variety of boats moored in the bay. The town is surrounded on the north-eastern side by bush-covered, rolling hills.

We rode slowly into the bay and parked just to the north of the jetty. I sat under a tree programming the GPS (Global Positioning System), while Burglar went and bought lunch. It was all very pleasant.

All good things must come to an end sometime though and, so it was with lunch at Russell. We reboarded the Seadoos and headed out to the north towards Cape Wiwiki, but Burglar was having trouble with his auxiliary fuel pump cavitating, so we called into a beach south of Wiwiki to check it out.

We found that the fuel filters were being blocked by residual aluminium filings from the construction and installation of the tanks. The last thing you should do before installing tanks is clean them thoroughly. The fact that it wasn't done was to end up causing problems and extra expense for the entire ride around New Zealand. It would be unfair to apportion blame here though because the installers did a fantastic job and were working flat out under time constraints, so it just wasn't considered.

We had continued on just past Cape Wiwiki, when Burglar informed me that his pump still wasn't working very well. I made the decision to turn back towards Cape Brett and Whangarei, so that at least we were heading in the right direction if our problems got worse. As we passed Home Point on Whangaruru North Head we decided to call into a deserted bay to have another look at the pump problem. Burglar checked his filter and found it clear, but the pump still sounded like it was cavitating. While he was doing this I drifted nearby in calm crystal clear water where I could see the bottom 6 m below.

Now I want you to think about this carefully......it's not a trick question. Where does the smoke come out first when there is a fire inside a Seadoo? You are wrong. It comes out the end of the handle bars on the control column.

It was obvious to me from watching Burglar that the tempo had lifted somewhat. He was jumping around on the Seadoo as if he was being attacked by a swarm of bees. As I watched with amazement he stood up, spun around, unclipped the seats and threw them into the water. Immediately a large cloud of smoke enveloped him, so that all I could see was the odd limb appear every now and then like a fight in a cartoon. If there were bees there before they would be gone now as they don't like smoke, so I relaxed a little.

Then he yelled at me, "Gosh (or something similar), the bloody thing is on fire". I suggested that he put some water on it as there was plenty around, but he reckoned he couldn't see where the flames were. If it wasn't so serious it would have been funny, but at that moment we could both see our grand adventure about to flounder in a deserted bay *before the first ball had even been bowled.* Eventually the smoke subsided on its own and it became obvious that the fire had been caused by the auxiliary fuel pump. The pump had overheated and self destructed. The smoke had been caused by the burning of the fibreglass of the hull next to the pump. The fire had gone out when the heat had melted the wires connecting the pump to the battery, stopping the pump. The conclusion of an electrician we consulted the next day was that the pump had been faulty.

After retrieving all Burglars' discarded bits we made our way into Bland Bay, just around the corner to the south. Burglar went up to the campground to borrow a drum and we set to work siphoning fuel from the aux. tanks to the main. Siphoning is not my favourite thing as petrol tends to get in your mouth and, although it's cheaper than bottled water, it doesn't taste as good. Once the fuel transfer was done we zoomed off again towards Whangarei. We had a good run down to Tutukaka, then the afternoon wind came up to about 40 km/hr with associated head on chop. We had already been riding for about 6 hours so were getting tired but, as we told each other, this was the time every day when we would need to dig deep and we might as well start training for it now.

This was our first new type of sea condition of the many we would encounter on the ride. I call this one the *bone shaker*. It's a half to 1 m, tightly spaced, oncoming chop with a strong headwind. If you ride slowly enough you can go up and down the waves but you never get anywhere. The best way to ride the bone shaker is hard out bouncing across the tops at between 50 and 60 km/hr. It rattles your bones, and the hull of the Seadoo. Your arms and wrists get tired from holding on, but at least you get somewhere. We did two and a half hours of bone shaking all the way back to Parua Bay, arriving there about 5pm after eight and a half hours riding.

We had been wearing full face helmets on this ride. I always do on any ride. I can't understand why it isn't compulsory. With the speeds that the Seadoos are capable of, it just doesn't make sense not to wear a helmet, yet most people don't. If you fall off and hit the water at 100 km/hr, that water will be as hard as concrete. And the number of times that we hit our chins or faces on the handle bars in rough conditions during the actual trip made us appreciate the chin guards as well.

One of the things we noticed on this first training ride was that, with helmets on, the head support portion of our life jackets tended to push our heads forward and made it difficult for us to look up and forward. As a result we asked Hutchwilco if they would replace the lifejackets with water ski jackets. They were more than happy to help and, as always, a pleasure to deal with.

All in all, this had been a great test ride and we had also proven two important things: That we could physically handle the long days and that fuel transfer would not be as simple as we would have liked.

The next day was a day off at Whananaki. We still needed to exercise so I suggested a bit of swimming would be useful, especially if we were to fall off the Seadoos during the ride. We decided to swim the length of the beach a few times. There are a lot of things Burglar does well. Swimming is not one of them.

If you have ever been swimming in a lap pool you will have noticed swimmers who seem to glide along effortlessly as if driven by an invisible propeller. I am not one of these people but over the years I have perfected my bastardised style and I get along ok, albeit in an ugly way. Below me and at the bottom of the scale are those swimmers who look like they are towing an invisible sea anchor. In fact, one of my old triathlon buddies was proudly known as *Sea Anchor Griffiths*.

As far as swimming goes, Burglar is a *subspecies*, or in more ways than one, a *bottom feeder*. When he swims he looks like he is towing out a heavy trans-continental telephone cable from a huge reel. The more it rolls out the more weight there is to drag him under. Being fit and strong, Burglar thrashes around like a shark attack victim and creates his own whirlpool action around him. As we swam along the beach this is what he did now. New Zealand campers are a creative lot and they don't miss many chances. It was not hard to imagine all the camp's mothers rushing to gather their dirty washing and some soap powder and then all congregating at the waters edge, discussing nervously and excitably whether they should risk a shark attack and throw all their dirty washing into the heavy duty wash cycle being created by Burglar.

Because I was so far ahead I can't confirm whether any one did or not, but what I can tell you is that everyone looked to be wearing cleaner clothes for the next few days.

In the week before we started the actual ride we did two more big training rides. The first we did on the Sunday. We put in at first light at Takapuna ramp on Auckland's North Shore and headed out between Rangitoto and Waiheke Islands. Conditions were again fairly good as we made our way towards Cape Colville on the tip of the Coromandel Peninsula. From Cape Colville we headed north-east to Cape Barrier on the southern tip of Great Barrier Island. There was an easy 2 m swell across the channel. When we were about 2 km from Cape Barrier we encountered a new sea condition that I'll refer to as *steep and nasty*. It's where the normal swell hits a shallow patch and the swell turns into waves that are steep, almost breaking, and fast moving. They are also closely spaced. The only way to approach these waves is straight on. Each wave involves climbing up the face and dropping off the back; recovering just in time to face the next one. Progress is very slow. At times your forward speed reduces to around 12 km/hr and, if you watch the land, it doesn't seem like you are moving at all. We dealt with 3 m *steep and nasties* for about forty minutes before we got clear and started up the east coast of Great Barrier Island.

The east coast of Great Barrier Island is rugged and beautiful. It has an intricate, rocky coastline with several offshore islets and pinnacles. The coast has been shaped by millions of years of easterly swell that comes from thousands of kilometres away, across the Pacific Ocean. From south to north the island measures about 40 km in length.

Known to the Maori as Aotea, the island is a detached piece of the Coromandel Peninsula. Since being discovered by Captain Cook in 1769, Great Barrier has been exploited for timber and minerals. Its present permanent population is around 300. Its highest point is Mt Hobson, at only about 630 m, but the island is generally very rugged, with rocky bluffs rising steeply from the sea, especially on the western shore. The centre of the island is difficult to traverse because of deep ravines, steep cliffs and jagged pinnacles. There are excellent walking tracks all over the island.

Two thirds of the way up the coast of Barrier, and about 5 km off shore from it is Rakitu Island. Just beside Rakitu Island we got to test out another procedure we had talked about and planned for. I needed to go to the toilet. There aren't many public toilets on Rakitu Island. Actually there are none. Number ones we had already sorted out. I had ordered wetsuits with longer front zips that opened from both ends. The procedure was to slow down to idle, stand up, leaning your legs against the handle bars for balance, unzip, find it (not easy given the cold wet conditions) and Bob's your uncle. This procedure worked well, as you could even steer while you went by moving the bars with your legs. This meant that you could continue on clocking up metres in the right direction at idle speed, which was about 5 km/hr. We worked out that we probably did this procedure about three-hundred times on the whole ride, so we covered some serious ground peeing.

Number twos was a different story, as it took a good three minutes to undress sufficiently, and even longer in bad conditions. So we first had to undress and then the procedure was to climb over the back and reverse down the boarding ladder into the water. We had agreed for safety reasons that the other bloke would stand off at a close, but mental health preserving, distance and be on the lookout for trouble; such as a shark mistaking a tough forty-six year old butt for something edible.

You have to be fairly comfortable with your buddy to do this and I'm sure the whole procedure has created a dubious strengthening of the male bond between us. But I have to say that no matter how well you know someone, during this particular event it is inevitable that you have the exact same stupid look on your face as a dog does when it is caught crapping on your lawn.

So Rakitu Island was where the procedure was tested and

signed off and the water around the Island was declared a Hazard
to Shipping. We then continued on to Needles Point at the northern end of Great Barrier Island. We rounded the point and had
an excellent ride down the west coast of Great Barrier into Port
Fitzroy, where we had a lunch date with Roger and Sherrin
Mortimer on their 36 ft Riviera. The weather was improving and
lunch was delicious.

Roger and Sherrin lived right below, and in between, Colin
Bower and us when we lived in Clifton Road. Roger also has a
Seadoo, but it would be worth more in a museum than on the
market. It is propelled, for the most part, by noise and rattle.
In spite of that the three of us formed a convenient Seadoo 'Triad'.
In addition to the Triad, just around the corner in Oban Road lived
the inimitable John Devine who also owned a Seadoo. The four
of us would go riding frequently. The group had an average age
in the early fifties, (thanks gratefully accepted for my contribution to lowering this average) were fairly responsible and never
caused much trouble. I think the worst thing we ever did was
when the other three were waiting for me with their Seadoos on
their trailers and they inadvertently pulled up outside the Browns
Bay Bingo Club. As the story goes, while they waited they leaned
against their cars wearing muscle shirts and chatting and caused
a riot in the club.

It would normally take at least three bullock teams to separate
an old bingo player from her bingo card, but in this case cards
were deserted wholesale. Colin had his muscle shirt completely
ripped off and even now he still receives texts from a couple of old
girls called Ruby and Iris.

Back on the Riviera, Roger cooked us fresh fish on his barbecue, so by the time we left there we were feeling pretty con-
tented. We regrettably said our goodbyes and headed west from
Port Fitzroy around the northern side of the nature reserve of little
Barrier Island before tracking to Cape Rodney, and then south
past Tokatu Pt and west into Kawau Bay.

We then tracked south past the boating mecca of historic Mansion House Bay on Kawau Island to the stunning Motuketekete Island, where we found a nice little sheltered beach for a break and a snack. From Motuketekete we headed south again through the Whangaparaoa Passage, past the bird sanctuary of Tiritiri Matangi Island and then back to Takapuna. We had completed another long range ride. We had taken eight hours and had covered some 300 km. We were gaining confidence.

We did one more long ride for training on the Wednesday before departure. We again put in at Takapuna ramp and headed out to Cape Colville. We had a pretty good run to the cape. Once we rounded the cape and headed south towards the Mercury Islands it started to rain fairly heavily. We were initially concerned about this as the rain stings when it hits your face, but after a while we became used to it and decided it wasn't that bad after all. The sea conditions were very good. They always seem better in the rain. Burglar had asked me why this was so. I said that I supposed it was because the rain fills up the hollows in the waves and makes them less steep. Sadly, he was happy with that explanation and, in the absence of a better one, it is the one we will stick to.

With the rain came poor visibility and at times we were completely surrounded by a white horizon and a murky grey sea. My GPS was lulling us into a false sense of security on this ride by actually working. *It rarely did on the main ride.* Burglar didn't have a GPS, so he didn't know whether he was Arthur or Martha and was zooming all over the place. Eventually Slipper Island came in to view. This was our turn around point and we had made very good time. Slipper Island is a beautiful tropical-style island a few kilometres off Pauanui. There are chalets right next to the golden sand beach. The water is crystal clear and it is worth the effort to get out there and spend a weekend, as we have done in the past. We had lunch on the Seadoos just off the beach at Slipper and then headed back north.

We soon encountered a new type of sea condition that we'll call *bastard glass*. *Glass* is where the sea is so smooth that it looks like glass and is good for high speed riding. *Bastard glass* looks like glass, but still has an underlying wave in it that is very hard to judge when you are riding on it. The reflections and optical illusions caused by the smooth water mean that you don't know when you will hit a wave, or if you are about to drop off one, so you don't know when to brace and injury is more likely.

We rode on *bastard glass* for some time before an easterly wind sprung up which helped define the waves better. We rounded Cape Colville and headed south-west. The easterly wind was getting stronger as we approached Rakino Island and we were subjected to our second new sea condition of the day. We'll call this one *slap in the face*. It's where you have a following sea of about 1 m, but it's steep and the wavelength is short so that, as you surf down the front of one wave, it is impossible not to dive into the back of the next wave. This causes water to be forced into your face at high pressure, kind of like someone throwing a bucket of water into your face at high speed. It varies from just being cold and wet to hitting you so hard that water goes up your nose and into your sinuses and ears with such force that you can't hear anything for a few minutes. On the odd occasion, it does so with such force that the water entering the front of your helmet snaps your head back. Occasionally our goggles would be forced out from the goggle cavity in the helmet and off our heads completely. They would end up having to be retrieved from the water. I lost a pair this way.

We rode slap in the face conditions all the way from Rakino to Takapuna ramp. This had been another good ride overall though, with us covering 350 km in just over seven hours.

The Burglar Brothers were ready.

At Great Barrier Island on our second training ride.

Chapter 3
Final Preparation

In the last few weeks leading up to the ride I wanted to make sure we had as much done as we could. I figured that if it could be organised beforehand then it should be, as I knew I wouldn't have too much energy left for organisational things while on the ride.

Cath Saunders had organised a meeting with Bill Francis at the Radio Network to sell the idea of me doing radio interviews all the way around the country. The meeting went well and Cath then organised a schedule for daily, or sometimes twice daily, interviews. The radio network organised an initial interview to set the scene, and I was advised of it the night before it was due to happen. I was on my way to Sydney to take out a flight to some exotic destination and would have to be up at ten to six Sydney time for the call. I arrived in Sydney late the night before and didn't sleep well. I was also just recovering from flu, so had a continuous tickle in my throat and was worried that I would break out into uncontrollable fits of coughing mid interview. If you are thinking that I am setting you up to tell you that the interview didn't go that well, then you are right. It was not one of the finer performances, not helped by the interviewer who had made no effort to research the background of the event. But it was a start and gave us something to work on. By the time the event was over I was, even if I do say so myself, quite the pro at radio interviews, having done them from Seadoos, cars, while aimlessly wandering the streets and from toilet cubicles. If the listeners had only known!

Cath also organized some media training for both Burglar and I at the Juice TV studios in Parnell. Here we learnt how not to look like a complete goose on TV, and other useful skills. There had been a fair bit of effort put into getting TV stations interested in the event. Nick Dooner from TVNZ had passed on the concept to management, who had then filed it somewhere where it couldn't be found. This is actually quite understandable when you look at the shenanigans that were going on there at the time. There was obviously a game of *management musical chairs* going on and the managers were all too busy walking slowly around eyeing the remaining chairs and each other, while waiting for the music to stop. David Libeau from Qantas had some friends at TV3 and when they heard about the ride they jumped on it. We had a meeting at Qantas with Cath Saunders, Phil Briars, David, Kathy Gera, Burglar, myself, and John Campbell and Carol Hirschfeld from *Campbell Live*. John and Carol were totally enthusiastic about the event and committed to covering it. Carol also agreed to loan us a TV3 video camera so that we could film some of the ride as we went along.

I had a couple more meetings with the good folk from the Cancer Society. We came to the conclusion that the event should not be used to raise money, but to raise awareness of skin cancer. The Cancer Society is very aware of not being seen to have their hand out too much and they already had their *Relay for Life* fundraiser happening at the time.

While we are talking about the Cancer Society, I have to say I am totally overawed by the quality of the people that work there. They are all very impressive people. Everywhere we went around the country they were there to meet us and offer support. We got to spend time with some of them, which was an absolute pleasure. They do great work in a difficult field and New Zealanders are lucky that such a fabulous network exists to support people with a disease that affects so many of us at some time in our lives.

There was a lot of equipment that needed to be bought and

organised. You would not believe the amount of gear you need for an event like this. Clothing, maps, lists of radio frequencies, ropes, tow ropes, fuel drums, nose hair clippers, radios, phones… the list goes on and on. I spent two days researching and book-ing accommodation all around the country. I spent another two days researching local knowledge on things like the Greymouth River Bar and where you come ashore at Haast. It will later be revealed that I could have spent some more time on researching Haast landing sites.

Burglar and I spent a few hours printing out coastal charts and, while I put all the radio frequencies and navigation waypoints on them, he laminated them so as to make them waterproof. All of this good work was effectively negated by good housekeep-ing and even better intentions. When we started off, Jeff from our ground crew had organised all our information into a ring binder for quick reference. In an amusing, but frustrating, turn of events this unfortunately included the maps. It's a sad, but inescapable, fact that waterproof maps with holes punched through them are no longer waterproof. Most of them ended up getting soaked and having the ink run until it looked like we were riding around Australia. We enjoyed bringing this up with Jeff from time to time using varying and minimal degrees of subtlety.

I organised a satellite phone through Wright Technologies in Albany. The satellite phone industry is not very competitive in New Zealand and there is a certain air of arrogance about it. There was no way any company would consider a discount even though it was a charity event. We needed the phone though, for out of the way interviews and safety, so we went ahead and signed up for it. I asked for the phone number in advance so that it could be distributed to everyone who might need it. The day before we were due to leave I picked up the phone and was informed that it would be a different number. Someone had dropped the ball and given our number to another customer. An indication of how arrogant they are at Wright Technologies was that they thought

I was being unreasonable asking for my original, promised, number. They couldn't understand why I couldn't just change the number with all of my contacts. In the end I insisted on the original number and they got it for me, but it was a battle.

Burglar and I had to prepare the Seadoos to a configuration that we thought would be best for the ride. We had had trouble before with batteries on our Marlborough Sounds ride, so we wanted to be prepared this time. Burglar installed permanent jumper leads in both Seadoos, so that if one battery died we could instantly jump start from the other. In a stroke of pure genius he also set up the front compartment so that it would carry two extra ten litre fuel drums as a reserve, thus increasing our total fuel capacity to 190 litres each. The system was extraordinary to look at, very effective and reasonably fail safe. These extra drums were to prove very useful at times. He also put his building skills to good use building a box for the front of the trailer to hold ten, 20 litre fuel drums for remote refueling on the ride.

We stocked up on anti-inflammatory drugs and creams for repairing wear and tear. The anti inflammatory drugs proved very useful as I reckon my entire body was inflamed the whole way. We had been recommended to use 3B cream for wear and tear. The manufacturer of 3B cream markets this cream as being for the 'breasts, buttocks and between the legs'. We feel that they are missing a major marketing opportunity here. If a guy walks into a chemist shop, he doesn't want to tell the pretty sales assistant that he has chafed balls because he's been on a jet ski for eight hours. He wants to see loud and clear on the packaging that this cream is indeed for chafed balls. Therefore, what we intend to do is first buy shares in the company and then write to them suggesting they change the name to 4B and add balls to the packaging. Sales will skyrocket.

I finalised our ground crew. It's not easy finding ground crew for an event like this. It's hard to find people who can get the time off.

It's also important that your crew know how to run a military style operation. For this event we had to run a very disciplined operation for it to be successful. Ground crew would also need to be easy to get on with and hard working. I was fortunate to find four stars who fit the above description and I sold them on the idea by waving glossy tourist brochures of exotic New Zealand locations in front of their faces and talking endlessly of nights out drinking with Scandinavian backpackers until the early hours.

In the end these four guys were the absolute unsung heroes of the trip. They made the whole thing work when we were too exhausted, and Burglar and I will always be grateful to them.

The first was an American (this doesn't make him a bad person); Jeff Stangl. Now living permanently in Torbay, Jeff is an entrepreneurial type, originally from San Diego, who has a good sense of humour and a passion for number crunching. He is also a fine chef, whose forte is scones and strong coffee. Jeff was given the nickname *Chinashop* (as in a bull in a china shop) early on as nothing was done without a lot of noise. I would have hated to have been the poor tourists next door to us at 5am every morning when we were getting going. We briefly considered calling Jeff *HolePuncher*, but *Chinashop* won out.

Next was Kiwi Peter Robertson from Te Puke. Peter missed his true calling and should have been a roadie. He is the ultimate ground crew. He was so hard working and dedicated that it was embarrassing. There was almost nothing (by civilised standards) Peter wouldn't do to make life easier for us. Peter got given the nickname *Pete* along the way, as we couldn't find any peculiar traits to suggest a better one.

Then came South African-born Michael Bridger who is a construction guru for a local Auckland company. The man with the golden tongue, Michael was a joy to listen to when he was negotiating discounts, or asking for assistance. He has that knack of asking in such a way as it is impossible to say no. He is also a fine chef. Michael gained the nickname *Chainsaw* along the way because of his prize winning snoring. His snoring sounds like a very powerful chainsaw in need of a tune up, only worse.

Last, but not least, was Captain Matthew Gray, one of my compatriots from Qantas and a man who has done some of New Zealand's great walks with me. Matt, nicknamed *Mateus* because of his extensive knowledge of viticulture, is also a great chef. He has about as dry a sense of humour as you will find outside Death Valley, which is a good characteristic on an event like this. Matt is also a melanoma survivor. But more on these guys later.

So as you can see, the last few weeks were very busy, with interviews, photo shoots and organisational stuff. I also had to deal with the inconvenience of going to work. I had an eight day London trip rostered to finish just over a week before the ride was to start. I had two good reasons not to do it. I had a problem with both my eyes, and my heart. The eye problem was that I couldn't see myself going to work, and the heart problem was that my heart wasn't in it. Professional pride took over though and I went to work as planned, which ended up being helpful as it gave me a break from organising, and a chance to recharge my enthusiasm levels before the start.

In the end, the eve of the trip arrived and we finished final preparations at about 9pm that night. We felt ready. We couldn't wait to just get going.

I spent ages preparing the maps.

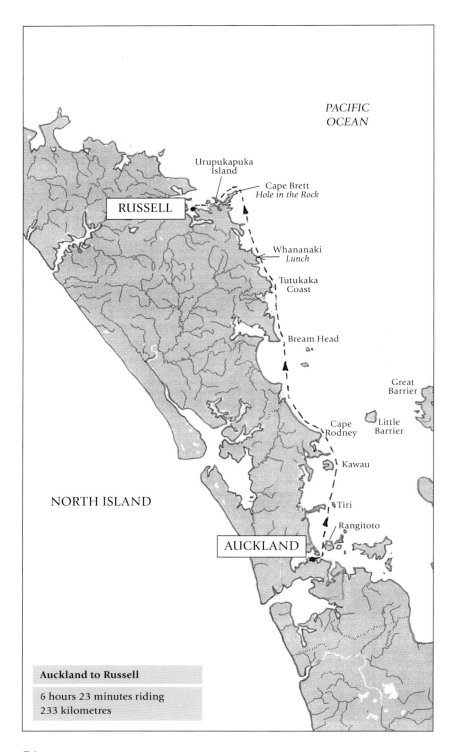

PACIFIC
OCEAN

Urupukapuka
Island

Cape Brett
Hole in the Rock

RUSSELL

Whananaki
Lunch

Tutukaka
Coast

Bream Head

Great
Barrier

Cape
Rodney

Little
Barrier

Kawau

NORTH ISLAND

Tiri

Rangitoto

AUCKLAND

Auckland to Russell

6 hours 23 minutes riding
233 kilometres

Chapter 4
The Ride: To Russell

Sunday 5th February 2006

On Day 1 we woke pretty early because we wanted to have the Seadoos at Auckland's Americas' Cup Viaduct Basin by 8am.

We had had a full house, as my old mate Colin Bower and his wife Rae (*Who-Rae*) had come to stay. We had had a discussion the night before about songs that we would like to have played at our funeral. People apparently do this as they get older, but Colin had kept pushing me for mine which shows just how much faith he had in us completing the adventure in anything but a pine box. I eventually pulled a song out of nowhere, which he had forgotten by the time we reached Tauranga on the ride. And for the record it's *Flying Without Wings*, but I reserve the right to change that without notice, or recourse.

I had promised to embarrass Colin with my pre-departure speech so he wasn't going to miss that for any amount of money and he also wanted to ride out with us for a while on the leg to Russell. Rae just wanted to get a good look at me before I headed off to "certain death". Peter Robertson was part of our initial ground crew, so he stayed over too. Our other initial ground crew guy, Jeff Stangl (Chinashop), lives just down the road from us so he didn't stay and he was too busy anyway, digging the tunnel between our houses so that when bird flu arrives we can still get together even with a full lockdown in place. Americans like to be prepared for these things you know!

My wife Manola was busy getting things ready and the boys were out doing their paper runs early so they could get to the Viaduct too.

We had loaded the Sorento the night before so we were all ready to leave at about 7.15am. We headed off and did another $400 refuel. We then drove to the Westhaven Marina where we launched and then rode around to the Viaduct. Phil Briars from the Cancer Society and David Libeau from Qantas had everything organised by the time we got there. *The Loaded Hog* had been dressed in Qantas signage and we were all set to go.

For the next hour we talked to guests and well wishers and I did a couple of radio interviews. At 9.15am we were herded upstairs at the *Hog* for breakfast, which was quite exceptional. Phil Briars then got the speeches rolling. Former Governor General Dame Cath Tizard was there and she gave a great speech which included nominating us for her "Order of Confirmed Nutters". I was honoured to be nominated and said so in my speech. Colin wasn't disappointed either as I embarrassed him by telling the *shared fuel drum* story. Cath Saunders, our media planner was frowning at me from the side and pointing to her watch as departure time approached. Zella Briars said a karakia (Maori Prayer) for us to keep us safe and finally it was all done. We headed downstairs and went to get changed. Once changed we made our way down the ramp to the waiting media. We did a couple of TV interviews and were photographed so many times that I wanted to call my broker and order Kodak shares.

After a lot of fussing and carry on we eventually made it on to the Seadoos. David from Qantas had told me to bring my Captains hat and wear it for the departure. I was resisting putting it on as I feared that if any Qantas pilot ever saw a photo of me wearing it I would be subject to frequent harassment and sound thrashings in toilet cubicles when I returned to work. I eventually relented though and put the hat on for a brief moment much to the delight of the crowd who roared their approval. You wouldn't believe it, but some whacker took a photo of me wearing it, and that was the one that made the Herald the next day. I am still wearing a false nose and moustache and one of those beards that hooks over your ears when I go to work.

When we were finally ready, Dame Cath fired off a loud portable air-horn and the crowd went mad!! (Later having to be put into a home) We took off at a break-neck 10 km/hr. "Why so slow?" I hear you asking. And, since you ask so nicely, I will tell you.

Well I know it's popular for people who own other types of boat, or people who live near the water, to talk negatively about Personal Water Craft. I hear it all the time and sometimes I think the perspective taken is fairly narrow. Sure they can be noisy and sure some people ride them in an unsafe way and in the wrong places, but these are the minority. In the right hands and used within the rules PWCs are no different than any other boat. Indeed, there is frequent evidence of stupidity on all types of boats. What we really need is a bit of judicious policing of maritime trouble-makers in general.

We had decided beforehand that one thing we didn't want to do was give anyone any reason to froth at the mouth about PWCs, so we were determined to set an example by not breaking any rules. Hence the 10 km/hr departure all the way out of the Viaduct, much to the disappointment of the crowd who were expecting a wheelie, or a burnout, or at least the marine equivalent. But better to disappoint the crowd than give someone with too much time on their hands an excuse to write a letter to the editor about jet-ski hoons.

So we puttered out of the Viaduct Basin. The Coastguard; who had been taken over at gun point by the TV cameramen; were right next to us. There were about six other people on PWCs accompanying us, including Colin and Tasha Bower. We had been asked by TV3 to go past Kelly Tarltons because there would be another cameraman there. Once out of the Viaduct we rode at high speed in an easterly direction down the harbour. I had no idea where Kelly

Tarltons was exactly so I was just hugging the southern extremes
of the harbour. We zoomed past Bastion Point and then headed
north through the Rangitoto Channel. There was quite a strong
south-westerly breeze blowing and we were already experiencing
mild *slap in the face* sea conditions (steep following seas that cause
the Seadoo to nose dive, and water to spray in your face).

We passed to the west of the volcanic cone of Auckland's icon-
ic extinct volcano, Rangitoto Island. Sea conditions were getting
worse and so I suggested that the accompanying riders turn back
before the going got too tough. Now we were on our own and
finally underway. And we felt pretty damn good about it too.

We set a heading which would take us through the Whangaparaoa
Passage to the west of Tiri Tiri Matangi Island and directly to the
east coast of Kawau Island. Kawau Island was once the home of
former Governor General Sir George Grey. It was he that transformed the Mansion House at Mansion House Bay into what it is
today. He was also responsible for importing many overseas birds
and animals to the island including wallabies and kookaburras.

As we passed Kawau some fishermen in a boat who had obviously heard about our attempt came up to us waving and cheering. Once we realized Brad wasn't on fire again and the fishermen
were just being nice our spirits were lifted somewhat. On we went,
past Omaha Bay and around Cape Rodney with Little Barrier
Island towering majestically out of the water 20 km to the east.

From Cape Rodney we skirted around the diving and snorkel-
ing paradise of the Goat Island Marine reserve. Goat Island got its
name from the nineteenth century when most travel was done by
boat. Seafarers of the era of Captain Cook, and later, introduced
domesticated animals whenever they could to provide future food
sources. To release these animals on the mainland would make no
sense because the animals would wander off, but islands would
pen the animals so that they could be hunted easily. Some islands
had a dependable supply of running water so cattle could survive

there, but the smaller islands without fresh water were only suitable for goats since goats don't need to drink water. Hence, these islands were of a type labeled goat, or goat islands. Around the coast of New Zealand four or five Goat Islands exist. In the past this particular Goat Island has been stocked with goats and pigs. The pigs, however, escaped by swimming (or flying) to the coast, which goats don't do. We kept a good eye out for pigs wearing swim goggles and togs and also for goats, but saw neither.

We then hugged the coast to shelter from the wind all the way to Mangawai heads. At Bream Tail we had to leave the coast and head across Bream Bay, past the Hen and Chicken Islands and the entrance to the Whangarei Harbour near Bream Head.

Across Bream Bay the wind was getting up and the following seas were rising. We started to frequently nose dive and we both took many face-fulls of water. My sinuses were getting the cleansing of their life. One thing I have noticed from surfing and riding Seadoos is that my sinuses are very good at storing salt water, sometimes for hours, and then later suddenly releasing a couple of gallons of water at the most embarrassing time. I amused myself imagining how my currently full sinuses would contrive to embarrass me after we reached Russell. Given that it was Waitangi day the next day, the most likely scenario I could come up with was that the Queen, or the Prime Minister, would be up there for the ceremonies and be staying in the Top 10 Holiday Park in the bunk room next to us. On hearing of our exploits their people would talk to our people and they would arrange to be invited over to our place for afternoon tea. I would be leaning over saying "more tea your majesty" and my sinuses would let go into her cup of tea. Naturally she would be too polite to say anything.

Snapping back to reality we passed Bream Head and hugged the beautiful Tutukaka Coast. This made the riding slightly easier and we made reasonable time to a lunch stop at Otamure Bay, just north of Whananaki. The golden sand beaches and magnificent hanging Pohutukawa trees make this bay one of my all time favourite spots. We spent a very pleasant twenty minutes eating tinned rice pudding, oranges and Snickers bars.

Then, with energy levels recharged we again headed north past Rimariki Island and Whangaruru Harbour, and then on past Home Point and the site of Burglar's fire drama of a few weeks earlier. Cape Brett was clearly in sight and that gave us more energy, as we knew that that was the turning point in towards Russell in the Bay of Islands.

Our plan had been to go through the Hole in the Rock at Cape Brett and film with TV3's camera, but the turbulence caused by tidal action around Cape Brett made holding a camera steady almost impossible, so we continued on.

The magnificent Bay of Islands is an expanse of water with several long inlets and over one-hundred-and-fifty islands. The first European visitor was Captain Cook, who named the bay in 1769. From Cape Brett to Russell is about 25 km so we had counted on a quick ride in, but on turning towards the west and Russell we encountered a howling south-westerly wind again and had to battle *bone shaker* seas all the way in. This was hard work and we were not impressed. We bashed past Urupukapuka Island at about 40 km/hr and turned north-west towards Tapeka Point.

Eventually we rounded Tapeka Point and the sea conditions improved. We increased speed towards Russell, which was now very close. Because it was Waitangi Day the next day, the whole New Zealand Navy was parked between Paihia and Russell. She looked magnificent and fearsome at her moorings, and I was comforted by the fact that we New Zealanders were in good hands.

Paihia is the sight of the Waitangi Treaty Grounds. It is New Zealand's pre-eminent historic sight. It was here on February 6th 1840 that the Treaty of Waitangi was first signed between Maori and the British Government.

Russell was the original capital of New Zealand, but in 1841 Governor Hobson moved the capital to the shores of the Waitemata

Harbour, where he founded Auckland. In 1865 the seat of government was moved again, from Auckland to Wellington. Every now and then the politicians talk about moving again. A few years back, Rodney Hide, an Act politician, as a joke, suggested in parliament that they physically pick up and move the Beehive (New Zealand's current parliament house), probably so that the politicians could be closer to the beach for their lunch hour and the Prime Minister could get to try out her new bikini. Later, after a committee had been formed and serious money spent on investigating the proposal, Rodney stood up and told everyone what a stupid idea it was. The pro-move people responded by saying, "But this was your idea in the first place", whereupon Rodney said "But I was only joking".

The sight of Russell was very welcome as we slowed to come into the bay past all the moored pleasure craft, to a rousing welcome from our ground crew, Chinashop and Pete, and Phil Briars from the Cancer Society who was accompanied by his wife Zella. All the event flags were blowing in the breeze and a few locals and tourists watched with interest as we arrived. It had taken us six hours and twenty-three minutes to ride 233 km.

At the launch ramp Chinashop and Pete pulled the Seadoos out of the water. The Sorento was full of gear, so there was no room for us inside. We decided to ride on the Seadoos on the back of the trailer through Russell to the service station to get fuel. We must have looked like a couple of prize turkeys, but I've always said if you're going to look stupid you might as well make a good job of it so we kept our helmets on and gave the royal wave to all the passers by.

After refueling we drove back to the Duke of Marlborough Pub for more refueling in what has to be one of the finest settings for drinking beer known to man. The pub has a garden bar that sits overlooking Russell Bay and drinking there is quite simply one of the great pleasures of life.

After a few beers we drove to the Russell Top 10 holiday park where we were staying for the night. The Russell Top 10 is a top quality park, in a great setting and is clean, tidy and well organised. The staff at the park were very helpful to us and donated the room free of charge, which was much appreciated. Chinashop cooked up a great meal and Phil had a bottle of wine, so we dined well and retired happy, but tired, at about 8.30pm hoping like hell that the Queen and the Prime Minister wouldn't make too much noise in the room next door.

Dame Cath Tizard set off the air horn and we 'took off'
at 10 km an hour.

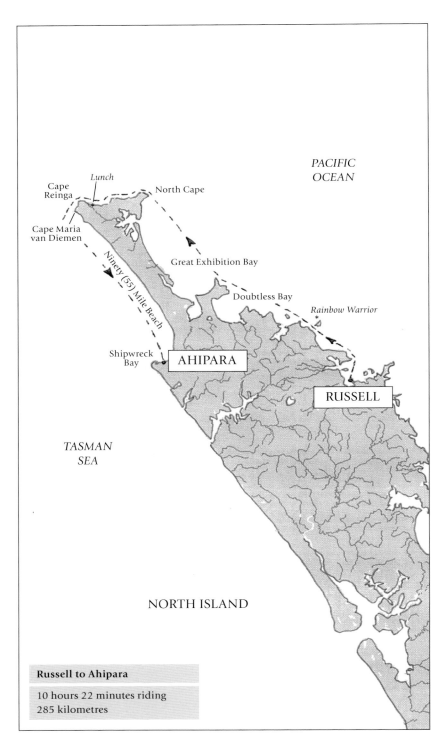

PACIFIC
OCEAN

Lunch

Cape
Reinga

North Cape

Cape Maria
van Diemen

Ninety (55) Mile Beach

Great Exhibition Bay

Doubtless Bay

Rainbow Warrior

Shipwreck
Bay

AHIPARA

RUSSELL

TASMAN
SEA

NORTH ISLAND

Russell to Ahipara

10 hours 22 minutes riding
285 kilometres

Chapter 5
The Ride: To Ahipara

Monday 6th February 2006

We woke at 5.30am and wandered over to the camp kitchen to see what delights Chinashop had conjured up for us for breakfast. I don't know about you but I find it hard to eat that early in the morning, so it has to be very appetizing. Thankfully, Chinashop had excelled himself and had made fresh scones and an unknown, but tasty, American version of eggs. We had a big day planned, so we tried to stuff as much food in as we could. Russell to North Cape to Cape Reinga and then to Ahipara at Kaitaia would be one of our bigger planned days, but at this point we were blissfully unaware of just how big it would turn out to be. Chinashop had also made a big pot of Altura coffee. He likes it strong and in this regard he was true to form. I sliced myself off a cup of coffee and downed it waiting for the first telltale sign of my heart starting up. Good coffee never fails and soon my heart was pumping regularly, but in protest, and the blood had started to flow.

With breakfast out of the way we went through the first of eighteen painful daily rituals of putting on wet wetsuits and boots and all the other gear that we wore. There is only one word to describe how it feels to be donning wet gear at 6am in the dark and that is UGLY.

This task completed, we headed down to Russell ramp for a daybreak launching. The weather looked pretty good, so our

spirits were high as we waved goodbye and motored quietly out of
Russell Bay and then noisily past the navy who were still parked in
the channel, guns fully loaded with tomatoes and eggs and trained
on the Waitangi Treaty House in case things got out of hand there
during the day's ceremonies.

The sea was fairly flat in the Bay of Islands, so we felt great as we
zoomed past Moturoa Island towards Cape Wiwiki. Rounding the
cape to the north the sea chopped up a bit so we bounced our way
towards the Cavalli Islands where the former Greenpeace vessel,
the *Rainbow Warrior,* has been laid to rest. The *Rainbow Warrior* was
sunk in Auckland Harbour by French agents in an attempt to stop
Greenpeace from protesting French nuclear tests in the Pacific.
It was later moved to its current location. We thought about planting a French flag on the islands to stir up the locals, but sadly there
wasn't one in our spare parts case. We stopped just off Matauri
Bay for a radio interview using the satellite phone. The sun had
just risen and everything was looking good, so the interview was
fairly upbeat.

From Matauri Bay the coastline heads north-west past
Whangaroa Bay. The scenery was magnificent and we were enjoy-
ing ourselves. The GPS was showing signs of losing interest.
I assumed it must be batteries, so I turned it off. I identified Cape
Karikari as our next target and headed for it using the *Mark One
Eyeball* for guidance. I started off my flying career as an air force
navigator which was to prove very useful throughout the trip, but
particularly when the GPS stopped working.

We had to cross the entrance to Doubtless Bay to get to Cape
Karikari. Doubtless Bay is quite big and, from our low lying perspective, Cape Karikari looked like an island. This can be quite disconcerting when you are navigating visually, so you have to back
up with other cues if they are available and trust your judgment.
I looked on the map and saw that there were no large islands in this
area, so I was confident that we were heading the right way and would
not end up in Fiji or Tahiti (worse things could happen though).

Incidentally I am not the only one to be uncertain about Doubtless Bay. When Cook sailed past it he wrote in his diary, "doubtless a bay", hence its name.

Burglar's knowledge of navigation was slightly less than bugger-all, so he just had to trust me and, to his credit, he never hassled me about it during the whole trip

We stopped off Matai Bay on Cape Karikari and called the coast-guard to let them know we were okay. The coastguard remarked that conditions on the West Coast were less than ideal. Looking back I would have to say that this was the understatement of the trip. The forecast had been for a 20 km/hr south-easterly down Ninety Mile Beach, which we considered would give us a good run from Cape Reinga to Ahipara if we stuck close to the coast. I suppose we should have known not to believe the forecast. Ever since my air force days; when the base meteorologists were famous for planning barbecues that got ruined by rain, snow and tornadoes; I have never trusted forecasts.

From Cape Karikari we could see some of the Aupouri Peninsula leading up to North Cape. The whole peninsula was once covered in massive Kauri forests. Some fifty- to sixty-thousand years ago it was gradually buried beneath peat swamps and encroaching sand dunes. The ancient wood is mined for making ornaments and furniture, with the land now partly farmed and partly forested with exotics.

Leaving Cape Karikari I had no intention of following the coast of the peninsula to North Cape, because Great Exhibition Bay is shaped almost like a half moon and to follow the coast would add about an extra 40 km to our ride. The GPS was issued with a summons and given a good stern talking to and then we set a heading direct for North Cape. This heading would have us up to 20 km off the coast at times. We had quite a strong south-westerly blowing and a one metre following sea, but it wasn't steep so we made reasonable progress and rounded North Cape at about 11.30am.

This was our first major milestone, so I got out the TV3 camera and told Burglar to ride back and forward past the cape while I filmed. He zoomed around for a while like a dog that's been let off its leash (I'll bet that his tongue was hanging out too) and then a short while, and quite a bit of fuel later, we regained our focus and started to head west.

The top of New Zealand stretches from North Cape in the east, about 40 km to Cape Reinga in the west. There are pretty bays dotted all along the top. As we rounded North Cape the wind suddenly strengthened to about 35 km/hr. We had to battle *bone shaker* seas and hug the coast to avoid the worst of it. I was starting to think conditions around Cape Reinga may be pretty nasty, so we pulled in to a little bay just east of Cape Reinga for lunch. It was pretty rocky and we were unable to land, so we turned off our engines and drifted around while we dined *alfresco* on tinned rice pudding and oranges and Up & Go energy drink.

We were also carrying Camelbaks, which are strap on backpacks that carry liquid. They have a tube that extends out of them that you suck on to retrieve the drink. It all works very well. In our case we could fit two litres of liquid in them. Our favorite drink was Raro Lemon Lime with electrolyte solution added and if the Raro company wishes to acknowledge this endorsement with a new Porsche, or a Townhouse in Queenstown, then let the record show that I am ready to accept it. But needless to say, the Camelbaks were very important to the success of the operation, as remaining hydrated was critical. In the same manner as a hardcore drinker stands at the urinal in a pub peeing and drinking beer at the same time, we found ourselves frequently standing and peeing on our trip while simultaneously drinking Raro.

Having finished eating we paid the bill and made our way over to a huge nearby cave, where I filmed while Burglar backed tentatively into the cave as if he was expecting to find bears in there. We mucked around there for a little while longer and then headed towards Cape Reinga.

Cape Reinga has great spiritual significance for Maori as the departing place of souls (Te Rerenga Wairua) on their journey to the homeland, Hawaiki. Te Reinga means *the leaping place of spirits.*

The Cape Reinga lighthouse is where tourists tend to visit, even though North Cape is further north, because Reinga is easier to get to. There are always busloads of tourists there. The lighthouse sits about 290 m above the sea and has a great viewing area which is perfect for photography.

As we approached the lighthouse I could see that there were large numbers of tourists there. They were all watching us and I began to get that familiar feeling that something was about to happen. The cape is where the Tasman Sea meets the Pacific Ocean. As we rounded the Cape it became very obvious that the two seas don't like each other. The seas also become very shallow at the Cape, which just makes thing worse. What we saw ahead of us was like a nightmare. Closer to the Cape the sea was a turmoil of breaking 6 m surf. It was almost totally white water for a kilometre, with occasional patches of deep blue showing as the water churned. Further out, towering 6 m waves marched in formation towards us at high speed. They were almost vertical and occasionally some were breaking. The wind had increased up to a howling 40 km/hr. Burglar and I looked at each other and mouthed the word "gosh" (or something like that) at the same time. Meanwhile, up at the lighthouse I could imagine all of the tourists falling over themselves to get photos that they were sure would be sought after by the press once we had disappeared.

Quite frankly I haven't been that frightened since I narrowly avoided crashing an aeroplane into a hill in Papua New Guinea in 1982. That was a short-lived fear though, fixed by a change of underwear and a beer. This nightmare seemed to go on forever.

There was no discussion about whether or not to continue on. We just did it. We moved closer together in order to support each other in case of falling off, and rode into battle. The waves were fearsomely big and riding up the front of them seemed to take an eternity. As we would crest a wave it would suddenly disappear from beneath us and we would drop around 2 to 3 m through thin air with our machines at a 70° angle to the horizontal. The back end of the Seadoos would hit the water making a loud plunking sound and then we would be off again up the face of the next wave. Sometimes the Seadoos would get a bit off centre if the top of the wave was uneven and they would still come down on the 70° angle, but leaning 30° left or right. Although this made it physically exhausting to hold on, the Seadoos were amazing at handling these conditions. No matter which way they came down, they would always right themselves and plow out in the right direction.

We never fell off the Seadoos throughout these harsh conditions, but I sure came close a few times. On one occasion I was washed almost completely off my Seadoo, but managed to still hold on to the handle bars. My lower body was dragging through the water on the left side of the machine. It took an extreme effort to pull myself back up onto the side while still moving forward at a good pace. I managed it a split second before the next wave hit, very nearly getting wiped off again. I was grateful for all the time spent weight training in the gym; it was certainly paying off now.

We took an hour to cover the 7 km from Cape Reinga to Cape Maria van Diemen. Rounding Cape Maria we slowly got further out to sea. The deeper water meant that the 6 m waves dropped to 4 m and were generally, but not always, less steep. The wind continued its assault on us at a steady 40 km/hr. We had about 90 km to go to Ahipara from here and we set ourselves to the task. There was no chance of rest as we would be wiped out if we stopped, so we continued on. It is amazing what the human body can endure. We certainly found new levels of endurance we didn't know we had. We were continuously taking spine crushing impacts from falling off the back of waves. This was so continuous that the insides of my shoes started to compress out of shape from the impacts. Frequently we would be blinded by spray as we were falling off the back of a huge wave and we would fall blind, not knowing when, or how, we would hit the water below. Thank God for the helmets, as my helmet saved me a few times from a broken jaw when my face slammed down onto the controls in front of me. One time, in spite of the helmet, I hit my head so hard that I suddenly remembered what I was in my last life, (it's a secret)and later found that I could recite *pi* to 1,323 decimal places.

We were now tracking southwards parallel to Ninety Mile Beach. Ninety Mile Beach is not ninety miles long. Whoever named it that was stretching the truth a tad. Maybe they wanted the American tourists to think they were getting their moneys worth.

Its about 90 km, or 55 miles long, but its certainly worth seeing. It is a vast arch of fine white sand backed by immense dunes, broken by rocky outcrops and shallow streams.

The sand dunes along the beach go inland as far as 6 km and, in some places, are as high as 150 m. The sand hills are the highest at the northern end, and gradually decrease in height at the southern end, where they are about 60 m high. On the eastern fringe of the dunes is a series of lakes, which are used for various water sports. The whole area is a bit of an adventure playground.

As you approach Ahipara from the north, the beach curves towards the west. We didn't want to waste more fuel by following the coast exactly, so we wanted to track direct to Shipwreck Bay at Ahipara. The GPS was on a 'rostered afternoon off' and refused to work, so I had to set a heading for Shipwreck by keeping a set distance off the coast. Our pace was so slow that it seemed we weren't moving relative to landmarks on the beach and Whakatehaua Island took about an hour to go past.

We ploughed on oblivious to the other dramas playing out on land. At 3pm while we were still 40 km short of Ahipara, Pete, Chinashop and Phil and Zella Briars had worked out that we would be out of fuel by now. I never asked how they worked it out, but I suppose it would have involved the Pythagorean Theorem, the specific gravity of fuel, Archimedes Principle and the standard deviation of the Dow Jones Industrial Index. Whatever…we are getting way too technical here and I don't want you falling asleep, so we'll move on.

So they worked out we were out of gas and decided to run in the Sorento at high speed up *fifty-five* mile beach looking for wreckage. Their concern was heightened as they saw the sea conditions and everyone feared the worst. They asked a local Maori fisherman if he had seen us. His response was to say, "If they are out in that that's very serious. It's not good at all". To make matters worse, because we were outside the coverage of Hereiam's GPS tracking system, we disappeared off that at Cape Reinga. People following our progress, such as my family and the long suffering Colin Bower, (who was hunting through his records for my funeral song), were having kittens as, first we disappeared, and then they tracked the Sorento screaming up fifty-five mile beach, obviously on a rescue mission.

Meanwhile, back at the coal face it was 4.30pm and we were within 15 km of Shipwreck Bay. Burglar was running low on fuel and every now and then came alongside, gesticulating wildly and mouthing "fuel". There was nothing for it but to continue on. We couldn't beach the Seadoos because the surf would have been a good 4 m and we would have been history, so I kept pointing towards Shipwreck and plowed on.

Finally we made it to within 3 km of Shipwreck with nothing but vapour in our fuel tanks, and the satisfaction of disproving one of Pythagoras' constants. We phoned the team on our Vodafone mobile to get guidance as to the retrieval point. It was a very relieved and weary pair of Burglar Brothers who arrived at Shipwreck Bay at 5.15pm and shook hands with an equally relieved ground crew team. Zella Briars had bottles of water for us which were like gold, as we had run out of Raro some hours earlier.

I had just come out of the water when sports commentator Peter Montgomery phoned for a radio interview. I remember doing this interview totally wasted and crouched down behind the Sorento to shelter from the wind. We had been on the Seadoos for ten hours twenty-two minutes, and had covered 285 km. The last 90 km had taken five hours.

Once the Seadoos were on the trailer we headed to the Ahipara Motor Camp. The camp is rustic, but clean, and the owners were once again very helpful and provided the accommodation for free.

We had a few beers and a feed and a post mortem, then retired gracefully and early to bed totally exhausted and mentally shattered.

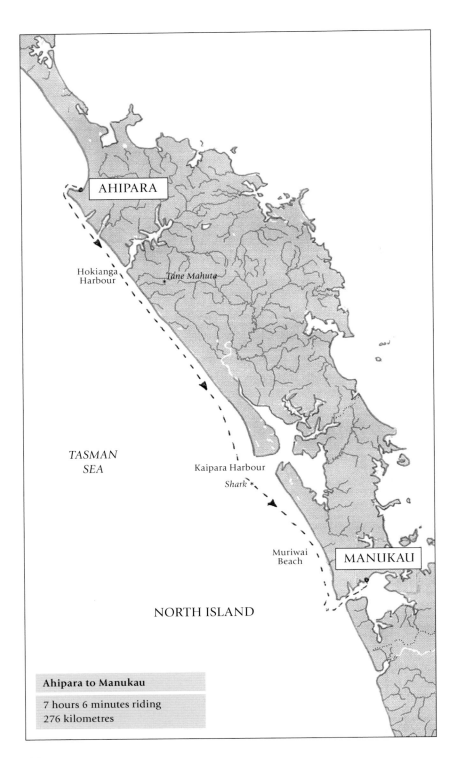

AHIPARA

Hokianga
Harbour

Tāne Mahuta

TASMAN
SEA

Kaipara Harbour

Shark *

Muriwai
Beach

MANUKAU

NORTH ISLAND

Ahipara to Manukau

7 hours 6 minutes riding
276 kilometres

Chapter 6
The Ride: To Manukau

Tuesday 7th February 2006

We woke early again as we were expecting another long, hard day. The weather forecast for our ride down the west coast to Auckland's Manukau Harbour had not been the best and we were dreading going out in similar conditions to the day before. I couldn't eat anything and I could see Burglar was struggling as well. Mentally we were shattered and we would have rather been anywhere else other than in Ahipara, getting ready to do it again.

Prior to the event we had pictured ourselves having a nice scenic ride around New Zealand with a majority of good weather. February is known for its good weather and that's why we chose to programme the ride for then. We also had the impression that every night would be quite social with a few beers and a chat, but that wasn't happening either, as we were too exhausted to stay up and were hitting the sack straight after dinner.

The ride from Russell to Ahipara had been a bit of a shock to our systems and now, rather than being optimistic about the rest of the ride, we were quietly dreading it. I've always tended to not expect too much from anything, because I find that it's less disappointing if it doesn't turn out well. I was definitely in that mode now.

As the days went by on the ride we found that the weather was rarely as forecast. Whenever we thought we were going to have a good day the weather would turn crappy and we would have a bad day and, in most cases, when we psyched ourselves up for a bad ride in bad weather, the weather would be better than forecast and we would have a good day.

And so it turned out on this day. As we made our way back down to Shipwreck Bay to launch we could see that there was no wind and the sea was dead flat. It is astounding how quickly the sea conditions can change from one day to the next in New Zealand. They can go from okay to completely nasty in the space of an hour, which is why boating around New Zealand can be so dangerous.

While our crew was getting ready to launch, Burglar approached me for a quiet chat.

There is nothing more sacred to a burglar than jewels, and there is nothing more sacred to Burglar than the Burton Family Jewels. Burglar informed me that he had a painful left gonad. I asked him if the other one was sore, because if they were both sore this could be explained away by the fact that we had been away from home for a while. It wasn't. I asked him if the left one was still actually there and he informed me it was. I then told him that he must have sat on it sometime the day before and, given the conditions that we were riding in, he was bloody lucky that it hadn't been rammed back up behind his shoulder blades from whence it had come some twenty-something years ago. I gave him the 3B cream and refused his request to apply the cream for him, telling him that our friendship hadn't quite developed to that point yet.

With spirits slightly improved we headed north-west from Shipwreck Bay in very good conditions. As we rounded Tauroa Pt and changed direction to the south-east, to head down the Kauri Coast, we encountered the leftover swell from the day before. This was coming from the south at about 2 m, so we were pretty-much head on into it but we were pleased that, apart from the swell, the sea condition was otherwise smooth. I call this sea condition the *bouncer,* because you get airborne off every wave and either land in the following trough, or on the face of the next wave. After a while it can be pretty annoying continually bracing for the landing impact. Eight hours of it is boring enough to give you brain damage on its own. Fortunately the scenery down the Kauri Coast is spectacular and we distracted ourselves from the bashing by admiring the coastline. The hills are steep and quite high in this area and every now and then a stunning inlet opens up between them, leading into an equally impressive harbour. The weather was fine, the sun was up and there was even a bit of mist snaking down the valleys on the hills. All this beauty is quite overwhelming and seeing it from the ocean you can't help but think how lucky we are in New Zealand. There is such a variety of magnificent scenery to be explored.

We continued on and soon the towering sand hills at the northern head of the Hokianga Harbour came into view. The bleached sand hills tower up to 170 m high in places and are a favourite spot for sand tobogganing. The Hokianga Harbour is quite an impressive harbour, extending more than 30 km inland. It has had an interesting history.

In 1837 an eccentric Frenchman called Charles Phillipe Hippolyte de Thierry arrived in Hokianga Harbour with a group of colonists and proclaimed himself Sovereign Chief of New Zealand. He was ridiculed and deserted by his followers; probably more because of his name than his ambitions; but both Maori and English were worried about French colonising ambitions. He was later talked out of his ambitious scheme with a bribe of some land near Hokianga. And ever since then the French approach to diplomacy with New Zealand has continued in a similarly dubious fashion (see the Chapter 5 reference to the Rainbow Warrior). On the southern shore of Hokianga Harbour is the town of Opononi. Opononi became world famous in the summer of 1955-56 when a playful dolphin swam with children and gave them rides on her back. Named Opo, she was to have been given protection by law, but died in mysterious circumstances before this came into force. She was memorialised by writers and artists, and there is a sculpture at her grave.

Ten kilometres further on is the Waipoua Forest. In this forest is the giant kauri tree *Tane Mahuta* (translated as *Lord of the Forest)*, which is one-thousand-two-hundred years old and stands 52 m tall. It has a girth of 13 m. It's sobering to think how the world has changed since *Tane Mahuta* started growing. The whole of the Kauri Coast is of historic importance to New Zealand and there is a very impressive museum at Matakohe, south-east of Dargaville, which commemorates both the kauri industry and the early white settlers.

Further south, as the scenery slowly became less spectacular, I found my mind wandering and thinking about some of the things I had been through in my life to get to this point.

A name that usually springs to mind when I look back on some of the people that shaped my life is that of Norman Burns. Norman Burns was the ultimate bullshit artist and conman and to this day he serves the purpose of defining that end of the integrity scale for me. Norman doesn't occupy that space all on his own, but he is definitely the benchmark.

When myself and Bruce Bartlett left the New Zealand Air Force and went to Sydney to study aviation related subjects and look for flying jobs we needed part-time employment so we answered an advert for taxi drivers, which necessitated attending the *Taxi Training Centre for Sydney*. It was run by Norman Burns. Norman was about fifty, with curly dyed hair and more jewelry than Liberace .The whole taxi training centre was a scam. The instructor was a big dumb Swiss bloke called Lucien who couldn't speak English; then again, most of the trainees couldn't either. Norman was a master at changing the subject to avoid the issue. One of his favourite methods was to start talking about his hemorrhoids, which was a prize conversation stopper. The Burns 'rhoids were apparently plentiful, colourful and thriving and, over the course of our conversations, they developed a full personality of their own.

When we complained to Norman about Lucien's English he informed us that Lucien's brother was a general in the Swiss Army, which I suppose made everything okay. We complained about other deficiencies. Norman would point to a Justice of the Peace certificate on the wall and ask how we could accuse him of dishonesty, and then immediately start to tell us about how he could get three cups of tea from one teabag.

Norman organised our license medicals. We had to pay Norman AU$10 and then he sent us down the road to his mate Dr Fox. Dr Fox invited us in, enquired as to our health and then, after we paid him another AU$40, he signed us off.

I always get a laugh when I think about Norman and, as I rode, I found myself snickering quietly to myself and feeling better as a result. Incidentally, I did end up driving taxis in Sydney for a while. I would have to say that this was a developmental experience for me. You pretty much get to see and experience it all and it leaves you with a new found maturity and a slight nervous twitch that strangers find quite off-putting.

As we passed the Kaiiwi Lakes and the Maunganui Bluff the sea conditions improved even more as the swell became more westerly, so that the bashing stopped and we were able to make better progress.

We encountered a baby Killer Whale just off Ripiro Beach, which appeared to be on its own. This was our first real wildlife encounter and it helped lift our spirits even more.

It had turned into a magnificent day and we decided to stop just north of the Kaipara Harbour's North Head for a lunch of rice, apple and snickers again. With the sun shining, and almost no wind, we enjoyed our break immensely.

The Kaipara Harbour is the largest harbour in the Southern

Hemisphere, with over 800 kms of coastline. Its waters have provided sustenance and shelter, as well as being the predominant trading route north and south, since the Maori arrived in the fourteenth century. The first European traders in sailing ships entered the harbour around 1838 to serve the mission stations and to trade for timber. From this time an increasing trade in timber, and later gum, led to an influx of shipping that, at one point, made this harbour the busiest in the country. At the height of the timber trade as many as twenty-six ships left the harbour on one tide in the course of a day, all carrying timber from mills around the shores of the harbour. Of the thousands of ships that came in and out of the entrance, at least forty-five were wrecked, the remains of them showing up in the shifting sands from time to time.

After lunch we charged on to the mouth of the Kaipara. I had seen the Kaipara Harbour entrance many times from the air and it always looks spectacular and dangerous. There are sand bars everywhere and huge tidal rips as tall as houses extend for kilometres. For as far as we could see, there were large breaking waves with seemingly no way through. The alternative to going through this area was to take a huge diversion out to sea of about 15 km to go around it all. This was an option we weren't keen on and, given our confidence in the maneuverability of the Seadoos, we decided to try and find a way through. In the end it wasn't really that bad. We ran between the breaking waves and, as we were forced closer in we would look for a way of edging out again by finding gaps in the waves. After we got used to it we actually started to quite enjoy the challenge.

We had made arrangements that my wife, Manola, and son, Dean, would fly out with one of my flying mates, Vern Reynolds, in his Cessna, and film and photograph us from the air. Because we had made such good progress I was concerned that they would head too far north in their search for us and miss us completely, but they had checked our position with the Hereiam website and came straight to us just off Kaipara Harbour. It was great to have company and we put on a good show, jumping waves and generally hooning along at a great pace.

When we had made it past the Kaipara Heads we set a heading for Rangitira beach, with our air support still circling above us. It was then that I saw the shark. The shark was slowly making its way along on the surface and I couldn't help but be inquisitive, so I signaled to Burglar to come and have a look. The shark was huge. Its fin stuck out of the water a good half metre. We got to within about 10 m of it and watched with our fingers ready on the throttles. The shark circled slowly and I imagine it was thinking, "If these guys come a metre closer, or lose concentration for just one second, I'm having burglar burgers for lunch". Eventually the shark started to turn towards us and I said to Burglar, "Lets get out of here, Mate. What do you say?" Our departure was a bit like a fire drill in a lunatic asylum and, in our haste, we turned into each other and had a mini collision. Just at that exact moment the plane flew over and photographed the whole thing. It's an impressive photo. We showed it to a Kaipara Harbour fisherman and he said that he reckoned it was a great white shark. Great whites are apparently quite common in this area. I can imagine the conversation in the plane at the time too. Vern and Dean would have been willing us to get away and my wife, Manola, knowing my insurance policy was up to date, would definitely have been rooting for the shark.

We made our way further south and waved goodbye to the plane as they waggled their wings and disappeared towards the south-east and Auckland's Dairy Flat Aerodrome. We could see Muriwai Beach thirty minutes in the distance, so we made our way in close to the shore. The underlying 2 m swell was still there and, with the calm conditions, the surf near the beach was predictable and awesome. We rode along, playing chicken with the waves; waiting until they would almost break on us before riding up the sides of the steep faces on an angle and then dropping over the back. This was quite exhilarating and some of the best riding fun we had on the whole trip.

After passing Muriwai, the spectacular Waitakere Regional Park loomed above us as we rode. We made our way past Bethells Beach, Lion Rock and Karekare. Approaching Whatipu we saw that the Manukau harbour entrance was going to be as difficult to negotiate as the Kaipara had been, so we diverted out to sea about 5 km to clear the worst of it. The safest path in then became fairly obvious and we entered Manukau Harbour with a sigh of relief. The water in the harbour was flat calm, so we had a high speed ride up the harbour to Titirangi's Jenkins Bay ramp where our support was waiting.

We saw the Sorento on the beach with people around it, so we screamed in at maximum speed. We were quite close now and I made a spectacular arrival running my Seadoo up on to the smooth slippery rock right near the Sorento and jumping off while the Seadoo was still sliding; running the last few metres to the Sorento with the Seadoo nipping at my heals. Phil Briars reckoned I had stuffed it up and misjudged my speed and the depth of the water. I told him it was all planned and I was just entertaining the sponsors. Don't tell Phil, but he was right. Fortunately there was no damage to the Seadoo.

David Libeau and Kathy Gera from Qantas had come down to welcome us in, and David showed his superb situational awareness by turning up with a box of cold Crown Lagers. We all stood around on the beach and told shark stories and *Burglar Brother's Getaways* stories, while toasting a very successful day. We had ridden for seven hours and six minutes, covering a distance of 276 km. When there was no more beer to drink we drove across Auckland to my home for our overnight stay. Battling Auckland's traffic was by far the most painful experience of the day.

Time and tide wait for no man. Telling one too many war stories at Jenkins Bay, Manukau Harbour.

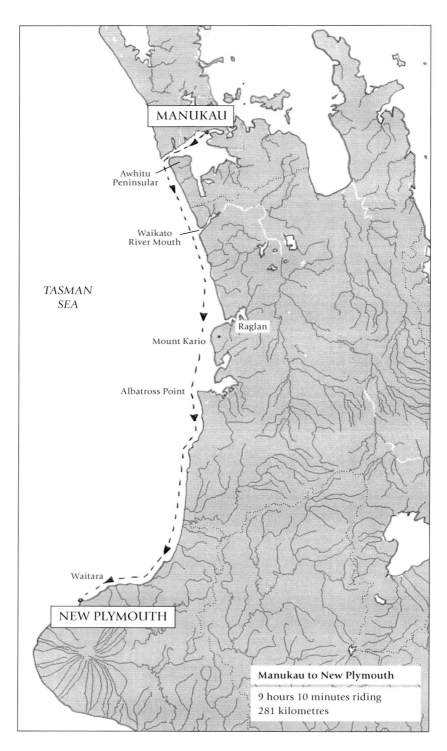

MANUKAU

Awhitu
Peninsular

Waikato
River Mouth

TASMAN
SEA

Mount Kario

Raglan

Albatross Point

Waitara

NEW PLYMOUTH

Manukau to New Plymouth

9 hours 10 minutes riding
281 kilometres

Chapter 7
The Ride:
To New Plymouth

Wednesday 8th February 2006

The alarm was not a welcome sound and I wanted to ignore it, but self discipline took over and I rolled out of bed. I made a cup of coffee and sat there vacantly staring into space trying to work up an interest in getting the crap beaten out of me for another day, but the mood wouldn't take me. The weather forecast for today's ride to New Plymouth wasn't good, with 40 km/hr northerly winds and heavy rain south of Raglan. I struggled through breakfast yet again. My body didn't seem interested in food.

I don't want to sound like I'm complaining at all, but we had ridden twenty-four hours in the last three days and our bodies were showing signs of wear and tear. My insides were all shaken up and I felt like I had had a random organ redistribution. At that point it wouldn't have surprised me if my kidneys were beating and my heart was filtering last night's beer, and trying to coordinate with my liver which had shifted into my head to fill the space recently vacated by my brain. My brain having no where else to go would have relocated to my butt, thus setting me up for continuous mild concussions every time I sat down or passed a medium strength, or greater, fart.

We had organised to meet some of our team at Onehunga

Wharf at 6.30am, but we fluffed around trying to avoid the inevitable and ended up getting caught in Auckland's traffic. The good thing about being stuck in Auckland traffic is that just about anything else seems quite appealing in comparison, even ten hours on a Seadoo. Politicians have dithered on the traffic problem for years, citing cost as one of the major issues. The real issue is dithering politicians. Obviously no-one has factored in the economic cost of all those people sitting idle, burning gas and polluting the atmosphere.

We eventually made it to Onehunga half an hour late and launched with subdued levels of enthusiasm. We put in at the Manukau Cruising Club and had an excellent ride down Manukau Harbour to the Manukau entrance. We were pleased to see that the entrance was relatively calm and that there would be no problem getting out.

An interesting fact about the Manukau Harbour is that the Waikato River used to run out into it. About three million years ago; even before Colin Bower was born; lava flows erupting from the Pukekohe-Bombay area diverted the river to the west, and its current outlet at Port Waikato.

Six local riders had put into the water at Waiuku where the Waikato River used to run through and were going to ride with us as far as Port Waikato. This was a bonus. Company was much appreciated on our rides, as it helped make the whole event more interesting.

We had a radio interview organised with Paul Holmes for 7.50am, so we stopped just outside the Harbour for the call on the satellite phone. We waited for a good ten minutes and then I checked the phone to see how the reception was, only to find that the satellite coverage was very low and they probably couldn't reach us. This turned out to be the case and Holmes was pretty dark about the whole thing, but he had stuffed up and missed our previous interview the Friday before we left, so although it was disappointing from a coverage point of view it was declared a draw as far as incompetence goes. I put the phone away in its waterproof container and we headed on south.

We rode alongside the spectacular Awhitu Peninsula, where the strong, predominantly westerly winds have drifted sand dunes up to a present height of around 300 m.

We had a slight *slap in the face* following sea as we rode on enjoying the interaction with our new companions. Sadly, the Waikato River came up far too soon. We waved them off and continued on.

The visibility was still pretty good and I could see a large symmetrical mountain further down the coast. It looked just like Mt Taranaki, which is just behind our destination New Plymouth. My spirits lifted. If you can see your destination it sure helps and it didn't look that far away, either. It's amazing the tricks the brain can play on you. I wanted New Plymouth to be close so I assumed that the mountain was Mt Taranaki, but all logic should have told me that it wasn't. We still had about 200 km to go. I discussed it with Burglar who asked me what I had been smoking and said it couldn't possibly be our destination. A quick check of the map showed that it was the 756 m high extinct volcano, Mt Karioi at Pirongia just south of the surfing *Mecca* of Raglan. Mt Karioi dominates the coastal town and is said to be almost hypnotic. I am forced to agree.

I rode on slightly deflated and considered how good life would be if distances were shorter. Think of the time and money that would be saved. I might write a letter to the Act party asking them to consider adding to their election manifesto that, if elected to power, they will immediately legislate to make distances shorter. They'll get my vote.

Raglan is a summer marine resort that serves the nearby city of Hamilton. It is world renown for its black volcanic sand and famous left hand surf break at Manu Bay. It is said to have a laid back bohemian lifestyle and has become the place to be seen and a lifestyle for the famous, infamous and the downright trendies.

I haven't been there, but having read that description I see that I have no choice but to go there, and soon.

My GPS was feeling seasick by the time we made Raglan and was refusing to work, so we had resigned ourselves to manual navigation for the rest of the day. We set our heading from Woody Head, direct to Albatross Point 30 km to the south. This put us about 8 km off the coast. By now the wind was rising and the seas were getting bigger. It was hard to avoid the inevitable bucket of cold water in the face once every thirty seconds or so. We charged on and I noticed that the sky over Albatross Point was black, with heavy rain approaching. I told Burglar we had better get to the point before the rain or we would get lost in the reducing visibility. Without the GPS we needed to be in sight of land at all times. We went hard and just made it to the point as the storm hit. It was like being in a nightmare. The wind strengthened to 45 km/hr and the rain was pelting down. Daytime turned to almost night conditions and as the visibility reduced to about 200 m, we were forced to remove our goggles. With conditions so dark it was difficult to see with the goggles on. This increased the danger of eye damage from being hit in the face by water. The seas increased in size to about 2 m from the north-west and became very untidy and hard to handle. At times the whole surface of the sea was white with foam for as far as we could see.

I was starting to wish I was back in Auckland's traffic, with all the pleasures that that implies. I reminded myself that I was married with three children and asked myself what I was doing here. And all the time the conditions just kept getting worse, until we were both asking ourselves if there was some alternative to this. There wasn't. There was no where to go but on. We ploughed on unable to stop to eat, unable to identify where we were, and taking an absolutely harsh physical pounding.

Having very low visibility made life even more difficult, as we had to stick close to the coast or risk getting disoriented. This added all sorts of extra problems like submerged, or semi-submerged rocks, and sea conditions that were all over the place like a dog's breakfast, as the driving swell hit the coast and bounced back towards the incoming swell. On top of this, as we followed the coast south, we would periodically come across a headland and be forced to head westward into the oncoming sea and rain to get around it.

We battled on for some hours in these conditions. At one stage I lost concentration for a moment and rode down the face of a wave too fast, plowing into the back of the preceding wave and causing the Seadoo to become completely submerged. The force of the impact wiped me off into the water and I found myself swimming for all I was worth to get back to the Seadoo before it was washed away by the following wave. It was comforting to see Burglar hovering nearby. Our system of watching and supporting was working well.

As we reached Mokau visibility improved and, although the sea was still very rough, we were at least able to enjoy the magnificent scenery. The hills were beautiful and green and all along the coast huge waterfalls fell into the sea. There was more time to reflect on things and it was inevitable that the question of why are we doing this should arise. I thought about this for a while and in the end it was very simple. Brad and I are not quitters and there were also a lot of people and companies that had invested in this event and we didn't want to let them down. But the most important reason from my point of view was that my son Douglas' class at Torbay School had started a project following our progress and the whole school had got involved. There was a map of New Zealand in the foyer and our progress was updated everyday. There was no way I wanted to let them down. It was important that we showed the kids that you don't quit when the going gets tough. You finish what you started.

The coast was starting to curve slowly around towards the west now and the seas were more side on. If the GPS had have been working we would have tracked direct to New Plymouth, which would have saved us about 40 km, but as it was we were stuck following the coast. We had been going for seven hours without food and our only sustenance had been the Raro drink (I'll take both the Porche and the townhouse now thanks).We felt and looked like drowned rats and exhaustion was setting in.

My arms had lost all their feeling and were tingling like pins and needles. Because of this, I was unable to stand for great lengths of time because, without the feeling in my arms, I was unable to maintain balance properly. This problem would continue to get worse throughout the trip. Having to sit down for long periods raised the problem of wear and tear on the butt. This is a very unpleasant thing which is, *on the whole*, not good.

Butt wear and tear was to become a major issue involving much planning and nursing, and litres of Vaseline on top of the good old 3B cream. As we would compensate for wear in one patch, another would develop somewhere else. I got very good at weight shifting and springing up from a sitting position to avoid a large impact.

Another issue was that my index finger, which I used to work the throttle, had failed. It just refused to follow instructions from the brain, as if there was no longer a connection, so I had started to use the middle finger. I calculated that at that rate I would be out of fingers about two thirds of the way around and would finish undeterred and in grand style using my nose to operate the throttle. Burglar was also feeling the pain, but thankfully his severe testicular trauma had abated.

As we approached Waitara we turned towards the north-west for a while and had to ride into the swells. This was soul destroying and Waitara seemed to take forever to reach. But reach it we did (or I wouldn't be talking to you now) and we then headed south-west again towards New Plymouth, which we could now see in the distance. True to form, *lead-foot* Burglar was running out of petrol once more and was starting to get that *I'm being attacked by bees* look again. As we approached New Plymouth the cloud cleared and we got an awesome and welcome view of the splendid Mt Taranaki in the distance. A few local riders came out to meet us and we arrived in Port Taranaki relieved and feeling very old. We did a few interviews and photo ops then Chinashop and Pete dropped us at the Top 10 Holiday Park and went off to get the Hereiam trackers fixed. Burglar and I were famished, so we ordered a large pizza each and sat in the spa eating pizza and drinking coke. It was all very decadent and enjoyable and, what made it even better was that we knew we deserved it.

It had been a big day of nine hours and ten minutes riding, covering 281 km.

At 6.30 pm Chinashop and Pete were still out, so we walked back to our rooms totally exhausted, threw our clothes on the bed and fell asleep draped over the clothes horse.

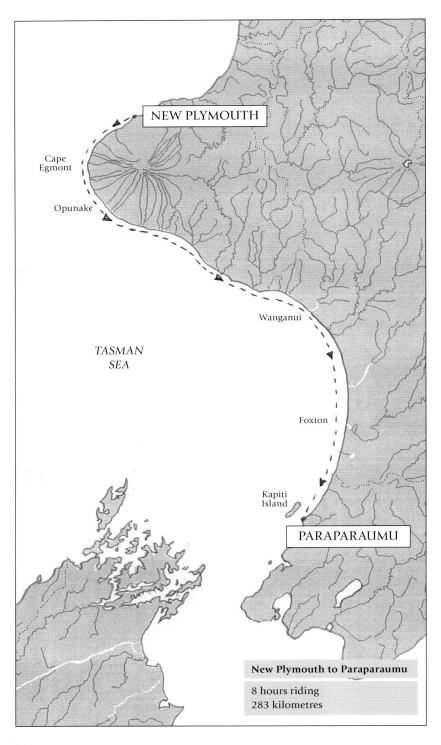

NEW PLYMOUTH

Cape
Egmont

Opunake

Wanganui

TASMAN
SEA

Foxton

Kapiti
Island

PARAPARAUMU

New Plymouth to Paraparaumu

8 hours riding
283 kilometres

Chapter 8
The Ride: To Paraparaumu

Thursday 9th February 2006

I am not a morning person and for a while, after yet another rude awakening, I couldn't work out where I was or, for that matter, who I was. My entire body was still sore from the previous day. My butt was still very sore after the extra wear from the day before and I understood what it must feel like to be the new boy in a prison. To make matters worse I had developed a rash all over my back that was both itchy and sore. It was caused by the continued rubbing of the wet wetsuit rubber on my sensitive bare skin.

We walked like zombies across to the camp kitchen to see what culinary delights Chinashop had conjured up for us. As usual it was very impressive, but we still couldn't get interested and, apart from pizza, we hadn't eaten much food in days. This was a little worrying, as we still had a long way to go and we had to remain disciplined about how we took care of our bodies. We managed to stuff a couple of scones in each and then went back to the room to start the ritual of preparing gear and putting our wet gear on our already sore and damaged bodies. I wasn't taking any chances today. I had inserted a couple of litres of Vaseline into my sensitive areas and was wearing two pairs of bicycling pants with an extra pair of thick shorts over the top. I am sure the fashion police are still looking for me now, with a view to locking me up and throwing away the key.

While sorting all the gear I made an annoying discovery. We had been given a waterproof container for the satellite phone, but somehow in the mayhem of yesterday's ride water had got into the container and completely destroyed the phone. There was water behind the glass faceplate of the phone. Burglar made the observation that we could still use it, but only as a spirit level. We were relying on the phone as a safety backup, and also as a means for doing radio interviews from out of the way places. We would need to replace it, but we decided to wait until we hit Nelson to do so.

When we were ready we were driven down to Port Taranaki, where quite a group of people had gathered to see us off. The Mayor was there wearing all his ceremonial Mayoral *necklaces*. Why was he wearing the jewellery? You ask. I don't know and it doesn't matter anyway, because it looked impressive. We were to meet quite a few Mayors on the trip and they were all different, well intentioned and amusing in their own way. We have come to the conclusion that first and foremost, Mayors are just official meeters and greeters for anyone of importance that comes to town, just like the guy in a top hat and tails that opens the door for you at a posh hotel. I suppose they do other things too, but you don't tend to see the evidence of it unless you read the papers a lot, so for me they will remain the *bloke in the top hat.*

The same jet skiers who met us on the way in the previous day were there again to ride out with us, which was nice. What I didn't tell you the day before was that there had been a large great white shark hanging around just off Port Taranaki and generally annoying people in boats and on PWCs. He was becoming quite a nuisance and his anti-social behaviour had made the national news. We had received various email warnings about the shark, but in our agony the afternoon before we had forgotten all about it. Now we were heading out through his area, so we were determined not to fall off, or go too slow, lest he decide to have a nip at our ankles as we passed by.

When everyone was ready we all headed off together out of the port towards *Shark Central*. As we left the port a rogue wave came at us and we all had to turn and run to get away from it. By the looks on all the faces I could tell that we were all thinking that this would not be a good time to end up in the water. The wave was large and persistent but we eventually managed to slip around the side of it and continue on.

Once clear of the shallows we headed south-west towards Cape Egmont with the magnificent, snow capped 2,518 m Mt Taranaki to our left. Mt Taranaki is a beautiful volcanic cone-shaped mountain that looks somewhat like Japan's Mt Fuji, which is why it was used as a back drop for the film *The Last Samurai*. The last evidence of volcanic activity on Mt Taranaki was about two-hundred-and-thirty years ago which, in the grand scheme of things, is fairly recent. The mountain is a source for more than fifty rivers and streams, and is a favourite of hikers and climbers.

As we rode along a tidy 3 m north-westerly swell was coming at us from our right hand side. As it reached the shallows the waves would steepen and rise to about 4 m in height. Sometimes they would break. We had to stay on our toes, as every now and then a larger wave would rear up right next to us and threaten to crash down on top of us. We played chicken with these waves around to Cape Egmont, staying just close enough to the coast to keep the track miles down, but just far enough off the coast to avoid the waves.

We rounded Cape Egmont and started to head south-east past Opunake and Manaia.

Slowly the conditions improved as the large swells came around on to our tail and the sea became generally smoother. We were now almost surfing. The swells were now large, gently sloping walls of water that seemed to be moving at a very high speed. We were traveling at about 65 km/hr, and were struggling to keep up with them. We would slowly climb up the back of a swell and then zoom down the other side before starting the whole cycle again. It was quite good fun and we knew we were covering good ground.

My spirits were lifted considerably and I started thinking about what it was that was so attractive about being out on the ocean zooming along on a high powered machine. Eventually I decided that it was because there isn't much out there to bother you. Sure there's the odd man-eating shark, but there are dogs that live near me that have looked far more likely to bite my leg off than a shark ever has. And there is bugger all chance of catching bird flu out here and...... there are no Jehovah's Witnesses (mainly because no one would lend them a jet ski, and they would get their suits wet anyway).

We had made great time and were about thirty minutes out of Wanganui, where Pete and Chinashop were waiting to refuel us.

Do you ever get a sudden urge for junk food at really weird times? I did right now as my *Grease-low-level light* came on in my brain. Call me sick and depraved. Call me any thing you like (except late for dinner), but all of a sudden I had an unexplainable desire to eat a McDonalds Big Mac meal. I frantically waved Burglar down and we both agreed that it would be a fine idea to ring the boys and pre-order our grease fix for our imminent arrival in Wanganui. After all, we hadn't been eating much and we figured if we felt like eating something then we had better do it, in spite of the fact that we would be reducing our lives by a couple of weeks.

I phoned Pete and he was very receptive to our plan. I amused myself for the next half hour alternately dreaming first about the Big Mac, and then about the imaginary nightmare that Pete was going through driving for miles to find a Maccas and then queuing up behind twenty loud American tourists so wide that he couldn't see the menu around them. The one in front of him, with vital statistics of 36-24-36, and the other leg exactly the same, would step backwards onto his foot causing permanent damage. Another would unknowingly rest her 48F-cup breasts on his head from behind (he is only a little guy). All the while, as he waited in line he would be checking his watch to see if there would be time to have a play in the McDonalds playground, and once he made the front of the line he would have to deal with a pimply faced boy who looked like he had been eating all the profits and whose hygiene levels were less than exemplary. On the way out he would nearly get stuck in the door when another, even wider, American tourist came through it at the same time from the other direction. Add to this the fact that a statue of Ronald McDonald would have been staring at Pete the whole time, and it is easy to see just how unsettling the whole experience could be. And I want you to know that it would have been just as easy to cast this fantasy with local talent, but I thought that by using Americans I would avoid copyright, trademark, or union complaints from McDonalds.

All good fantasies must come to an end and I was snapped back to reality as Wanganui came into view. We were fairly wary of the Whanganui River bar, as the swells were big and fast moving, but in the end it wasn't a drama, as we easily made it into the river. What greeted us was the ugliest sight that we were to see all trip. As we made our way up the river a few hundred metres through the muddy water we saw evidence of decades of neglect. Rusting wharfs, or parts thereof, broken up hulls of wrecked boats and a mish mash of derelict facilities. There were mud banks dotted around and it was generally quite hazardous getting through it all.

Burglar and I had kayaked the upper Whanganui River in 2003 from Taumaranui to Pipiriki. This is a four to five day trip that is absolutely the best adventure in New Zealand. The river is magnificent and the scenery is out of this world. The campsites on the side of the river are well placed and well set up. I liked it so much that in 2005 I took a group of twenty-three scouts and parents down the river and I plan to go down again in 2007. The most satisfying thing about that expedition was the way that twenty-three inexperienced and under confident people changed over four days. I gave a full briefing each morning before setting out on the days paddle. On the last day everyone turned up for the briefing and I said, "No briefing today. You know what to do". And they did.

The river experience is even further enhanced because the river has a lot of history as a centre of Maori culture and is navigable by small boats for 200 km. The famous *Bridge to Nowhere* is an easy walk from one of the campsites.

The fact that the river is so beautiful upstream makes it all the more disappointing that it's climax is such an anti-climax, and I hope the locals do something about fixing it up sometime soon. It's a disgrace. Another thing they could sort out while they are at it is the spelling of Wanganui and the Whanganui River. I might be showing my ignorance here but I reckon one should be changed.

We made it in through the minefield and tied up the Seadoos before enjoying a good feed of grease that, for once, didn't leave me wondering why I had eaten it. We rested for about half an hour and then headed back out over the river bar and south towards Paraparaumu. Paraparaumu has special significance to me because I spent my school years there on the Kapiti Coast. It was, and still is, a great place for kids to grow up in; with the sea on one side and the bush covered Tararua State Forest Park on the other. I was looking forward to coming home with great anticipation.

We could see Kapiti Island from the time we left Wanganui so our spirits were high.

Kapiti Island is a nature reserve about 5 km off Paraparaumu on the west coast, just north of Wellington. Kapiti is one of the few relatively accessible island nature reserves. A marine reserve spans the gap between the mainland and the island.

Kapiti is the summit of a submerged mountain range created by earthquakes 200 million years ago. At one time, moa and kaka-po wandered the valley that lay between the mountains and the rest of the mainland. Several million years ago, most of this range was inundated by rising sea levels. It was, for a time, part of a land bridge that extended across what is now Cook Strait. What remains is an island about 10 km long and 2 km wide, of wind-blasted hillsides to the west and lush temperate rainforests to the sheltered east.

Over the centuries Kapiti has been home to a succession of Maori tribes. Kapiti was the stronghold of the famous Maori chief Te Rauparaha.

We made good time down the coast past Himatangi and Foxton Beach and by the time we passed Otaki Beach we could smell a victory of sorts, because we calculated that we would beat the ground crew to Paraparaumu. From Otaki south the sea chopped up to *boneshaker* status, but we wanted the victory so we went hard. I could see Paraparaumu Beach about 15 km away and I was going as hard as my beaten up body would allow. I knew Burglar was just behind me, or at least I thought I did. I stopped 2 km short of Paraparaumu Beach to let him catch up so that we could arrive together. When I looked around he was nowhere to be seen. I couldn't believe it. I rubbed my eyes and looked again, but he just wasn't there. I looked back where I had come from, but couldn't see him. There was nothing for it but to retrace my steps and see if he was back there somewhere. I was tired and sore and when you have nearly 5000 km to ride you don't want to do any back track-ing, so I was pretty annoyed. About 10 km back a spot became visible on the horizon and, eventually, I found the Burglar. He wasn't happy either. His Seadoo was broken and he suspected battery problems. We had connected a lot of extra items to the bat-teries for the trip and we could see that there would be a problem with corrosion and possible shorting of the battery. That's what it later turned out to be, but in the meantime the Seadoo was dead. We decided that I would tow Burglar to Paraparaumu Beach, so I threw him a rope and away we went.

Seadoos are quite heavy and they rely on lots of power to get them up on the plane. We struggled for some time to get up on the plane, but eventually managed to achieve it with the help of a few friendly waves. I was using maximum power to do this and the jet wash coming out the back of my machine was hitting the front of Burglar's machine, as well as Burglar. He had to keep his head down and trust that all was well, as he couldn't see a thing. We made a mental note to take a longer tow rope next time.

We eventually made it to Paraparaumu and the waiting ground crew. We did a couple of newspaper interviews on the beach and then the boys dropped us at our hotel and headed into Boyz Toyz at Porirua where Carl Lampe and his boys confirmed the battery problem and replaced it. That day we spent seven hours and thirty minutes on the Seadoos, and covered 283 km.

Burglar and I showered (even though it wasn't Sunday) and then carried out our daily ritual of phoning home, sponsors, and media connections. This could easily take an hour, as there were frequently up to fifteen messages on our phones. I was suffering from a painful left kidney and had told my wife Manola about it. She had called my new doctor, Andrew Murley. He had told her it was fairly serious and suggested I go and see a doctor. She was adamant that I do so. I explained to her that, with all due respect to Andrew, going to a doctor would not achieve anything, as he would tell me to take it easy which I wasn't going to do and prescribe anti-inflammatories which I already had. I didn't need to pay $60 and waste an hour to find this out. I promised to wear a kidney belt from then on and Manola was happy with that.

Communication duties completed, we walked down to the local Raumati pub with the intention of cooling down my kidney from the inside with *brown anti-inflammatories*. The pub was as dead as a doornail. For a while it was like being in a funeral parlour with a beverage service, but then things improved when a guy who appeared to be the consummate loser (and later proved this beyond reasonable doubt) turned up with his girlfriend of

too many times around the block fame. The two of them fought continuously for at least an hour, broken sporadically by his visits
to the toilet, whereupon the girlfriend would send shy drunken
smiles in Burglar's direction until *loser* returned. Burglar thought
that they were paid entertainment put on by the pub and when we
left he wanted to leave a tip, but I talked him out of it for the sake
of international peace.

The boys were still not back from Porirua so we dined on fish
and chips and went to bed early, but satisfied, and dreaming
of mountain ranges and deserts and other places where there are
no waves.

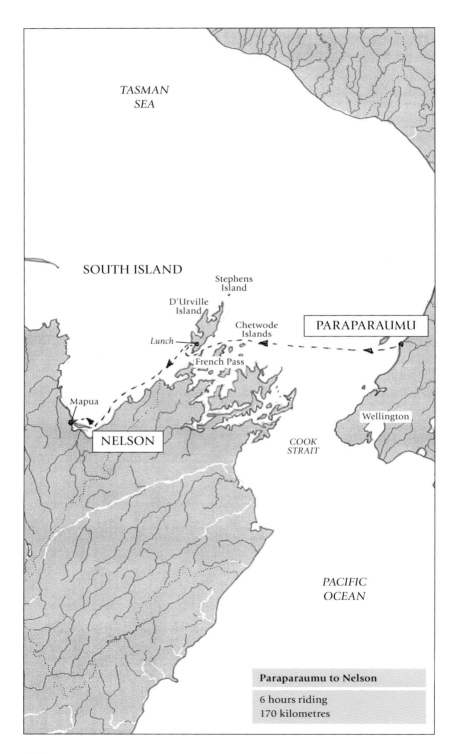

TASMAN
SEA

SOUTH ISLAND

Stephens
Island

D'Urville
Island

Chetwode
Islands

PARAPARAUMU

Lunch

French Pass

Mapua

Wellington

NELSON

COOK
STRAIT

PACIFIC
OCEAN

Paraparaumu to Nelson

6 hours riding
170 kilometres

Chapter 9
The Ride: To Nelson

Friday 10th February 2006

I could hear rain outside and I hoped it wasn't too heavy. Today we would cross Cook Strait and the GPS had proven it was completely useless in anything other than calm conditions. Chinashop had a GPS with him, but it wasn't waterproof so I didn't want to expose it to the joys of Cook Strait and risk destroying that as well as the satellite phone.

This was Day 6 and we were anticipating, and indeed looking forward to, an easy one before our day off in Nelson the next day. Five days of hard riding had taken their toll. My butt was sore and my old knee injury was showing up again. My arms and hands were completely numb, except for a permanent pins and needles-like tingling and some dull pain from my judo wrist injury. I had a huge hole on my left ankle from wear from the boots on the bare skin. It was getting deeper every day and was obviously not happy with being wet all the time. My left kidney was still a bit bruised, but feeling slightly better. Burglar was a bit better off than me, but was worn in spots (read here left nad) and generally sore.

Mentally we were improving. We had started to eat again and had started to get over the mental scarring from our two horror days. The weather forecast was okay and we could see that we had covered quite a distance already, so we were happy but cautious.

We had a good breakfast and then prepared the all important

Raro drink and poured it into the Camelbaks (I'll take the Porsche, the Queenstown townhouse and a 42 ft Riviera moored at Gulf Harbour, thanks). We geared up and jumped into the Sorento for the ride back to Paraparaumu Beach for launching. I did a radio interview from the back of the Sorento on the way there and then another from the beach. As I spoke I looked out to sea in the direction of Kapiti Island and Cook Strait and the rain started to come down hard, reducing visibility to a couple of kilometres. I could see that, without the GPS, this was going to be difficult.

Before we headed off I decided to call Trent from Classic Hits Radio in Nelson. In an interview with him a couple of days before, he had suggested I contact him about coming into the studio for a live interview while in Nelson so I was just calling to confirm this with him. I gave my name and asked for Trent and was put on hold. While on hold with Classic Hits you get to hear what's playing and, as I stood there waiting to talk to him, I heard him say, "Well everyone, I've got that mad bugger Jeremy Burfoot on the line again", and then he proceeded to interview me without warning. It wasn't really a drama as he is a great interviewer, but once I hung up I got to thinking, was I really a mad bugger? Once when I was nineteen and doing my Air Force Navigators course in Christchurch I went on a 30 km run from Wigram around some of the Port Hills and back. On my return I passed the Sunnyside Mental Home. As I passed by, a woman on the other side of the fence lay reclined on a chair in the sun. She yelled out to me, "How far have you run?" I told her about 30 km and she said, "You are maaaaaaad". On reflection she was right and it probably would have been quite appropriate for me to jog back to the main gate, turn myself in, and trade my running shoes for a recliner and a paper cup full of pills.

    With that thought clearly in mind we set out into the murk to cross the infamous Cook Strait in heavy rain and low visibility, and without navigation aids.

Cook Strait is the stretch of water separating the North and South Islands of New Zealand. It connects the South Pacific Ocean and the Tasman Sea through the centre of the New Zealand land mass. It is 20 km wide at it's narrowest, between Cape Terawhiti on the south-east coast of Wellington and Wellington Head near Tory Channel. Since the early years of European settlement, Cook Strait has been notorious for its treacherous currents and high winds, often of gale force. The tidal currents now generated in the strait reach a velocity of about 8 kn westwards and 4 kn eastward, but are very erratic depending on conditions of wind and weather. Wind velocities of up to 220 km/hr have been recorded in the vicinity of Wellington. The strait provides a natural channel for large air masses to accelerate and squeeze through between the North and South Islands.

It is believed that, during the last glaciations, the sea level in Cook Strait dropped about 100 m, thus joining the North and South Islands and forming a great sound in place of the strait. The sound appears to have had its northern end somewhere west of Kapiti Island.

Burglar and I have noticed that place names on the New Zealand coast are both varied, and fascinating. Many were named by and after explorers and many have Maori names. Some place names are just plain bizarre. An example of bizarre is Bonar Knob south of Haast. This must have been named by a frustrated explorer thinking about his good woman waiting at home, who named it after the first thing that popped up. I have a theory that Captain Cook got sick of naming every place after himself and very unselfishly decided to name places after men on his crew. Hence, Banks Peninsula and Young Nick's Head. By the time he reached Cook Strait he would have been well committed to this pattern and we speculate that Cook Strait was in fact named after his cook, and not himself as the history books claim (you heard it here first). This theme also applies to Cape Foulwind, off Westport. It was probably not named for the conditions, but more likely for one of the crew with a keenness for onions, garlic, curried egg and Polish sausage. But I digress.

Getting back to the job in hand, our proposed route from Kapiti Island to the Chetwode Islands 75 km away, would take us almost due west, meaning that we would avoid the narrowest part of the strait and most of the tidal rips. But we hadn't counted on not being able to see the Chetwodes. With the rain and the visibility getting worse by the minute, we headed out to the southern tip of Kapiti Island, narrowly missing a 2 m shark on the way.

From Kapiti we set a heading and noted the angle at which we were approaching the south-westerly swell. We kept attacking the swells at the same angle for sometime, hoping that the swell direction wouldn't change that much as we went further out in the strait. I started my aviation career as an air force navigator, and I found it amusing now that such a basic navigation skill as this would be so important to us. The wave conditions were reasonable and fairly consistent, so we had a bit of confidence in the technique. About half way across the visibility improved and we were able to make out the Chetwode Islands just to the left of the nose. We adjusted our angle to the waves but again the rain came, and we were navigating blind once more. Forty-five minutes further on we were delighted to come into sight of land again, about 500 m off track, off the northern tip of Te Kakaho Island in the Chetwode group. This was a victory for basic navigation and commonsense, and I could see that Burglar was impressed.

We had planned to visit my Aunt and Uncle who live on D'Urville Island for lunch, so the successful crossing had lifted our spirits markedly as we both started to dream about sitting on a nice, comfortable, non-moving seat and drinking countless cups of tea and just relaxing. The ride had definitely focused us on some of the simple pleasures in life.

We still had to go through Admiralty Bay and French Pass to get there though, so we went fairly hard towards the south-west.

In the prevailing winds Admiralty Bay should have been fairly calm, but it wasn't and we were fairly annoyed at getting beaten up yet again. As we approached French Pass the tidal current whipped up quite a chop, slowing us considerably.

The French Pass passage between Admiralty Bay and East Tasman Bay is a combination of churning currents and whirlpools, whipped up by reefs and a tidal flow which can prove treacherous for vessels. The nineteenth century explorer Dumont D'Urville was spun by its tumultuous whirlpools and almost lost his vessel. He didn't have the luxury of a high speed, highly maneuverable vessel like we did and we were able to negotiate the pass without hassle. It was tempting to even go back and have a play in the whirlpools, but the cup of tea was beckoning.

We saw some dolphins just after the pass and I wondered if they were related to the famous dolphin Pelorus Jack who, for twenty years in the early 1900s, accompanied vessels crossing Admiralty Bay. We were in too much of a hurry to stop and ask though and we zoomed around Sauvage Pt on the southern point of D'Urville Island and headed north into the group of bays known as Manuwhakapakapa. Try standing on your head and saying that five times quickly.

Iron Pot Bay is one of the bays in Manuwhakapakapa and, tucked into a bushy sheltered corner of the bay is the home of Pip and Jeanette Aplin. You would have to go a long way to find a more interesting and down to earth couple. Come to think about it, we did go a long way to find them! Jeanette is my Mother's younger sister. She is a well known author. Her most well known book is *The Lighthouse Keeper's Wife*, which is about her life as the wife of a lighthouse keeper on some of New Zealand's most inhospitable islands, including Stephens Island to the north of D'Urville and Dog Island in Foveaux Strait. It's a great read.

Pip is, you guessed it, an ex-lighthouse keeper. He is a qualified builder and handyman and all around good guy. He spends his time building on D'Urville Island, or working for the Department of Conservation on mountain hut building and maintenance around New Zealand. He only stands about 5 ft 6 in tall, but is more of a man than most. His general knowledge of New Zealand is astounding, making him a most interesting person to talk to. He often wears a tee-shirt that says, *The Lighthouse Keeper's Wife's Husband*.

The two of them live in *The House That Pip Built*. It's a small two bedroom house tucked into the bush, but with a view of the bay. The house has running water from a spring, but no power. They have a kerosene fridge and a wood-fired Shacklock 501 stove with a wetback. The walls of the living room have been wallpapered with newspaper articles from the early 1900s. They run a solar powered computer for communication. For food they have a huge veggie garden and there is plenty of fish, venison and pork to be had on the island. Old MacDonald had nothing on these guys; there are animals everywhere. They even have quite a few Kune Kune pigs. Kune Kune pigs are an old breed kept by Maori communities for years, which were rescued from extinction by the Rare Breeds Society about twenty-five years ago. They are hairy, short nosed, extremely good natured and have tassels under their chins.

Seventy metres along the beach is a huge shed full of tools, boats and machines for doing this and that. It would not surprise me to find a heart bypass machine in there somewhere. Attached to the shed is a sleep out for visitors to stay in. It's a pretty idyllic setup.

Burglar and I had visited here before on skis, so we rode confidently straight into the bay.

We parked just off the beach and anchored the Seadoos. There was no sign of movement from the house and for a minute we thought Pip and Jeanette must be away, but then Jeanette appeared along the path and all was well.

We took off all our wet gear and borrowed some dry gear of

Pips, and went into the house for a well earned and welcome cup of tea with pikelets that Jeanette cooked on the cooktop. It was wonderful to just sit and enjoy and chat. When we had arrived Pip had been building on the other side of D'Urville, but he made it back in time for lunch - wild venison steaks. It was fantastic.

Meanwhile, Chinashop and Pete, having dropped us in the water at Paraparaumu, had driven into Wellington. Pete then caught a flight back home courtesy of Qantas and Chinashop brought the Sorento and trailer across Cook Strait on a ferry courtesy of The Interisland Line. His trip across the strait and subsequent drive to Nelson would take a while, so we timed our departure from D'Urville so as to arrive in Nelson at the same time.

We said our goodbyes to Pip and Jeanette at around 2pm and headed south-west towards Nelson. A few kilometres into the journey we saw some quite major rocks sticking out of the water so we went to investigate and found a large hole through one of them. It wasn't as large as Cape Brett's Hole in the Rock, but it was impressive nonetheless so we spent some time zooming back and forward through it and filming each other doing it.

We rode in fairly good conditions down the coast on the eastern side of Tasman Bay, past Croisilles Harbour and then Pepin Island. We saw large numbers of dolphins and rode for a while with some of them. Eventually Nelson came into view and we rode the last 30 km or so at a relaxed pace because we could see that we were early and, clearly, Chinashop would not be there.

The Port of Nelson is not the easiest place to find your way around, but we had been there on our previous ride so there were no complications as we rode directly to our stop point. We were early, so no-one was there to meet us and we lay across the Seadoos and relaxed. Within five minutes though, a large group of people had turned up to congratulate us and it turns out that they had been watching our progress on the Hereiam website and had watched us come into the port. They were very friendly and helpful. Some of them even went and bought a pack of Kentucky Fried Chicken for each of us and refused to accept money for it. It is amazing what you will eat when you are hungry and, in spite of the grease and the ever present threat of bird flu (just ask Chinashop), we got stuck into it with great gusto. The local press came and went and then all our new friends had to go back to work (either that, or they got sick of hearing our war stories) ,and soon we found ourselves alone again. I called home and then David Libeau at Qantas and Phil Briars from the Cancer Society, who was now acting as our liaison man in Auckland. Then I rang Chinashop and found that he was delayed a couple of hours. How many coffee shops can you visit in a day?

Given that we looked like sitting around for another couple of hours we decided that we would continue on to Mapua, 15 km to the west, as that was where we were staying that night and, more importantly, there was a bar next to the boat ramp. We headed out of the port and along the northern coast of Rabbit Island. We were very wary of this area, because it can get very shallow, very quickly. The last time we had come here we had both run up on a sand bar at high speed and had taken thirty minutes to pull the machines off it. But this time we didn't have any problems and entered the Waimea Inlet, riding straight to the Mapua Wharf. We tied up at the wharf and spent some time talking to some young boys who had been jumping off the wharf and had seen us on TV a few days earlier. We encouraged the boys to sit on the Seadoos and we could tell they were impressed.

There's a lot to like about Mapua. We had stayed there on our last PWC adventure down this way. The locals had been very helpful to us. We had needed fuel, so we had borrowed some drums from a jet boat operator and were about to walk to the local service station to fill them up when a couple of old blokes who had been watching us threw us the keys to their car. I can guarantee you that wouldn't happen in a big city.

Once the boys had had their fun climbing all over the Seadoos we went to the bar at the top of the wharf where the boss recognised us as well and gave us free beer until Chinashop turned up at 6pm and ruined it all. We pulled the Seadoos out of the water and drove across to the Mapua Leisure Park which would be our home for the next two nights.

It had been a good day, with about four hours riding, and we had covered 170 km. We were looking forward to our day off and after dinner we went down to the beach front bar to celebrate our progress so far. It was a nice night and over the course of the evening we consumed and enjoyed a substantial amount of aged fermented crushed grapes.

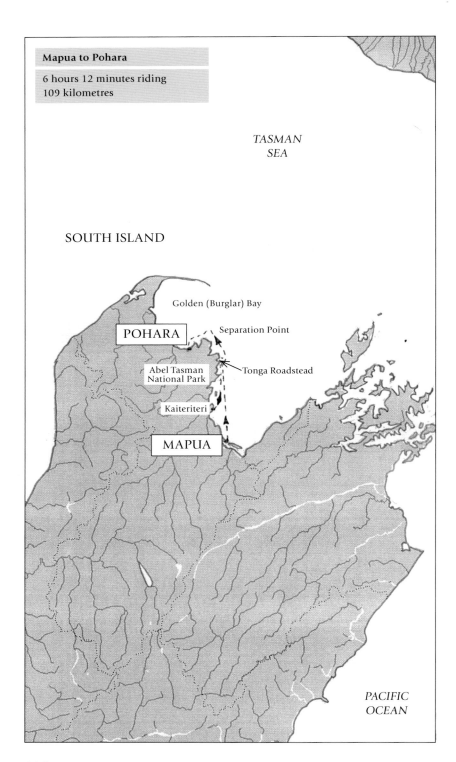

Mapua to Pohara

6 hours 12 minutes riding
109 kilometres

*TASMAN
SEA*

SOUTH ISLAND

Golden (Burglar) Bay

POHARA

Separation Point

Abel Tasman
National Park

Tonga Roadstead

Kaiteriteri

MAPUA

*PACIFIC
OCEAN*

Chapter 10
Nelson

Sunday 12th February 2006

If you don't like nudity close your eyes before reading this section, because it turns out that the Mapua Leisure Park at Mapua just west of Nelson is *clothing optional* during February and March. For the uninitiated this means that inside the confines of the park you don't have to wear clothes. The Prime Minister would be happy to know she can leave her bikini at home if she ever comes to Mapua.

Now you may well ask why people on a skin cancer awareness drive would stay at a sun bathing park. And my answer to you is that we were on an evangelistic mission to educate about the dangers of the sun, so where better to go. Where else would you find more potential skin cancer victims?

That is our story and we're sticking to it. We were missionaries, no less, and someone has to be prepared to do the dirty work.

But actually it's not quite as bad as it seems. Nudity only really happens in certain parts of the park, namely the beach and pool, and it's a very civilised place to have a day off, what with the nice setting and its great beach bar and the excellent restaurants at the Mapua Wharf. The only complaint we had was that the rooms we had been given were way too small. They were so small that you had to go outside to change your mind and, if Burglar and I were in our room at the same time, we had to ensure that our breathing was coordinated so that we didn't both breath in at the same time. One time when Burglar bent down to pick something up he got stuck.

The showers were interesting though as they were mixed. You could be standing there quietly enjoying a nice shower and the next thing you know, a person of the opposite sex would be standing next to you doing the same. It took a while to convince Chinashop that this was the case, but once he experienced it himself he was a convert to the whole concept and readily agreed to a roster to watch the shower entrance and give the others a *heads up* as to a good time to take a shower. Burglar was also inspired with the concept, and ended up the cleanest I have ever seen him.

We had a nice relaxing day planned for our day off. Burglar was going to head to the beach and rub sunscreen on all the nudists (except all the men and the women over thirty-five) and Chinashop and I would go in to Nelson Airport and pick up Pete's replacement, Michael Bridger; soon to be known as Chainsaw, because his snoring was like a badly tuned V8 chainsaw. In the end Burglar reluctantly came too, because it was raining and there was no-one on the beach.

We arrived at Nelson Airport at about 11am and picked up Chainsaw, who had flown down from Auckland. We then headed into Nelson itself to do a bit of shopping and look for a new GPS. I had decided to buy a replacement because we really needed it. We got a good deal on the replacement, which is just as well because a few days later it ended up with the same bad attitude and refusal to work as its predecessor.

While in Nelson I had a call from my old mate, Colin Bower, who had been following our progress closely on Hereiam. He was convinced we were dead when we disappeared off the screen at Cape Reinga, so the phone call was very earnest and I told him to relax because only the good die young. It was nice to hear from him. We had a lot of support like that as we went around. There were lots of phone messages wishing us good luck and lots of texts too. The Qantas staff in both Australia and New Zealand were particularly supportive, which we greatly appreciated.

I found a post office and phoned Andrew from Wright Technologies to tell him I was about to courier his dead satellite phone back, water and all. He tried to take advantage of our situation by saying that if we wanted a replacement phone it would cost us $2,700 plus GST. He was generally very arrogant about the whole thing and I ended up deciding we could make do without a satellite phone, and that I would sort it out with him later. Incidentally, when I got back and he had noticed how much publicity we had got, he informed me that the real price of a new phone was only $2,000 plus GST, and that that was what I owed him for the dead one. Later, while we were still arguing over who was responsible for its death, (a question of whether the waterproof container failed, or I misused it) he just debited my credit card for the outstanding amount plus a little more, and without my approval. It was very disappointing.

On a nicer note, Nelson is a lovely, mid-sized town with friendly people and a great atmosphere and we enjoyed being there. We could see why people love to live there. It is very relaxing and, even though the weather was ordinary that day, it is generally known for its sunshine and good weather. It is also home to the famous Macs Brewery, so it was inevitable that we should decide to make a visitation and acquaint ourselves with the brewery's product.

Finding said brewery is not as easy as we would have liked. It is almost like they don't really want to be found. We went here and there and asked a few people and ended up somewhere near Picton, refueled and then drove back again and asked someone else and got sent up a garden path, and all the while we could see a gaggle of wild geese right in front of us. Then suddenly it struck us. We were asking women! What woman knows where a brewery is and, for that matter, what woman cares? So we asked the guy at the service station, who was refueling us for the second time, and were sent straight there. We arrived outside touring hours, but were offered a tasting instead. Devastated as we were, we settled for the tasting and enjoyed some fine brews over the next hour or so.

Tasting completed and box ticked we wove our way back to Mapua where we found the technician from Hereiam working on the trackers on the Seadoos. We helped out there for a while by standing around and asking stupid questions and then we departed for Mapua Wharf where we had a delightful dinner at one of the restaurants there.

The meal was one of the best I have ever had and if it wasn't for the fact that I forgot my glasses and ordered the wrong thing, it would have been perfect.

If you are in your mid-to-late forties, stay with me. The rest of you can talk amongst yourselves for a while. This is about eyesight. Trying to read the menu at the restaurant was the continuation of a personal disaster that had been developing lately. My eyes have been getting steadily worse all year. Apparently this is inevitable at this age, so don't fight it, and don't forget to give your mother a call and tell her she was right all along.

After dinner we returned to the leisure park. It had been a good day off and we were relaxed, but we had seen the next day's forecast and it wasn't good, so we went to bed anxious and slept poorly.

We woke at 5.30am and stuck our heads out the door. There was a very strong northerly wind blowing and a bit of rain around, so we wandered over to the kitchen where Chinashop and Chainsaw were already preparing breakfast and informed them of the decision not to go. It would be a long day around to Karamea on the West Coast and in these conditions we wouldn't make it. Once you get around Farewell Spit there is really nowhere to go except on or back. There is no pull-out point. That stretch of coast is very rugged and devoid of roads.

We had a bit of breakfast and then went back to the hut for a bit more sleep. We woke again at about 8.30am and looked out the door. The wind appeared to have died down and the sun was shining, so we optimistically decided to give it a go after all.

Within half an hour we had launched at Mapua Wharf and were heading out the entrance of the Waimea Inlet into Tasman Bay.

Tasman Bay stretches from Nelson in the south to Separation Point in the north-west, and then across to D'Urville Island in the north-east. It was discovered by Abel Tasman in 1642, but not named. In 1770 Cook named it Blind Bay, which is a name still used occasionally. We made our way up the western coast of the bay past Moutere Bluff and on towards Motueka. Sea conditions weren't too bad and we bounced along at a good pace past Kaiteriteri and then past Marahau, the starting point of the Abel Tasman Coastal Track.

The Abel Tasman National park stretches from Marahau in the south, to Wainui Bay in the north. With its mild and sunny climate, curving beaches of golden sand, large tranquil lagoons and tidal estuaries, with forested hills stretching down to meet the clear blue coastal water, the park is a coastal paradise. It is New Zealand's smallest national park, but one of its most famous. In the interior of the park beautiful Beech forests, bizarre marble karst landscapes and a spectacular system of caves can be found. The park is best known for its 52 km coastal track and its sea kayaking. The track is magnificent. It is gentle enough that people of all ages can do it and, if you want, a boat will carry your gear for you from campsite to campsite. Burglar and I walked the track a few years back. We particularly liked that, every hour or so, the track would come down to an idyllic golden sand beach and we could go for a cooling off swim. We have done many of the great walks of New Zealand and are unanimous in voting this one the 'greatest of the greats'.

We made our way now inside Adele Island and up the coast past magnificent Torrent Bay and then further north, passing kayakers all the way. We paused for a while to enjoy the stunning beauty of Bark Bay and then headed into the Tonga Island Marine Reserve and on towards Tonga Island.

Just as we were about to pass inside Tonga Island my Seadoo started to play up. The engine would stop and I would have to start it again. As soon as I would get started, the engine would stop again. I signaled to Burglar that I was having problems and that we should head into the beach. We headed into the bay known as Tonga Roadstead. Don't ask me why its called Tonga Roadstead. My interest in place names only goes so far you know. What do you mean you want to know?? Okay. Hands up all those who want to know where that name came from. There you are. You are the only one and, be honest, you really don't care either. Every one else is happy to continue, so we will.

I limped into the beach, where the engine finally gave up all together. Burglar and I considered this to be likely a battery problem again, so the only thing for it was for him to tow me back to Kaiteriteri where we would rendezvous with our ground crew who had a spare battery. First we had to contact the boys and let them know that a rescue was required, as they were heading southwest towards Karamea to meet us there. Mobile phones don't work well in national parks, particularly in bays with strange names, so I got out the marine VHF radio and called Marine Radio. They were good enough to ring the boys and divert them back to Kaiteriteri. That done we hitched up a long rope between the Seadoos and commenced the 20 km tow.

The tow was uneventful, but exciting. Seadoos don't like being towed much. (They don't say as much but it's patently obvious from their behaviour.) Once we finally got up on the plane my Seadoo lurched and surged like a bucking bronco. It was a great ride, which I thoroughly enjoyed, and the time passed quickly. Soon we were entering beautiful Kaiteriteri. We anchored and waited for the boys who arrived about ten minutes after we did. We then put my Seadoo on the trailer and pulled it up onto the esplanade. Then *Burglar the Builder* went to work. Seeing Burglar approach a job with a hammer and a mouth full of nails is a sight to behold. He gets a look of determination on his face and goes off into a world of his own. We quickly suggested alternative tools for a battery change and then stood by to watch and offer useless and annoying advice. A battery change would normally not be a drama except that we were running a lot of extra gear off the battery, such as auxiliary fuel pumps and the Hereiam tracker system, so there was a bird's nest of wires going in all directions. While Burglar struggled with this, Chainsaw and I refueled both Seadoos.

About half an hour after he started, Burglar's head emerged from the engine compartment to announce that the job was done. By this time it was after midday and we decided to have another crack at getting around to Karamea, knowing full well that it would depend on the weather. Chainsaw and Chinashop were briefed to stay within mobile coverage for the next two hours in case we couldn't get around Farewell Spit. In that case we would turn back into Golden Bay, which we rated as about a fifty-fifty chance.

We headed off again and retraced our route towards Tonga Island, steering clear of the colourful fleets of kayaks as we went. As we reached Tonga Island the wind strengthened markedly and the sea started to change to *steep and nasty*. We battled on past Awaroa Head, going north towards Farewell Spit. Now the wind was up to around fifty km/hr from the north and the seas were steep; between 1 and 2 m; and coming straight at us at high speed. We could see that we were making only about 15 km/hr forward speed and we knew that at this rate we would be hours just reaching Farewell Spit. We decided to give it away and headed slowly north-west towards Separation Point, and then into Golden Bay.

Golden Bay was also discovered by Tasman in 1642. After losing four men in a battle with the local Maori he named it Murderers' Bay. In 1770 Cook included it as part of Blind Bay. In 1827 D'Urville renamed it Massacre Bay. Following the discovery of coal at Takaka in 1842 it became known for a time as Coal Bay. The name Golden Bay became established following the discovery of the Collingwood Goldfields in 1857, and in 2006 Burglar changed its name to Burglar Bay. Watch for this appearing on maps soon.

We made our way southwest towards Takaka and found a sheltered marina in Pohara. We knew it would be a long wait for the boys, so we tied up in a vacant spot next to a large yacht. The owner of the yacht, whose name escapes me now, came out to see what the commotion was all about. He was a tremendously friendly and helpful guy who had heard about us on the news. He made us a very welcome cup of tea and we talked about sailing and other noble pastimes for a while. It was very civilised.

Finally the boys arrived and we pulled the Seadoos out of the water and drove to a little town just to the east of Takaka where we found accommodation for the night, had a few beers and a feed and retired early to bed, but behind schedule for the first time.

The rooms at Mapua were so small that you had to go outside to change your mind.

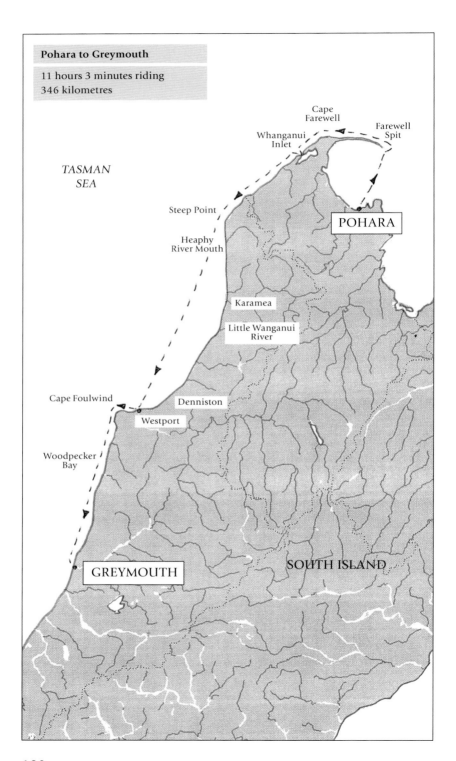

Pohara to Greymouth

11 hours 3 minutes riding
346 kilometres

Cape Farewell

Farewell Spit

Whanganui Inlet

TASMAN SEA

Steep Point

POHARA

Heaphy River Mouth

Karamea

Little Wanganui River

Cape Foulwind

Denniston

Westport

Woodpecker Bay

GREYMOUTH

SOUTH ISLAND

Chapter 11
The Ride: To Greymouth

Monday 13th February 2006

The forecast for today's ride was for moderate westerly winds, so we had decided to try to cover two days riding in one, bypass Karamea and go on to Westport and then Greymouth, a distance of 350 km. The weather was continuously keeping us guessing. If it was bad, progress would be slow and we might only cover 100 km in a day, but if we waited a day and then left in better weather we could conceivably cover that same 100 km in the first two hours and then go another 250 km in the same day. We wanted to cover the distance, but we didn't want to get too badly beaten up doing it. We were in self preservation mode. We wanted to get to the finish line in some semblance of good health.

With this in mind we launched at Pohara Marina at first light. The sunrise was a good twenty minutes off yet. Burglar (Golden) Bay was flat calm as we set off and followed the GPS towards Farewell Spit.

We identified a light in the distance which we thought was the lighthouse at Farewell Spit, but which turned out to be a fishing boat, so we gave him a wide berth and continued on.

Farewell Spit is about 25 km long and is formed entirely from quartz sands, derived from the erosion of granites and other rocks on the west coast and transported northwards by coastal drift. The spit is about 800 m wide and comprises shifting sand dunes up to 30 m high.

It's only about 30 km from Takaka to the spit and we eventually had it in sight. As we drew closer the sea came up a little and we started to bounce again. We aimed for a spot just to the right of the lighthouse but, to our annoyance, the tide was out and the shell banks were exposed to the east for at least a couple of kilometres. That meant we had to ride east for a while until we were brave enough to attempt a high speed, shallow draft crossing and then turn to head west.

Without the shelter provided to us by the spit we were now subjected to westerly winds of about 25 km/hr and *steep and nasty* seas of between 1 and 2 m. We found this pretty tough going and hoped that, as we headed further around the coast and onto a more south-westerly heading, conditions would improve. We battled on until we reached Cape Farewell where we thought conditions might improve.

At Cape Farewell the coastline changes direction towards the south-west and our hoped for improvement in the conditions did not eventuate. It became obvious that any westerly wind and swell that hit the coast would be diverted towards the north-east and straight into us.

Fifteen kilometres southwest of Cape Farewell the fuel in my main tank was getting low, so I turned on the auxiliary pump to transfer fuel from the aux. tank. I immediately became concerned because I couldn't hear the fuel pump operating. I informed Burglar that we would need to call into the Whanganui Inlet and find a calm spot to have a look at it.

The Whanganui Inlet is an example of a drowned valley. This is not as tragic as it sounds. In this case the valley drowned due to a rise in sea level. Twenty thousand years ago the sea level was 100 m lower than it is now. Ten thousand years ago it was still 30 m lower, rising to its present level about five-thousand years ago. It was this rise that produced many of the sheltered and beautiful harbours throughout the world, of which the Whanganui Inlet is a stunning example.

The entrance to the inlet is about a kilometre wide and if you could get to it, it would be a surfing paradise. The waves sometimes span most of the entrance and are almost perfectly formed. Sometimes they run for 500 m into the inlet. We had a great ride on the waves into the inlet and found an unbelievably beautiful beach to pull up to.

Burglar went to work on my machine and identified a corroded part on the fuel pump switch which would require a bit of manipulation every time we needed to transfer fuel. But at least we had identified the problem and could continue without having to transfer fuel by more primitive means.

With this problem sorted we relaxed for a while in the beautiful setting. The whole Inlet is surrounded by bush covered rolling hills that descend down at various intervals to golden sand beaches. The water was as clear as glass and flat calm, the sun was shining and it felt like we had arrived in paradise. We dined on snickers bars and tinned rice pudding and sucked away on our thirst quenching Raro (the townhouse, the Porsche, the boat and, perhaps, an all expenses paid world trip, thank you)

Eventually we conceded that we should get going so we reluctantly remounted and zoomed out through the entrance, both vowing to return sometime in the future. As we turned south-west again we encountered more of the same bashing that we had been getting before.

We loosened more fillings for the next two hours as we followed the coast down, passing Kahurangi Point and then Steep Point. At Steep Point the coast starts to head directly south and we quietly celebrated the fact that we had indeed made it to the West Coast. To add to our delight at this achievement the sea conditions improved markedly and we began to make excellent time.

Before long we had passed the entrance to the Heaphy River,

which is where the Heaphy track hits the coast. The Heaphy track is located in the Kahurangi National Park and, at 82 km, is the longest of New Zealand's *Great Walks*. Starting from near Collingwood in Golden Bay it snakes over expansive tussock downs, through lush forests and Nikau Palms and down the Heaphy River to the roaring seas of the West Coast. The scenery along this part of the coast is impressive to say the least, and we enjoyed it immensely.

We continued on at high speed past Karamea, which is known as the *winterless north* of the West Coast and is one of the many adventure centres of the region. The entrance to the Little Wanganui River flashed past soon after and then, in no time at all, the curve of the coast where Westport is situated appeared from below the horizon.

As we approached Westport we passed the historic coal mining town of Denniston. For those of you who care, between 1880 and 1967, the Denniston Incline brought coal down from the Rochfort plateau and the mines at Coalbrookdale, Wharatea and Iron Bridge. The incline, with its steepest section at an impressive gradient of 1 in 2.2, carried fifteen wagons an hour (with a total capacity of 120 tonnes), to the railway at Conns Creek at the foot of the incline. In its time, over thirteen million tonnes of coal went down from the plateau to the ships at Westport. The locals fondly referred to the incline as the Eighth Wonder of the World.

I know you'll agree that this is intriguing stuff. If you search the internet for the Eighth Wonder an extensive list pops up which includes, but is certainly not limited to, the Sydney Opera House, the monastery of St. Lawrence of Escorial Spain, Geoff Capes the British shotput champion and twice the world's strongest man, and the fictional King Kong. If you ask me, it's a wonder the Sydney Opera house was ever finished; I suspect that the Olympic shotput champion, who no doubt beat Capes, is quite miffed about missing the list; and King Kong could be knocked off any time by a bigger fictional character, so the list is obviously a work in progress.

The people of Denniston can only live in hope.

With Denniston left in our wake we approached the entrance to Westport's harbour and the Buller River. They must get some pretty nasty weather here, as the entrance has huge vertical walls on it and, as you enter, it feels like you are entering a protective fort. You almost expect large iron doors to slam shut behind you and to hear large sharks hitting the outside of them in frustration. But, of course, none of this happened and we sedately cruised up towards the port and into the launch ramp where Chainsaw and Chinashop were waiting. We met Stewart, the local Cancer Society Rep, and spoke to a reporter and posed for photos and generally fulfilled all our obligations so that there was really nothing else to do but eat.

Eating involved a trip into the metropolis of Westport. Burglar and I again had McDonalds in mind but, alas, there was none. Can you believe that? How does a town survive without a McDonalds? The very concept of it is mind boggling. The reason I say this is that McDonalds is not just for giving people fat butts, although at this it is a prize winner, but McDonalds is first and foremost a landmark, relative to which people give directions. For example "Good afternoon capitalist infidel pig can you tell me the way to the Army Surplus Weapons and Ammunition Store?" Why certainly my fine middle eastern looking fellow, mount your camel and then afterwards, if you have time, just ride the sorry looking beast down past McDonalds then take the first on the left and it's three stores down",…. or…. "Excuse me sir, can you assist me by directing me to the Jenny Craig weight loss centre?" "Certainly Mrs. Lardass. Go down to McDonalds and its right next door. In fact there are adjoining doors between the two! The Mayor owns both franchises!"

We drove down the main street of Westport looking for the food outlet that appeared most likely to satisfy our needs without giving us food poisoning and there were none that satisfied both requirements, so we settled on a small takeaway bar. The woman running it was old and Chinese. Perhaps she came here during the 1860s gold rush and never left. I don't know, and it doesn't really matter, because she made a reasonable burger.

While we were waiting for the food we stood on the main street of Westport and watched the dynamics of the town. Westport is the commercial and administrative centre for the northern West Coast area. The primary industry in the area is coal mining but, given the tourism opportunities in the area, it is a base for these as well.

I know I'll risk having a Westport native dump a truckload of coal on my doorstep for saying this, but Westport as a town did not impress us. Admittedly we only spent a short time there, but looking back on it, it was probably about enough. It looked like a large wild-west town that had had a complete makeover in 1942 and hadn't been touched since. I'm sure if you had the inclination, you could explore Westport and find something interesting, but for me Westport is certainly the poster boy in favour of global warming and the subsequent rise in the sea level that would result. The saving grace for the town is that the surrounding area is quite magnificent.

We ate our burgers in the car, spilling sauce and beetroot down the fronts of our wetsuits as we went. When we got back to the port we found three other riders getting ready to go out with us. They were planning to accompany us as far as Charleston, about 20 km down the coast. We all zoomed out through the breakwater and into the open sea and turned west towards Cape Foulwind. I was disappointed to find that the wind had come up and the sea was more chopped up than before.

We had become used to setting a continuous hard pace. It was the only way we could cover the required kilometres each day so, within a kilometre of leaving the port, our three friends had tucked into our wakes to get a bit of shelter from the waves. Just before we reached the cape we looked around to see if they were okay and they weren't there. They must have found the going too tough and turned back. Burglar and I felt quite guilty about dropping them like that but we didn't even see them go, so there wasn't much we could do about it.

We rounded Cape Foulwind and headed south past the town of Charleston, which was the site of a major gold rush in the 1860s and is now famous for its extensive limestone caves and caving experiences. Next we passed Woodpecker Bay, which is another one of those places, no doubt named after one of Cook's crew who had obviously had an unfortunate accident sometime in his life.

The coast from Charleston to Greymouth is quite stunning to look at and it helped our moral as our tired bodies took another beating. There are bluffs and magnificent bush all the way along. We saw something that looked like a smoking volcano, but was probably a mine of some sort. Eventually Greymouth hove into view and we dragged our tired and sad butts towards the entrance of the Grey River.

The Greymouth bar is one of the most dangerous port entrances in the world. If you do an internet search on it, it comes up with a list of accident reports for the bar. The bar is particularly hazardous because it is the point where the mountain-fed Grey River meets the huge *roaring forties* swells that come from the Atlantic Ocean, south of South Africa, across the Indian Ocean and south of Tasmania, to hit the West Coast. The tidal changes and shifting sand and silt in the bar make it even more tricky. Whenever we told someone we were planning to go over the Greymouth bar, they would suck air through their teeth and say, "You're not, are you?" An Auckland taxi driver had warned me against it, which really made me sit up and listen, given that taxi drivers are such authorities on just about everything.

So it was with a certain amount of respect that we approached the bar. Our first clue that this was no ordinary bar was the colour of the water. It was like dark chocolate from the silt that had been churned into it. We continued on slowly and rode in between the swells. As we approached the entrance, I remember thinking, "This doesn't look too bad", and then I suddenly found myself being lifted high in the air as the swell underneath me reared up from nothing to about 3 m in the space of a couple of seconds. For a moment I was tempted to ride down the front of it, but something told me not to and I backed off the throttle and sat on the back of it. It was just as well because the wave imploded in front of me in a monstrous turmoil of surging and boiling water. The noise and power of the wave was unbelievable. Burglar and I followed the wreckage of the wave into the main river and then motored slowly around into the port. There was quite a crew waiting there to meet us as we made our way through the muddy water towards the boat ramp. We were interviewed and photographed and then Chinashop backed the trailer into the water for our retrieval.

Now if there is anything more half-witted than revving the motor on a Seadoo in shallow muddy water then it doesn't occur to me right now, but that is exactly what I did now.

I decided to ride the Seadoo on to the trailer, but as I did so the Seadoo's powerful jet sucked up a bucket full of stones off the river bed and into the jet intake. This made an loud ominous high-pitched rattling sound that reportedly woke the napping residents of an old people's home in Wellington and unsettled dogs as far away as Napier. I shut down quickly to avoid any further damage.

Once we had loaded up we made our way to the Greymouth Top 10 Holiday Park and checked in. We had been on the Seadoos for eleven hours and covered 346 kilometres, and we were feeling it. I took a long hot shower. My rash on my back had got worse and many other parts of my body were worn and sore. After the shower we ate another fine meal cooked by Chainsaw and then checked the weather forecast on TV. The forecast was awful. There wasn't much chance of us going anywhere tomorrow and what better place to be stuck for a couple of days than Greymouth. We were beside ourselves with excitement.

Burglar in the Whanganui Inlet.

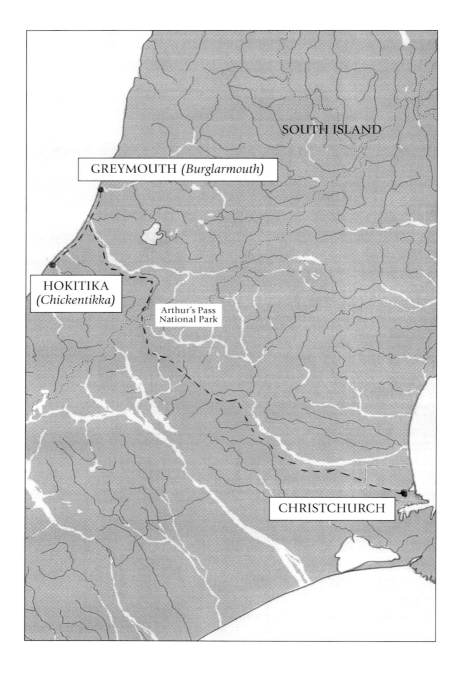

SOUTH ISLAND

GREYMOUTH *(Burglarmouth)*

HOKITIKA
(Chickentikka)

Arthur's Pass
National Park

CHRISTCHURCH

Chapter 12
Greymouth

Greymouth is an agreeable enough place in a, praise the lord for not having to live here, sort of way. It is situated on the northern part of the Westland Plain, close to the south bank of the Grey River mouth. The main part of the town extends along a narrow coastal plain. Immediately east of the town the country rises to bush clad hills. The town relies on coal mining, tourism and farming for its primary industries. In the past gold and greenstone have been found in the areas around it. The town is orderly, well maintained and pleasant to spend time in. With a population of around nine-thousand it is a nice size. It has one of each of the main grease franchises, including a strategically positioned McDonalds. In fact, on reflection there might just be too many franchises for a population of that size, but better to be prepared than sorry. Who knows when the population will triple overnight?

Greymouth was first known as Crescent City, later Blaketown, then Greytown and, finally, Greymouth. Obviously it is okay to rename places willy-nilly in the South Island and until they pass a law against it we intend to honour the tradition. So, without further ado, and in keeping with the current tradition of only changing half of the name at a time, Greymouth shall be forthwith known as Burglarmouth and Hokitika shall be known as Chicken Tikka.

We had a restless night. The Top 10 Holiday Park is close to the beach and all night we could hear large waves pounding on the shore. After some of the beatings we had taken, the sound was most unwelcome.

We woke again at 5.30am, still tired and sore, and slowly swung our feet out of bed and placed them on the floor. Three minutes later we were still in the same position trying hard to get some inspiration from the carpet. Finally I made a move. Burglar followed and we dressed and headed over to the kitchen for breakfast. The wind was quite strong from the south-west and we had doubts about the day ahead. We ate a bit of breakfast and then checked the weather on my laptop. It wasn't pretty, so we made the decision not to go. We would have to wait a day in Greymouth.

The Mayor of Greymouth was supposed to see us off so we drove down in the Sorento without the Seadoos to meet him and make our excuses. He was there with the local Cancer Society Rep., Danielle Smith. His first question was, "Where are the jet skis?" We told him they were still sleeping and explained our decision, whereupon he gave us a good briefing on all the local attractions, including the brewery. His version was an improvement on that of a Greymouth website that says, and I quote, "Greymouth hosts an <u>enticing</u> (my underlining) range of activities including the Art Gallery, History House and the walk on the flood wall which protects the town from the <u>mighty</u> (me again!) Grey River".

Thus, fully briefed, we then drove back to home base and Burglar and I slipped back into bed for an hour.

We rose again at about 8.30am. Chinashop and Chainsaw were out walking, so we decided to go for a drive to explore the town. We found a nice coffee shop and enjoyed the luxury of sitting on a non-moving platform and savouring a fine cup of coffee. I had a call from Danielle Smith inviting us all to her home near Hokitika for dinner that night. I told her I would talk to the boys and get back to her. Burglar and I then went shopping for snacks to take along on our rides and then we headed down to the offices of the Cancer Society.

We spent some time talking to the girls from the Cancer Society and using their internet connection to catch up on emails. We confirmed that we would love to come for dinner and then headed off in search of Chainsaw and Chinashop so that we could all go to the Monteiths Brewery for a tasting and tour. They were keen to go and we readied ourselves. It was disappointing that in all the preparations for the trip none of us had thought to pack cocktail shirts, so we just wore our plain t-shirts for the event.

Have you heard the joke about the American, South African, Aussie and Kiwi who went to the brewery together? Well that was us and it's all true, and I can categorically state that we were fine ambassadors for our nations and we would have made a percentage of our populations very proud.

When we got to the brewery we again found that we couldn't get on a tour, but that a tasting would be available. There were a few other tourists in our group as well, as the tasting got underway. The bloke running the tasting was friendly and helpful and, after we had sampled all the beers, he foolishly announced that we could have a period of 'helping ourselves'. We launched into this with great gusto and commendable enthusiasm and it wasn't long before the boys and I were pulling beers for all like old pros. Everyone was generally agreed that we had missed our true calling. It is possible to drink quite a lot of beer very quickly under these circumstances and a festive air rapidly developed. Everyone in the group was chatting loudly and enthusiastically to each other as if they had known each other for years. Chinashop was talking even louder than normal, Chainsaw was acting like a bit of a dag, Burglar was acting like a whole sheep's bum, and I wasn't much better. At one stage I started to spill beer down my shirt, so I moved closer to my glass and smugly advised the less experienced drinkers to do the same. A tour group of older European tourists with an average age the same as their average weight; this number was closer to one-hundred than fifty; joined us in the bar. We had drunk enough beer that language problems were no longer a problem and complements were coming and going thick and fast. Burglar spent his time being mobbed by old ladies trying to give him their daughter's, or their grand-daughter's, contact details and everyone was having a lot of fun. Eventually the wall opposite us had ceiling tiles on it, however, and the staff were looking concerned, so we knew it was time to go. Chainsaw hadn't been drinking much so he drove us back to the camp for a loud afternoon snooze.

At 5pm we loaded into the car for the drive to Danielle's place at Hokitika. It's about a 30 km drive from Greymouth to Hokitika and it's quite pretty all the way. About a third of the way down, the road crosses the Taramakau River. So does the railway line, and they both use the same bridge. The railway tracks run along the centre of the road. When we got to the bridge there was actually a train on it, so it was quite an experience to watch.

Hokitika is a small town of about three-thousand-five-hundred people. The good people of Hokitika are probably quite unaware that someone is offering their services and generally speaking for them on a website. While researching Hokitika, Burglar and I came up with the following quotes:

'In Hokitika visitors are welcome to rub shoulders with West Coasters and to experience the stories of nature, history and culture that are Hokitika'.

'Such a special place! Hokitika is a small friendly town of 3,500 folk, sandwiched between surf and river'.

With our aching bodies we fancied a shoulder rub, but I can tell you that it was never going to happen, although I can also tell you that the locals were friendly, if not great storytellers.

The website then goes on to say (and I'm guessing there were more than a few whiskeys downed during its creation):

'In Hokitika we get as many sunshine hours as Auckland and Wellington, but at 2,800mm per year, we <u>enjoy</u> much more rain'.

The writer then downs the last couple of inches straight out of the bottle and writes:'*Coasters quietly grumble and tell stories during wet weather*', etc, etc.

The writer then, mercifully, falls off his chair and the piece ends abruptly.

Incidentally the highest recorded annual rainfall in New Zealand was over 18,000 mm (about 60 ft),measured at Cropp River near Hokitika. I imagine the quiet grumbling that year would have risen to a crescendo much like the final of a contest to see who can whisper the loudest.

So there we have it; three-thousand-five-hundred friendly, shoulder rubbing, storytelling, sandwiched folk who enjoy rain, but grumble about it. They've got my vote!

We arrived at the house of Danielle and Lindsay Smith, where we were made very welcome. Lindsay had cooked a magnificent roast pork and for dessert we had blackberry and apple crumble. It was all very pleasant. The Smiths knew a local fisherman at Haast, which was our next destination, so we rang him to ask his opinion on the weather for the next day. He was very negative about it, suggesting that even he would not be able to go out fishing for at least the next two days. This was not good news, as we were already one day behind. The prospect of being three days behind was very depressing. We made a decision there and then to stay in Greymouth at least another day.

We drove home at 9.30pm tired, but well fed, and went to bed. Chainsaw had been given the separate room because of his snoring, but the door wasn't thick enough and we other three lay awake listening to the orchestra. It was strong, powerful and melodious. Every now and then he would choke a little and then stop. We would all wait for a minute wondering if he was dead, and whether we should get up and check, and then suddenly he would cough and start up again. The most annoying thing about snorers is that not only are they keeping you awake, but at the same time they are sleeping.

Meanwhile, in our room, other things were happening of an equally disturbing nature. Beer and roast pork are a volatile mixture and I won't tell you what was happening, because you might be eating or something, but all I can say is that we had closed the window to block out the surf noise. This meant that within a short time the air in our room was so dense that if you hung a seed potato on a string from the ceiling, by morning you would have a fully grown potato plant.

The next morning the weather was foul, as expected, so we contacted everyone to let them know that we were stuck there so that they could adjust our schedule. Poor old Cath Saunders was pulling her hair out trying to keep the radio interviews on track, but she was doing a great job. We decided to have a maintenance day where we would get a few things done. I did a load of washing for everyone and cut my nails.

My next job was to cut my nose hairs. Older guys will know what I mean when I say that nose hair grows at least three times faster than normal hair. Don't ask me why but it just does. I believe Newton was contemplating making it his fourth law. You go away from a mirror for a few days and then the first you know about it is when you are talking to someone slightly shorter than yourself and slowly you notice their eyes start to go cross-eyed. It might be ever so subtle at first, and it might be accompanied by a slight swaying of the body, or tilting of their head to one side. The conversation may lose its flow, such that you wonder if your friend is actually listening at all, and then suddenly their eyes will start to completely rotate in their sockets and they will start to stagger around the room as if they have been hit on the head with a hammer. They eventually fall over a chair and throw a mini fit on the ground. Don't be alarmed; they will get over it. This is all just an indication to you that it is time to get out the nose hair clippers. And you need to do it twice too, because there is always one hair that is at least a foot long that appears hours after a clipping.

Some people get around this problem by having a moustache. The moustache can then be made up of moustache hair and long nose hairs and this should be, I believe, a criminal offense.

One of the most disappointing things about our delay in Greymouth was that my wife Manola and the three boys were planning to fly down to meet us in Stewart Island for the weekend. We had planned to arrive there Friday night and have two days off. But now, with this delay and the prospect of further bad weather coming, we just couldn't see ourselves getting there until at least Saturday night, so we made the decision to cancel their trip. It was a major disappointment for everyone.

We stuffed around for most of the day doing odd jobs. Burglar spent some time on the Seadoos. The long range tanks were starting to rattle a bit and we discovered that the baffles inside them were starting to fall off. The baffles were put in to stop the fuel from surging too much as we rode in bumpy conditions. With 80 kg of fuel on the back we wanted to keep its movement down to the absolute minimum.

At about 4pm I decided to give my Seadoo a run to make sure all was okay after the ingestion of river stones from two days before. I probably should have done this sooner, but it didn't occur to me. I started it up and it rattled a bit and then Burglar waved at me to turn it off. He was pointing at a whole lot of material that had been spat out the back of the jet. At first I thought it was the Prime Minister's bikini. But how did it get there? Did she have it next to her on the beach at Mapua and a gust of wind blew it into the water? Or did it blow off the parliamentary clothesline and end up in Cook Strait?

On closer inspection we found that there was no Labour Party insignia on it, so it probably wasn't hers, and it actually appeared to be shavings of plastic or fibreglass. We looked inside the jet intake and found that there were large stones up to 5 cm in diameter stuck in the impeller that were grinding away at the wear ring around the impeller. This would need to be fixed before we left in the morning, so we put in an emergency call to Brad Clarke at Mike Phillips Jet Skis in Christchurch. Brad told us to come over and he would fix it. Rather than tow the Seadoos all the way to Christchurch we decided it would be easier to remove the damaged jet unit from the Seadoo. We borrowed a set of tools from the Top 10 maintenance man and Burglar set to work removing the jet unit. We then threw it in the back of the Sorento and headed off.

It's a very scenic 250 km from Greymouth to Christchurch. You drive south towards Hokitika and then branch off to the east at Kumara Junction, to head up through the magnificent Arthur's Pass National Park. From there you travel past Lakes Grasmere and Pearson and then out onto the Canterbury Plains. Our touring atlas has the journey time listed as four hours and ten minutes, but we managed it in three hours. It had crossed our minds that people would be checking our position on Hereiam and wondering what we were up to, so we decided that we would tell anyone who asked that we had driven over to go to the casino.

We arrived at Mike Phillips' at 7.30pm and Brad was waiting for us. He was super-keen and knew what he was doing. In conversation with him it came out that the general opinion was that we had set too hard a schedule and would be unable to stick to it. Hearing something like this from people in the industry had two effects. On the one hand it made us more determined to achieve it and, on the other hand, we were worried that they might be right. It only took Brad thirty minutes to fix the jet unit. We thanked him soundly and jumped in the Sorento to head back.

I had driven over, so Burglar was driving back. Christchurch has a network of one way streets designed to be useful to locals, but totally frustrating for visitors. Burglar roared out of the driveway and turned left into Lichfield St. Lichfield St is quite long and a half kilometre in the distance I could see two lanes of traffic and both were coming our way. Burglar hadn't noticed yet, so

I said to him, "You know Mate. There are two types of people in this world. There are winners, and there are those who turn the wrong way down a one way street". It suddenly dawned on him what he had done and he quickly turned into an industrial estate and then went the right way.

We made our way out of Christchurch, stopping for a bite to eat along the way. As we headed out through the Canterbury Plains it didn't occur to us that there wouldn't be another service station to get fuel until Greymouth, so we didn't bother to refuel. As we entered the mountains it got dark and, without the scenery, the ride became tedious. We knew that we should be in bed already getting some sleep before tomorrow's ride. We passed through Arthur's Pass and already the fuel gauge was pointing at 'E'; for *enough*. Burglar backed off from his normal neck-breaking driving style to something more like a driving-grandma-to-church style to save fuel. We passed through Kumara Junction with the smell of an oily rag in the tank and still 20 km to go. We were both convinced we would run out of fuel and, to make matters worse, there was no cellphone coverage in this area. We were dreading having to walk 10 km with a fuel drum, and then finally ending up in bed at 3am, with a 5.30am wakeup. On and on we went and it seemed like we would never get to Greymouth but eventually the outskirts of town appeared and we finally turned into the street that the Top 10 is in, and ran out of gas. We managed to coax another 200 m out of the vehicle, stopping next to the Seadoos with not a drop left in the tank.

Chainsaw and Chinashop got up to help with getting organised. I worked on getting the rest of our gear ready. Chinashop set off on foot with a fuel drum to get fuel. Burglar sat down behind the Seadoo and started to reinstall the jet unit. Chainsaw took the nail gun off him and handed him the correct tools, and within half an hour it was back on and looking as good as new. This was an exceptional effort on Burglar's part because it's quite a complicated operation and it was done by torch light. There were no left over nuts or bolts which was a confidence booster as well.

We finally hit the sack at midnight with our alarm set for 5.30am and the waves still thundering ominously onto the shore in the distance.

Our 'rig' at the Top 10 Holiday Park in Greymouth just before
we discovered the damage from the river stones.

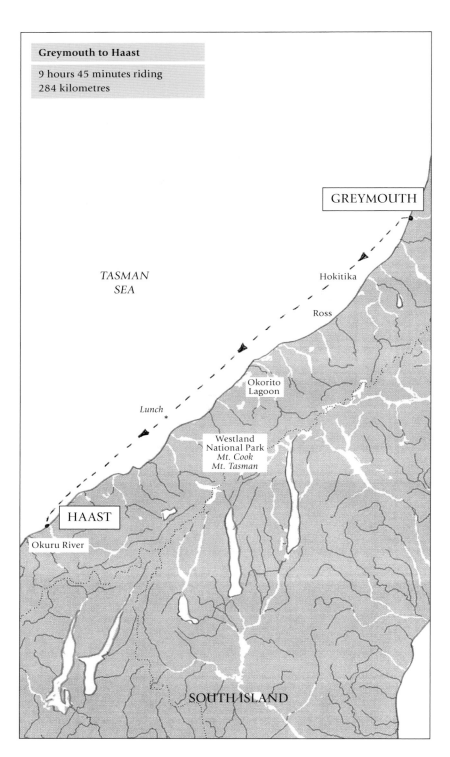

Greymouth to Haast

9 hours 45 minutes riding
284 kilometres

TASMAN
SEA

GREYMOUTH

Hokitika

Ross

Okorito
Lagoon

Lunch

Westland
National Park
Mt. Cook
Mt. Tasman

HAAST

Okuru River

SOUTH ISLAND

Chapter 13
The Ride: To Haast

Thursday 16th February 2006

After the late finish of the night before the alarm ringing at 5.30am was just plain bad news. Burglar hadn't snored too badly, and Chainsaw had his own room, but I still felt like I hadn't slept. The first thing I heard after the alarm stopped was the surf still pounding on the nearby shore, which again gave me that feeling of part-fear and part-nausea. I stumbled silently out of bed, as did Burglar. I could see that he was feeling the same way, but we had become used to pushing through this psychological moment and we did it again now.

We slowly dressed into something warm and headed over to the kitchen where Chinashop and Chainsaw were preparing breakfast. Both were way too cheerful for my liking. They were only trying to cheer us up, but we could never seem to communicate that we didn't feel like talking much. Mostly we just wanted to dwell on the day ahead and psyche ourselves up. Breakfast was fresh scones and eggs and the usual Altura coffee that you could stand a spoon up in. As always I found it hard to eat, but stuffed as much in as I could to help the energy levels for the day.

With breakfast over we headed back to the room to get dressed. I had dried our bike shorts in a camp dryer which made it easier than normal, but the suits were still damp, which added to our misery. By now the levels of gear we were wearing had increased, partly because it was getting colder, and partly to protect ourselves. We wanted to be able to survive in the water for a good length of time. Hypothermia would be a major problem this far south if we ended up in the water for any reason. Because my arms had lost their feeling, I was sitting down a lot more, so I needed more protection for my butt. I was wearing two pairs of underwear. Then on would go the titanium wetsuit. On top of that would go two pairs of padded bicycle shorts. Then I would put on the Hutchwilco lifejacket. On top of this would go another windproof jacket with a second lifejacket in it. I would then put a titanium hood over my head before putting on the helmet. Last, but not least, would be the gloves and boots. I was only wearing a glove on my left hand as I found that, with the loss of feeling in my arms, a glove on my right hand restricted my ability to operate the throttle.

All in all it was not an attractive look and it was a fashion statement that said, "I don't really care as long as I'm comfortable". Our main concern was that the fashion police might lock us up, but we considered this unlikely on the West Coast. We would have to watch it though when we reached the main centres.

We dressed, loaded up the car and headed off. It was just starting to become light and we could see it was going to be a reasonable day by the mist on the hills to the east of Greymouth. There was just a very light southerly breeze blowing and it was quite cold.

We launched the Seadoos into the muddy water, taking care to push them well out before starting them, and headed down the river towards the bar. We had been warned many times about the Greymouth bar and our experience on the way in had made us quite wary. But I have to say that, even though it's a bit scary, this sort of thing was when we had the most fun riding, as we got to throw the Seadoos around and take advantage of their maneuverability and stability. If you have to go over the Greymouth bar you couldn't ask for a better machine to do it on. As we approached it I noticed Chinashop standing up on the breakwater. He was obviously worried too. There was a 2 to 3 m break coming across the bar. It was dark brown in colour and it looked quite ominous. Brad and I looked at the bar and it was as if the bar was looking back at us saying, "Bring it on, boys". We looked at each other, nodded and charged into battle.

We approached quickly, as we could see a bit of a lull, but the bar was attempting to *sucker* us. Just as we reached it a large wave reared up in front of us. I turned and ran with it and looked back just in time to see Brad go straight up its almost vertical side and get airborne a good 2 m off the top of it. His Seadoo was vertical and I reckon he must have been close to going over backwards. He dropped behind the wave and out of sight. At the same time I saw a break on the south side of the wave so I spun around and zoomed across it. We both came together on the other side of that wave, only to see another one coming. There was a non-breaking section of that wave on the north side, so we raced over that, getting airborne for a bit because of our speed. We had to zigzag a few more times and run with one more wave before we were able to safely turn and mutter, "We beat you again, you bastard", then we set our heading to the south-west parallel to the coast; about 10 km off it; and into a fairly decent 2 m swell.

We found it hard to get back into a rhythm after two days off, so we weren't having fun as we plodded down the coast at a fairly slow pace. But soon the sun came up which raised our spirits somewhat and, as we went further south and passed friendly, shoulder rubbing, storytelling Hokitika, we started to get views of the Westland National Park, Mt Cook National Park and snow covered Mounts Cook (Aoraki) and Tasman. The Mount Cook National Park is a harsh land of rock and ice. Glaciers cover 40% of it. There are nineteen peaks of over 3000 m, including New Zealand's highest mountain, Mount Cook, at 3754 m high. The two parks, along with the Mount Aspiring National Park and Fiordland, are all part of the Te Wahipounamu South West New Zealand World Heritage Area.

The whole of the Southern Alps runs along the eastern side of the *Alpine Fault Line*.

Here the Australian tectonic plate is being pushed towards, and under, the Pacific plate. This compressing movement is causing the Southern Alps to be uplifted at a rate of approximately 7 mm per year. The average Kiwi would be quick to point out that this is just typical of the pushy Australian attitude generally, but I say bring it on. The more our mountains rise, the better skiing we get.

The fault line makes the West Coast a place of dramatic contrasts. To the east of the fault, mountains rise suddenly. High on the mountains, permanent snowfields feed a myriad of glaciers, including the Fox and Franz Joseph Glaciers , which descend right down to the lowlands. Dense rainforest dominated by rimu covers the lowlands west of the fault. Nearer the coast, there are scenic lakes, wetlands and wide river mouths. It is all quite spectacular.

We rode on with our towering backdrop of mountains and the view got better and better the further south we went. I spent my time wondering at the majesty of it all. After all, this is what we came for; to see New Zealand. And we were doing it in style, if not in comfort. I started to quite enjoy myself.

After a further couple of hours of bouncing we passed Okarito Lagoon. The lagoon is the largest unmodified wetland in New Zealand, covering 3,000 ha of shallow, open water and tidal flats. It is surrounded by magnificent kahikatea and rimu rainforest. The area is so green and luxuriant that it is often compared to the Amazonian rainforest. Many species of ferns and mosses adorn the towering kahikatea trees and wild orchids can be found in the forest. The lagoon is a bird watcher's paradise, with over seventy species of bird having been identified in the area. Kayaking on the lagoon is a great way to take in all it has to offer.

As we progressed to the south of Okarito Lagoon the swell dropped to about one metre and the water became as clear as glass, and a beautiful turquoise colour. There was hardly any wind. We were visited by countless pods of dolphins. This area was the most prolific area that we saw for marine life. All we had to do was slow down for a couple of minutes and dolphins would appear and cruise along with us. They are magnificent creatures and we spent a lot of time just cruising slowly along, watching them play and marveling at their beauty. They would swim so close to us that we were constantly getting splashed by them, and they were frequently bumping the bottom of the Seadoos.

We were very lucky at one stage to see some of the rare Hector's Dolphins. It's not hard to recognise them, as they look quite different to other dolphins, with their more rounded dorsal fins and nose. They almost look like a cartoon version of other dolphins. The Hector's dolphin is the smallest sea-living dolphin, as well as the rarest ocean species. They are only found in New Zealand waters, and only in specific areas within them. Between three-thousand and four-thousand can be found on the West Coast of the South Island and around Banks Peninsula, and between one-hundred and one-hundred-and-fifty Maui Dolphins (a close relative) can be found between Muriwai and Kawhia in the North Island.

We stopped for lunch about a kilometre off Heretaniwha Pt. It had turned into a glorious day and we really enjoyed sitting there eating peanut slabs and rice pudding and looking at the view. The beaches in that area have golden sand, and the hills behind them rise steeply and are totally covered with bush. It's spectacular to say the least, and it's one of the places we visited that I determined I would like to go back to and explore on foot with a tent and a semi-automatic .22 rifle with which to shoot the sandflies.

After lunch we carried on at a good pace because the sea was almost flat apart from the underlying swell. We were close to the coast now and we found a seal colony, so we went in to investigate and take photos. The seals were very inquisitive and we got some great photos while keeping a wary eye out for great white sharks that tend to hang around seal colonies making nuisances of themselves.

Having escaped becoming part of the food chain yet again we continued on and arrived off the Haast River mouth at about 2pm. I had spoken to a local fisherman by phone the night before and he had advised we use the Okuru River, rather than the Haast River, as it was easy to get into, so we continued on the extra 6 km.

At the Okuru River area we started to search for the river entrance. The wind had come up quite considerably from the south-west and there was a good surf breaking from about 500 m out so we couldn't get too close and, for the life of us, we could not find the entrance. After a while we decided to go back to the Haast River and go in there, so we rode back and searched for that entrance. To our utter amazement we couldn't find that either and then *lead-foot* Burglar informed me that he was running out of gas.

My initial reaction was frustration, as there weren't any obvious options. I was thinking about the beach, and then Burglar suggested we beach the machines. We could see an area of golden sand and there was a large group of people on the otherwise deserted beach, so we decided to run the Seadoos up on the beach next to the people and ask them to help us drag them clear of the surf. I went first and charged in through the surf, almost getting wiped out when I dropped off the front of a fairly big wave. But I recovered to ride hard up onto the beach in front of a very impressed bunch of Swedish tourists.

They were all dressed in motorcycle gear, as they had been attending an international Harley Davidson convention in Dunedin. The Swedes were busy videoing and taking photos of what they probably presumed is a normal thing to do in New Zealand. A few of the big blokes helped me pull my Seadoo up and then Burglar came in to great fanfare and much cheering as well.

Once the initial excitement had died down and I had finished trying out all the Swedish words that I knew (i.e., Stockholm, sauna, Bjorn Borg, etc.) we made a plan. We didn't know exactly where we were, so we decided that I would go in search of our ground crew, and possible rescue, and Burglar would stay with the skis and study Swedish. This was to prove an unlucky decision for both of us, for reasons that will become obvious later.

I plodded off up through the sand hills until I found a road, which could have been heading for Rome for all I knew (all roads do you know). I saw a service station a few hundred metres to the south, so I headed for that. The bloke at the station was very helpful, which was more than I could say for myself; I couldn't remember where we were booked into that night. After running through a list of all the up-market places, we moved to the down-market, and beyond, and we finally narrowed it down to the Haast Motor Lodge. My new buddy rang them and confirmed that our ground crew was there. The receptionist promised to send them out to us, which was a promise that she was never going to be able to fulfill, as Chainsaw and Chinashop had already snuck out to Okuru River to wait for us.

Happy that they were on their way, I headed back to wait on the road, inland from where we had come ashore. While I was standing there a Tour Operator's van pulled up and the driver said that he had been talking to our ground crew a while back. He offered me a ride as he had nothing better to do (and country folk are just plain nice and helpful), so we headed into Haast township.

Haast is only a small place. It consists mainly of tourist operators and accommodation. Add to that a couple of pubs and a service station, and there you have it. Its attraction is that it is in a beautiful setting. It has the Haast River and the beach right next to it and many magnificent valleys and mountains to the east. It is also the place you first start to see sand flies as a real threat as you are heading down the West Coast.

We drove to the Lodge to find that the boys had either driven past us without our noticing (they must have been wearing sunglasses), or they were well hidden at the lodge, because they were nowhere to be found. We turned around and headed back out to the south towards the Okuru River. As we passed our beaching spot I spotted the ground crew vehicle there, so my second new buddy of the afternoon dropped me off.

I walked down to the beach. Chinashop informed me that they had seen us heading back this way before the beaching, so had known pretty much where to look for us. The real worry now was that Burglar was a babbling mess. After I had left, the Swedes had all gone swimming naked, followed by sunbathing and, in their inimitable Swedish way had then decided it was okay to have sex on the beach, not 50 m away from Burglar. It had been a while for Burglar, and he's only thirty-one, so he was left visibly shaken and in obvious need of long term therapy. Had I sent him on the rescue mission things would have been a lot different, as my age and my considerable experience of European beaches meant that I would have coped a lot better and it would have, in the long term, saved everybody a lot of time and therapy money. As it is, all Burglar can talk about now is riding Seadoos around Sweden.

Getting back to less serious matters, we discussed our inability to find the entrance to either river and it turns out that both entrances have overlapping beaches, so you can only see the entrance from close in and from an angle. We decided to refuel the Seadoos and then we pushed them back into the water, bashed out through the surf and headed south again until we saw the Okuru River entrance. We entered the river and made our way to the launch area, where we were retrieved without drama.

We then made our way back to the Haast Lodge. The lodge is quite unusual in that its construction is like that of a tin shed. Indeed, from the outside it looks like a large tin shed. On the inside it is very spacious and effective for its purpose. There is a good atmosphere there.

We spent an hour or so at the lodge organising gear, checking the next day's weather and trying to make contact with our support in Auckland, in spite of there being no mobile phone coverage. When we were finally all organised we walked down to the pub for a well deserved beer. Then it was back to the lodge for a combined Chinashop/Chainsaw culinary creation spurred on by vicious pride and by good-natured ribbing from two hungry Burglar Brothers reclined in armchairs nearby with beer in hand.

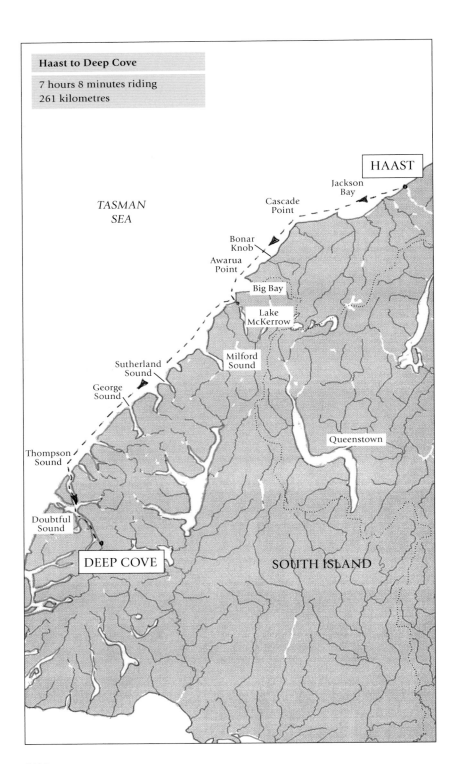

Haast to Deep Cove

7 hours 8 minutes riding
261 kilometres

TASMAN
SEA

HAAST

Jackson
Bay

Cascade
Point

Bonar
Knob

Awarua
Point

Big Bay

Lake
McKerrow

Milford
Sound

Sutherland
Sound

George
Sound

Queenstown

Thompson
Sound

Doubtful
Sound

DEEP COVE

SOUTH ISLAND

Chapter 14

The Ride: To Deep Cove

Friday 17th February 2006

We had to launch earlier than normal on this day because the boys had a long drive ahead of them. They had to drive about four hours to Queenstown, where Chainsaw would be dropped off to catch his sponsored Qantas flight back to Auckland. Then Chinashop would drive another two hours to Lake Manapouri, where he would catch a boat across the lake to West Arm, and then a bus across to Deep Cove where, we hoped, he would find us waiting impatiently for dry clothes, beer and dancing girls.

On top of the boy's routine, we had to leave early because we had changed our plans as well. Our original plan for the day was to ride to the Hollyford River and into Lake McKerrow. We would then cross the lake and follow the river again up to Lake Alabaster, having lunch at the Lake Alabaster Hut before retracing our steps to the ocean and whipping around the corner into Milford Sound for the night. But because we had lost two days in Greymouth we were going to try and cover two days riding in one by deleting the Lake Alabaster diversion and missing Milford Sound; continuing on to Doubtful Sound and Deep Cove.

We rose even earlier than usual, and Burglar and I watched the boys fighting over the cooking for the last time. Both Chainsaw and Chinashop are very proud of their cooking; and rightly so; and Burglar and I kept them on their toes by comparing their efforts.

With the eating ritual over we suffered the dreaded *dressing-in-wet-gear* ritual and then jumped in the car.

The weather looked pretty good, so we were hopeful of a good day. We arrived at the Okuru River launch point at daybreak and launched the Seadoos into the crystal clear water. But Murphy had apparently been watching all our preparations because the tide was dead low and the river too shallow to even start our machines. We ended up having to push them downstream for about ten minutes until the river got deep enough.

Once on our mounts we enjoyed a nice high speed run out to the river mouth, and then dashed out through the surf at the entrance and into the Tasman Sea. The sea was like glass but there was a small underlying swell that caused a light chop. So it was that we found ourselves dealing with *bastard glass* yet again, and wondering what it would take to find conditions that were easy to ride.

We headed south-west across Jackson Bay towards Jackson Head and then past that to Smoothwater and Stafford Bays.

In 1875 there was a major attempt to move settlers into this area. Two years later everyone had been driven away by the harsh conditions. Conditions weren't harsh there on this day though. The weather was stunning, and the scenery beautiful along the coast as we headed further south to Cascade point.

The cliffs at Cascade Point were superb and had magnificent waterfalls streaming off them. We stopped for a bit to do some filming. We were again visited by the ever present dolphins and the whole scene was very idyllic.

At Cascade Point the coast heads more towards the south and is more exposed, so the *bastard glass* was replaced by large swells with smooth surfaces and huge wavelengths. The height of the swells would have been about 4 m, but the distance between them would have been closer to 50 m. This made for great riding conditions, as we would power up the side of a swell and then zoom down the other side. It was like a smooth rollercoaster, except that we were heading into it instead of with it.

On we went past Cascade Bay and the curiously named Bonar Knob and then on to Awarua Point. Awarua Point is where the West Coast region ends and Southland starts. Around the corner is Big Bay.

I had been to Big Bay before in about 2001. I went there with my brother Dougal, Matt Gray (soon to join us on the ground crew) and Pete Fleming. We wanted to walk the Hollyford Track from the coast and then the Routeburn Track to Glenorchy near Queenstown. This story is worth telling so bear with me. We arranged to be flown in from Queenstown, as it is possible under normal circumstances to land on Three Mile Beach at Big Bay at low tide.

The four of us are all professional pilots with a total of about fifty-thousand hours flying experience between us, so it was with some amusement that we boarded the Cessna 207 at Queenstown Airport to be flown by a young pilot with about eight-hundred hours experience, onto a beach on the deserted West Coast, about an hour away by air.

We enjoyed the fine scenery and eventually arrived overhead Big Bay to find that, although the tide was out, a huge swell was rolling into the bay and running all the way up the beach. It didn't look too good, but the young pilot was confident that he could land far enough up the beach to avoid the water so he positioned us on final approach and made a nice landing. Unfortunately for him, his timing and positioning didn't match his confidence and a second after we touched down the *wave of the day* ran up the beach and crashed over the top of us. The spinning propeller sprayed water in all directions and we came to a grinding halt with the wheels buried a good twenty centimetres in the sand.

We all tumbled out of the aeroplane laughing our heads off because that was the funniest thing any of us had ever seen in aviation. Even the young pilot was laughing, although nervously I'm guessing. We did the Japanese thing and instead of dealing

with the crisis, we lined up for photos. With photographic opportunities exhausted, we then unloaded the plane. Once the plane
was unloaded we dug grooves in front of the wheels so that we
could push it out of the hole it was in. We briefed the young pilot
to find a thunderstorm on the way back to wash the plane and
then allowed him to strap himself in and start the engine. He
applied full power and the four of us pushed on the wing struts.
The Cessna finally started moving and then rose up on top of the
sand and, with it's now much lighter weight, was able to skim
across the top of the sand and get airborne.

In the same way that the fly is Australia's national bird, so too
is the sand fly the official bird of Southland and Fiordland.
Our guess is that Big Bay is named for the size and numbers of its
sand flies and, up until now, they had all been laughing too much
to have a go at us. But, with the aircraft and all chance of rescue
gone, they attacked viciously and in large numbers. We quickly
covered every piece of skin from head to toe and decided that the
only safe place to go to the toilet was in our pants. We then pitched
tents and made a fire on the beach. The sand flies at Big Bay are so
numerous that if you look into the distance it appears as if there
is a black haze over everything. If you go inside your tent they hit
the side of the tent with such force and evil intent that it sounds
like rain.

As the evening progressed and the port flowed, the conversation naturally turned to aviation themes and a discussion developed as to how so many sand flies could avoid midair collisions.
We decided that there must be some form of air traffic control and
that a standard communication might go something like this:

"Big Bay Control this is sand fly 6,346,234,001".

"Sand fly 6,346,234,001 this is Big Bay Control. Go ahead"

"Big Bay sand fly 001 would like to head low level towards
the campfire for a feed."

"Sand fly 001 Big Bay cleared as filed. Your traffic is 6 billion
other sand flies heading the same way. Have a safe flight. Big Bay

out." And so on.

The next day we walked south around the rugged coast towards Martins Bay. We passed a fisherman's hut on the way and then passed the seal colony at Long Reef, finally crashing at a Department of Conservation hut at the entrance to the Hollyford River. There are over nine-hundred-and-fifty DOC huts, and many more private huts, in New Zealand. It is customary to give these huts interesting names. No, not names like Roderick or Ignacious, but names that have something to do with the local area. I believe this hut was the Martins Bay Hut but I can't remember and it has been taken off the official hut register, so its name is lost.

While staying the night at the hut we were visited by the fisherman from further up the coast whose hut we had passed. His name was Dale and we guessed he was hoping we were women, but having seen the movie *Deliverance* we were all being fairly cautious. He had an ugly little dog with him named Sid, whose primary task that night was to stand in the doorway and allow sand flies in.

We live in a small world you know. About a year ago I was flying from Sydney to Johannesburg and the second officer started talking about Martins Bay and Dale and Sid. He'd been there, met them and stayed at Dale's Queenstown home. Astounding!

I could go on at length about the walk out to Queenstown, but I'm saving that for another book, so we can now get back to the ride.

We zoomed across Big Bay at high speed towards Long Reef. I wanted to video the seal colony there. Burglar was sitting a little further out from me as I approached Long Reef from the north. The swell was slowly getting bigger the further south we went, so by the time I reached Long Reef it was quite large and was being lifted further by the shallow waters. I tried to get in close to film the seals and then noticed I was surrounded by submerged rocks that showed themselves every time a swell passed over them. It was like being in a mine field and I couldn't get out of there quickly enough; with all thoughts of videoing gone.

Even though we weren't going up to Lake Alabaster I still wanted to show Burglar the Hollyford River, so we sat about 200 m out from the entrance to see how it looked. The entrance is quite narrow. It is about 50 m wide, but it has both visible and submerged rocks on the north side, and a sand bar on the south side. A huge volume of water was coming out of the river and large swells were coming in. For about 200 m the entrance looked very turbulent with large standing waves and chop everywhere like a dog's breakfast. The colour of the water was dark brown, making it impossible to see submerged rocks, except by the relatively greater turbulence caused by them.

This was one of those occasions where my head was telling me not to do it, but my heart was telling me to go ahead. We were gaining a lot of confidence, both in our ability to handle the Seadoos in any condition, and in the ability of the Seadoos to handle any condition so I decided to risk it and briefed Burglar to follow me with a good spacing in case I suddenly turned back. It felt a bit like being an ant on a grain of rice in a washing machine as I slowly made my way in, staying in-between the swells and, at the same time, negotiating the turbulent waters and watching for rocks.

I finally made it in and looked back to see Burglar following about 100 metres behind.

Once in we zoomed up the river and stopped on a nice sandy beach about 800 metres inland. The scenery was glorious. The water was clear and fresh. There were ducks, shags, gulls and terns scattered around the estuary. In the distance we could see the impressive Hollyford Valley and then, in the far distance, the Humboldt Mountains, which the Routeburn Track traverses.

The U-shaped Hollyford Valley was carved by a huge glacier about twenty-thousand years ago. It left behind the Donne Glacier on the eastern face of Mt Tutoko. Lake McKerrow was originally a fiord, which was cut off from the sea by sedimentary deposits at

Above: Phil Briars, Cath Saunders and John Loof from
the Cancer Society.

Below: Matt Kneesh gets ready to glue on the long range tanks
with molten licorice.

Above: Colin, Bevan and Matt spent a day and a half installing the tanks and deserve a medal.

Below: The Burfoot boys on a marketing mission just before the start.

Above: The home support team. From left, Dean, Jamie, Manola and Dougie Burfoot.

Below: Roadies. Ground crew Michael 'Chainsaw' Bridger and Jeffrey 'Chinashop' Stangl.

Above: The Bower Clan enjoy the pre-departure breakfast
and discuss the odds of us making it to the finish
in anything other than a pine box.

Below: Never let the truth get in the way of a good story.
Burglar was a natural on TV.

Above: Getting ready to leave.

Below: Arriving at Russell on day one with sinuses full
of sea water.

Above: Burglar eating lunch 'alfresco' just east of Cape Reinga.

Below: Getting ready to leave on day three from Ahipara.

Above: We were in such a hurry to run away from the shark that we collided.

Below: Still running from the shark.

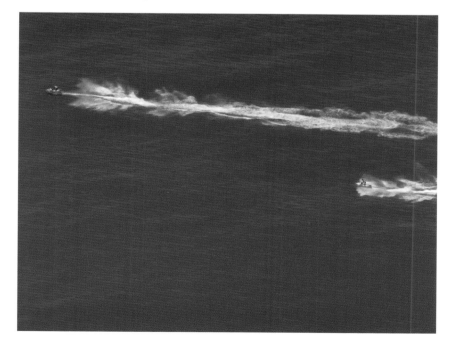

Above: Me after a spectacular arrival at Jenkins Bay involving
  a high speed grounding on flat slippery rock and a run up
  the beach.

Below: Here I've just told the boys that to make up time
  we would have to ride at night by moonlight.

Above: Burglar carries out repairs in the Whanganui Inlet.

Below: Off the West Coast with Mts. Cook and Tasman
in the background.

Above: Down the West Coast dolphins were everywhere.

Below: Me in the estuary of the Hollyford River just north
of Milford Sound.

Above: Deep Cove in Doubtful Sound.

Below: We arrive in Wellington after taking a beating
on Cook Strait.

Above: Chatting with Ron and Dorothy Terry shortly after arriving in Wellington.

Below: The team at Search and Rescue headquarters in Lower Hutt.

Above: Burglar investigates volcanic White Island.

Below: We meet up with the Tauranga group off Motiti Island.

Above: Coffee and pies on Waiheke Island while we lose time
so as not to arrive too early in Auckland.

Below: Our other ground crew, Captain Matthew 'Mateus'
Gray and Pete 'Pete' Robertson.

Above: Our arrival into Auckland at exactly 1:30pm
   on 27/2/2006.

Below: We were honoured with a Haka.

Above: There were a lot of questions from the media.

Below: Phil Briars tries unsuccessfully to screw up a photo
of us with David Libeau and Kathy Gera from Qantas.

Martins Bay. Schools of dolphins still regularly travel up the estuary to Lake McKerrow.

We sat on the side of the estuary snacking on peanut slabs and fruit bursts and I mentioned to Burglar that we had passed the old Martins Bay hut on the way through the river entrance. I told him that I was sure I had seen two Middle Eastern looking men wearing long nightshirts and tea towels and fan belts on their heads looking nervously out the door of the hut. One was tall with a beard and the other short and stocky, but also bearded. There were also camel footprints on the sandy beach in front of the hut. I mentioned to Burglar that it had been common knowledge in Auckland for a while that Osama bin Laden and Mullah Omah were living in Mt Roskill, a suburb of Auckland, and driving taxis for a living. They were confident enough that the US military would never find them there because New Zealand and the US don't share too much intelligence. But why had they moved to the Martins Bay hut? Burglar supposed they were hiding out from a much greater threat; bird flu.

We resolved not to bother them and finished our snack before heading back out through the mess at the entrance. It was even more difficult getting out than in, because we were going into the swell, and we had to turn and run a few times to avoid breaking waves. But eventually we made it and set our heading south again in good riding conditions, past Musket Bay and Yates Point, to the entrance of Milford Sound. From out at sea the entrance to Milford Sound does not show the beauty and magnificence hidden within.

Fiordland's Milford Sound is by far the best known of all the fiords, and the only one that can be reached by road. It is also the most northerly of the fiords indenting the south-west coastline of the South Island. It occupies the trunk portion of a formerly glaciated valley system, cut deeply below the surrounding mountains. The mountains rise almost vertically to heights of nearly 2,000 m above sea level and the deepest point of the fiord, near Stirling

Falls, is 400 m below sea level. Stirling Falls (150 m) and Bowen Falls (160 m) spout from hanging valleys over near vertical faces into the sound. Mitre Peak rises almost vertically from the sound to 1,695 m. It is so named because of it's resemblance to the shape of the bishop's mitre, when viewed from the south.

Milford Sound is where the Milford Track starts. It is probably the most famous of New Zealand's great walks, and one of the most spectacular. While on the walk one can view New Zealand's highest falls, the Sutherland Falls, which drop 580 m in three stages.

I think it's also worth mentioning that Milford Sound was one of the candidates for eighth wonder of the world. If it's a contest between British shot-putter Geoff Capes and Milford Sound I would have to say that I am leaning towards Milford, but then I am biased, am I not?

We bypassed all the Milford magnificence and continued on with great haste. Whenever the sea conditions were good we tried to take advantage of it, because the weather varies so much around the coast of New Zealand and there are so many local effects that conditions can easily change ten times in a day. As we headed further south the swell continued to get bigger and then, as we passed the entrance to Sutherland Sound, the wind came up from the south-west and whipped up the sea quite a bit. This was quite depressing for us, because we just wanted to have one day when the riding was good all day. We were determined to keep up our pace. It was either go hard and shake ourselves to bits, or slow down and lose time and risk the weather getting slowly worse all the time. We chose to go hard and we bashed our way past the entrances of Bligh Sound and George Sound and past Looking Glass Bay, which Cook no doubt named after the first thing he saw after he spotted the bay. Then we rode on past Two Thumb Bay (don't ask me!). Then it was bash bash bash past the entrance to Caswell Sound. We crashed past Charles Sound (probably named after the ship's navigator) and Nancy Sound (the ship's entertainment officer?). Of course I'm only speculating about these names and if you can come up with better reasons for the names, I'm happy to hear them. You also have to bear in mind that the names, in keeping with tradition, have probably been changed four times in the last two hundred years, so go easy on me.

Every thirty minutes or so we would stop and lie back on the Seadoos for a minute to straighten out our backs and rest our arms. Our backs were taking the pounding and our wrists and arms were suffering serious muscle fatigue from holding on in the jarring conditions. It would have been nice to stop for ten minutes, but with the distances we had to cover we just had to keep going forever forwards at whatever pace we could manage. After a minute of rest we would give our hands a good shake, take another slurp of the life giving Raro (I'll take the Townhouse, the car, the boat, the world trip and a lifetime supply of Tui beer: *Hey readers do you sense another endorsement opportunity here?*) and plow on.

Eventually we reached the entrance to Thompson Sound, which is where we needed to head into to get to Deep Cove. Never has a stretch of water looked so calm and inviting. It was flat calm and crystal clear once we entered the sound, and we were ecstatic. We rode standing up at a leisurely 60 km/hr with big smiles on our faces.

About 5 km in from the entrance we came across Deas Cove. Deas Cove is a beautiful spot about 100 m across, which has a small island in the middle of it. The island is covered in the most stunning flora and fauna and the whole cove looks like a Hawaiian fantasy painting, only real. It has to be one of the most awesome spots I have ever seen and I will have to go back there.

Five kilometres further on we found a large, magnificent waterfall that zigzagged down a steep mountain into the sound near a sandy beach. We stopped there for a few minutes and Burglar climbed up the waterfall while I filmed. He found a natural spa bath to sit in and seemed content to stay, but we still had a schedule to keep so we continued on.

At the end of Thompson Sound we turned right into the Pendulo Reach, and then left into the Malespina Reach, then riding right into the centre of the superb physical grandeur of Doubtful Sound. Known for its wilderness and wildlife, Doubtful Sound is the second largest of the fourteen fiords in the Fiordland National Park and it is three times longer, and ten times larger, than Milford Sound.

I had mentioned to Burglar to be on the lookout for dolphins, as the sound is famous for them, so we cruised along at a slower speed and kept a good eye out. As we went further east down the sound we came across a tourist boat loaded with tourists. It became apparent that they were watching dolphins and we kept well away to the north side of the sound and watched from a distance. The dolphins were putting on a great display for the tourists and we watched with interest. Then without warning they left the tourist boat and came our way. Obviously the sound of the Seadoos was something new and they were intrigued. Soon we were playing with about twelve large dolphins. They were a good 3 m long and as they splashed around us we got quite wet. Occasionally one would bump up under the Seadoo and give the whole machine a good jolt. It was quite something.

We were feeling just a tiny bit guilty at stealing the dolphins from the tourist boat, so we eventually rode off at high speed to leave them behind and give them back to the tourists. We later found out that the Captain of the boat had been really angry about it. Apparently a group of locals had got together recently and decided that jet skis should be banned from Doubtful Sound. The problem with this plan was that they didn't tell many people and neither did they put signs up so, when we organised our adventure and trip into the sound, the people we organised it with didn't know either. The other problem with this was, we gathered, that there was no legal ability for them to do so. It's like a group of people deciding cats should not be allowed in their street. I'm surprised they didn't vote to change the name of the sound as well.

Anyway, let's move on. We made our way to Deep Cove at the eastern extremity of Doubtful Sound. Deep Cove is where the water exits when it leaves the Manapouri Power Station. Following exploratory drilling in Lake Manapouri's West Arm, hundreds of men laboured through the 1960s in tough conditions, first tunneling into the solid rock, then carving out the massive underground chamber for the machine hall. Here seven generators were to be installed. Meanwhile similar work gangs tunneled from Deep Cove towards West Arm, creating a 10 km tailrace tunnel through which the waters of Lakes Manapouri and Te Anau; having dropped some 213 m down the penstocks to turn the generator turbines; would flow out to the sea on the West Coast. The Manapouri power station is the largest hydro power station in New Zealand, with an installed generation capacity of 850 MW.

We moored the Seadoos and wandered up the hill where we found Charlie Paddison, who runs the Deep Cove Outdoor Education Trust. He was very helpful and showed us to our accommodation in the trust hostel. The hostel is in a fabulous setting, on a bank looking down over Deep Cove. It was originally built to house the workers during the construction of the Manapouri Power Station. When construction was complete the buildings were donated to the Deep Cove Trust. Chinashop and I are trustees of a similar education centre in Auckland called the Sir Peter Blake Marine Education Recreation Centre. The Deep Cove Trust had agreed to give us free accommodation, as we were riding for a good cause.

We checked the weather for the next day on Charlie's computer. It wasn't the best, but we judged it okay to get around the corner to Riverton if luck stayed with us. Chinashop was still a couple of hours away so we sat with Charlie in our wetsuits and drank cups of tea. Charlie works two weeks on and one week off at the trust. I asked him if it was lonely work. He said a bit, but he was used to it and then he told us about the three years he spent setting up his own wilderness resort on the shores of Lake McKerrow.

He had done it by himself and had initially used a helicopter to fly the building materials in. When the money ran out, he rafted the materials down the Hollyford River. Eventually he discovered it was too far for paying customers to come so he sold the resort.

Charlie knew Dale and his dog Sid from Martins Bay. Apparently Sid was now dead, but had become something of a hero in the area a couple of years back when he had found a lost tramper.

We needed fuel for the next day, so Charlie got that organised. Burglar and Charlie used Charlie's truck to bring the fuel down in drums, and I filled the tanks. By the time fuel gets to Deep Cove it has lots of expenses to cover so it was $2 a litre. We took 270 litres. I hate the oil companies.

Just as we finished refueling, Chinashop arrived with beer, food and dry clothes, so we spent some time getting organised for the next day and cooking up a feed. I took a shower and found that we had neglected to bring towels. Burglar's shirt was conveniently lying on his bed, so I used that. When he complained about it being wet I told him that I didn't want to use my own because it was dry. Fortunately he saw the logic in that.

After dinner it was still early, so we took another beer and went for a walk down to the main wharf where the tourist boats were moored. It was quite an impressive setup. An overnight tour on Doubtful Sound on a cruise boat is definitely high on my *to do* list, and should be on yours too!

Burglar and Chinashop share a joke at Deep Cove.

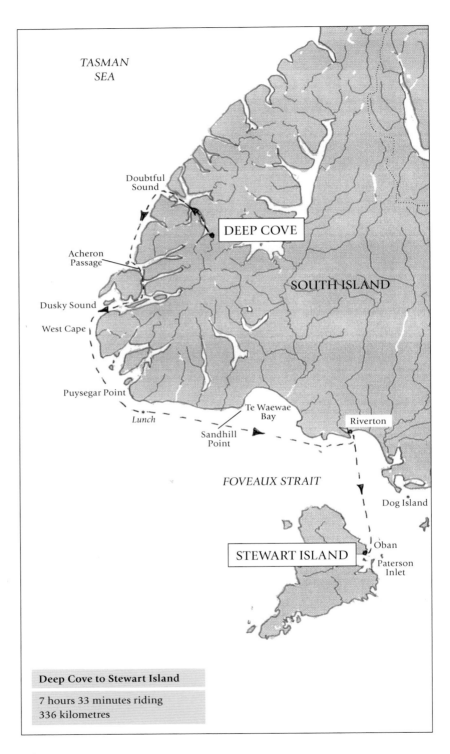

TASMAN
SEA

Doubtful
Sound

DEEP COVE

Acheron
Passage

SOUTH ISLAND

Dusky Sound

West Cape

Puysegar Point

Te Waewae
Bay

*
Lunch

Riverton

Sandhill
Point

FOVEAUX STRAIT

Dog Island

STEWART ISLAND

Oban

Paterson
Inlet

Deep Cove to Stewart Island

7 hours 33 minutes riding
336 kilometres

184

Chapter 15
The Ride: To Stewart Island

Saturday 18th February 2006

It was cold and still when we woke at the Deep Cove Hostel. Today would be a big day. We would have to ride 300 km around the coast of Fiordland and then east down Foveaux Strait to Riverton, near Invercargill. This is an area which is renowned for its bad weather and huge seas. We would pass around Puysegur Point, which is an area strongly influenced by the mountain ranges of the South Island. These ranges deflect the prevailing westerly winds of the middle latitudes, so that they pass around Puysegur Point as a strong wind from the north-west. On average, gale force winds of over 68 km/hr occur there on one-hundred days of the year. Today's forecast was for north-westerly winds of 30 km/hr north of Puysegur and down Foveaux Strait. The Puysegur region is also where the huge swells from the southern ocean hit the coast. Some bounce back into the incoming waves causing turmoil. Others are deflected north up the West Coast, or east down Foveaux Strait.

Add to this the complete isolation of the area and you have a recipe for trouble. If anything goes wrong there is no immediate rescue. You are on your own. There are no refueling points or roads there.

This was the big one and we knew it. It was this leg that the specifications of the long range fuel tanks had been based on. If we could get around Puysegur Point and into Riverton we would be well on the way to completing our journey. This day had been looming up on us for the last week and now it was finally here.

Our preparations had been as thorough as possible. I had spoken at length to an old mate of mine, Rodney Clark from Riverton, who had fished this area for years and knew all its bad habits. Burglar had family friends on Stewart Island, Alan and Lee Wadds, who also had good contacts in the area. He was given a list of points that we could shelter at if the weather turned nasty. We also had a list of fishing boats in the area. Mary Leask from Bluff Fisherman's Radio had radioed all boats in the area to keep an eye out for us.

We were as prepared as it is possible to be and now we just had to do it.

We had breakfast and then all got ready to do our thing. Chinashop was to catch the bus and boat back to the Sorento, then drive down to Riverton to pull the Seadoos out and refuel them so that we could continue on to Stewart Island if the weather was okay. He would then drive back to Queenstown, drop the Sorento with the Qantas manager there and fly back to Auckland. The Sorento would then be picked up by Matt and Pete and driven to Dunedin to meet us when we arrived there from Stewart Island.

Meanwhile, Burglar and I stuffed as much food into the Seadoos as we could fit and got, once again, into our wet gear.

We walked down to the water with just a hint of daylight appearing over the hills leading to West Arm. The air was cold and the water even colder. We were damp and cold but somehow there was a sense of *lets get this done* about both of us. Psychologically we felt good because the first 40 km would be in the calm waters of Doubtful Sound. We knew we would knock that distance over in a bit over half an hour and then only have 260 km to go to

Riverton.

We started our machines and motored slowly out away from the shore. We waved to Chinashop and Charlie and sped up to a comfortable 70 km/hr. The induced wind was bitterly cold, but the water was flat calm and crystal clear and we were enjoying the ride.

It was lighter now and it was a whole new world from that which we had seen the day before. A grey cloak of mist and fog hung over all the valleys. Even the water looked grey and it was as if, suddenly, the whole world had changed to a black and white movie. I looked down at my Seadoo and was comforted to see the red still there as it should be. Even in the murk, Doubtful sound was still impressive. It had an atmosphere of powerful solitude to it as we raced towards the coast. We slowed up a couple of times to ride with the dolphins, but we were on a mission and all too soon it was time to bid them farewell and leave them in our wake.

We continued past Bauza Island and then on to Febrero Point where the sound meets the Tasman Sea. We then headed south-west, straight into a large swell with a smaller secondary swell hitting us from the side. We bounced along over the secondary swell and rode up, and down, over the larger one. All in all it could have been better, but it could have been a lot worse, so we weren't complaining.

The large swells were huge walls of water. If I had to estimate their height I would say only about 6 m, but the length of them was what impressed us. Each wave would have been at least 60 m from trough to trough. The waves were almost large enough to have their own weather systems. We could feel the power in them. The sheer energy of that much water moving at that speed was awesome, such that riding each wave was an adventure on its own.

The sky was still very grey and, in the distance, the point where it merged with the ocean was impossible to pinpoint. Every now and then light showers of rain would reduce the visibility even further.

We rode further south past a place called Peninsula Point, which I suppose would be like naming a lake *Water Lake*. Then it was on past Dagg Sound. From there we pounded away for another hour until we reached Breaksea Island and the northern entrance to the Acheron Passage. The Acheron Passage passes to the east of Resolution Island and into Dusky Sound, separating Resolution Island from the mainland.

We had decided to take this detour so that we could have a good look at the sound. Dusky Sound is the largest fiord in New Zealand. It was discovered and named by Captain Cook on his first voyage. Cook returned to Dusky on his second voyage in March 1773 and stayed for two months, thoroughly exploring and charting the sound. Clearings were made in the bush and an observatory was established. There was also a blacksmith's shop, a sail maker's camp and, of course, a brewery.

We rode at high speed south through the Acheron passage enjoying a break from the thumping waves outside and enjoying the dramatic, but still mainly monochromatic scenery. We then turned south-west into the Bowen Channel. As we passed Passage Point we spotted a large ketch in the distance. We later found out that they had reported seeing us 'travelling at high speed' to Mary at Bluff Fisherman's Radio, so everyone knew that we were on our way.

We zoomed down the Bowen Channel past Duck Cove and Indian Island and saw in the distance a large cruise ship coming into the sound. We were heading straight for it, so we altered heading to pass about 100 m down its port side. It was an American luxury cruise ship, and it was huge and imposing alongside us. Many passengers were waving to us as we went past. I wondered how many of them thought to wonder what we were doing there so far from civilisation.

The ship was traveling slowly, but it still had a massive wake and we enjoyed a few good wave jumps as we passed around the back of it, then we headed on past the Many Islands, so named for obvious reasons. From there we rode to South Point and back out into the Tasman Sea. Ten kilometres further on we passed West Cape, which is supposedly the most westerly point in New Zealand, although from my map I can see places that are further west.

As we approached Providence Rocks; where the coast starts to curve around towards the south-east; and Puysegur Point, the sea conditions got markedly worse. The large swells started to hit the coast and bounce back out onto the incoming swells, creating all sorts of nastiness, until we found ourselves in sea conditions that we officially named *dog's breakfast*. This sea condition is where waves come from all directions and at varying heights, so that the only thing consistent about them is their inconsistency. It is hard work to ride because you can never get into a rhythm.

We aimed out to sea a bit to reduce the effect of the bounce back and battled on towards Puysegur Point. We could see it in the distance, and it always seemed to be the same distance away. The countryside around Puysegur is rugged and heavily forested. The whole area looks very inhospitable and the thought of having to take shelter in these parts for a few days was not attractive. There is said to still be a lot of gold in the area and you can see why. It's almost impossible to get to and, once there, it would take all of your energy just to survive.

We eventually rounded Puysegur Point and headed east towards Riverton. We were ecstatic to have got around, but we still had 120 km to go for the day. Ten kilometres further on the *dog's breakfast* seas had transformed into a much more user friendly, and quite tidy, following swell, so we stopped for a drifting lunch off the Green Islets.

To celebrate our successful rounding, lunch this day was Oysters Kilpatrick for entrée, pan fried fillet mignon on a bed of roasted parsnips with garlic and sautéed onions and béarnaise sauce for main and, for dessert, there was a choice of sticky date pudding and custard, or black forest gateaux with thickened fresh cream.

The meal was finished off with fresh brewed Altura Coffee with biscotti and liqueurs and a selection of seasonal cheeses and dried fruit. And then we woke up and had the old standard of rice pudding, oranges and a pee.

We made our way along the south coast of the Fiordland National Park. The countryside is incredibly rugged and well known for it's abundance of native timbers, birds and sea life. A coastal track was cut by government workers in 1896 to provide an alternative to the unreliable shipping service to the Cromarty and Te Oneroa gold mining settlements in Preservation Inlet near Puysegur Point. The Waitutu Track is now a popular tramping track. It takes four days to reach Big River, which is only two thirds of the way to Puysegur Point.

We started to enjoy the following swells that were pushing us eastwards down Foveaux Strait. These were relatively smooth and fairly consistent, so it was much like riding a tame rollercoaster, with an element of surprise thrown in. We were making good speed and were anticipating an early arrival into Riverton. The forecast strong winds had not yet eventuated and the sun had even come out to add some colour to the picture.

I hadn't seen my old mate Rodney Clark for twenty-five years, so we were both looking forward to the reunion. He was planning to come out from Riverton and meet us in Foveaux Strait with some of his mates on PWCs. I had told him to watch out for us appearing on the Hereiam screen as we came into phone coverage around the western end of Te Waewae Bay. He later reported that we had suddenly appeared on screen and we had been doing a lot higher speed than he anticipated, so that he barely had time to scramble his mates and make it out there in time.

We zoomed past Sand Hill Point and the old timber settlement of Port Craig. During the 1920s, Port Craig was the site of the largest and most modern sawmill in New Zealand.

The Marlborough Timber Company Mill employed over one-hundred-and-fifty men and produced up to 1800 m³ of timber a

month. Logs were brought to the mill along a high class tram-
way from the terrace forests to the west, between Port Craig and
the Wairaurahiri River. Large viaducts were constructed from
Australian hardwood to carry the tramlines over ravines. The largest, the Percy Burn viaduct, is 125 m long and 36 m above the
creek bed. It was fully repaired in 1994.

From Sand Hill Point we tracked direct to Wakaputa Point,
which is only 20 km short of Riverton. We saw quite a few fishing
boats and got an enthusiastic wave from the ones we passed close
to. Obviously the word was out that we were on the way.

We continued on past Oraka Point and across Colac Bay. Just off
Pig Island we spotted a couple of PWCs coming our way and soon
they were close enough to identify my old mate Rodney, who, in
his excitement, did a *Forest Gump* and jumped into the sea, before
swimming across to me and climbing on board. We rode together
into Riverton with him chatting all the way, oblivious to the fact
that I couldn't hear anything because of my helmet and hood.
I resorted to the, "Yep, yep, no way, extraordinary, yep, yep", routine that old blokes use with their wives when they are reading
and the wife is not. Once we got to Riverton we actually had a
decent conversation and it was great to catch up.

All sorts of people were there to meet us. There were a couple of
newspaper reporters and a local television station reporter. TV3's
freelance cameraman was there too, so we spent a good hour
doing interviews. Chinashop turned up shortly after we did
and refueled the Seadoos. We loaded some clothes into a dry bag
for our time on Stewart Island and then Chinashop disappeared
towards Queenstown. Meanwhile, Rodney had introduced us to
his wife Dee. Burglar had asked what had gone wrong with wives
A, B and C. Dee went off and got us some sandwiches and fruit
while we continued on with the interviews. All in all, it was a busy,
but fun, stopover in Riverton.

Rodney had hoped that we would stop over there for the night,
but we wanted to get across to Stewart Island while Foveaux Strait

was behaving itself, so he decided to catch the ferry across and join us with Dee on Stewart Island for the night. We phoned ahead to Alan and Lee Wadds to say that we were all coming and to keep the beer cold.

I would have liked to have had a good look around Riverton. It looks an interesting place.

The town is situated on the western bank of a lagoon estuary formed by the Aparima and Pourakino Rivers, and is the oldest permanent settlement in Southland. It has great beaches along the coast to both the west, and the east. Maybe next time!

We waved goodbye again and did a couple of runs past the assembled photographers before heading down the river and around the sand bar, then setting our heading for Halfmoon Bay on Stewart Island. It is about 65 km across Foveaux Strait to Halfmoon Bay and conditions were good, so we anticipated it taking us about an hour and a half.

We passed Pig Island again and then proceeded out into the Strait with the Port of Bluff on our left. My aunt and uncle, Jeanette and Pip Aplin from D'Urville Island, had once been lighthouse keepers on Dog Island, just south of Bluff, so I was keeping an eye out for it. During the day we had passed islands named pig, dog, bird, parrot, pigeon, duck and seal. It would be easy to be forgiven for thinking that sometime in the past *Old MacDonald* had cruised through these waters with all his farm animals and named all of these islands. Or perhaps it was *Dr Doolittle*. Who knows?

Eventually I spotted the low lying Dog Island. Interestingly (to me anyway), the New Zealand Government's Department of Statistics says this about Dog Island: "At the 2001 Census of Population and Dwellings the usually resident population count for Dog Island was 0". Then it goes on to say, "All population statistics are for the census, usually resident population count and have been randomly rounded to base three to preserve confidentiality. Percentages have been calculated against complete responses; that is, they exclude cases where no answers were provided and have been calculated on the rounded data so do not always total 100%". My best reading of this is that there may not be 0 people there in reality. It is highly possible that half a person lives there, or possibly even more than that if they failed to answer questions, or were not well rounded, or were possibly *unusual residents*.

When we had been riding down Foveaux Strait towards Riverton we had been unable to see Stewart Island because of poor visibility, but now the mountains of the Rakiura National Park were clearly visible and looking spectacular.

I could see the north-east coast of Stewart Island, where Halfmoon Bay was situated. Assistance from the GPS was, for once, not needed so it was working perfectly, as expected. Bastard electronics!

As we reached the middle of the strait the wind came up and we had to work a bit harder, but this only lasted twenty minutes and then we started to gain shelter in the lee of the island. We had a fantastic run past Horseshoe Bay and into the beautiful Halfmoon Bay, to the town of Oban.

The town of Oban is quite striking. As you enter Halfmoon Bay the wharf is on the right. Straight ahead is the beach. Right on the waterfront is the magnificent South Sea Hotel and behind that is the town. On the left are low-lying hills covered in bush, with houses scattered throughout. It's a lovely spot to come into. We rode up the bay at speed and parked in front of the hotel. We looked up at the hotel and could see Alan Wadds walking down towards us. Off to the left Lee was filming our arrival.

Alan came down and shook our hands and asked us how we felt. We were pretty damn happy because we had broken the back of the ride and got around Puysegur Point. We were also back on schedule, because we weren't due to leave Stewart Island until Monday morning and it was only Saturday night.

We could both see the hotel, and could almost smell the

beer (it was probably on Alan's breath), but we needed to get the Seadoos out of the water and this was not the place to do it. We ended up having to ride the Seadoos around Native Island into Paterson Inlet to a small launch ramp. There we were met by Alan and his mates, Bruce Ford and Trevor McLellan, who had organised a huge trailer to put the Seadoos on. The trailer was so large that the Seadoos fit on in tandem. We roped them on and then drove with them over the hill to Oban where we parked them on display in front of the hotel and settled down at a table for a few welcome cold beers.

The beer was cold and tasty, and the locals were friendly and welcoming. The atmosphere was great. Burglar and I voted the South Sea Hotel as one of our *all-time favourite pubs*, and the locals as being *the friendliest locals*. [Now it needs to be noted that we don't take things like this lightly. Before you vote on something like that you need to have seen a few pubs, which we have, and met a few locals, which we also have.]

While on the subject of voting for things, visitors to Sydney International Airport in the last couple of years might have noticed a big sign out the front that says, *Voted Worlds Best Airport 2005*. When I first saw this sign I asked, "Voted by whom, the management of Sydney Airport?" The only way this could have been legitimate is if all the voters had never seen another airport other than Sydney. At the risk of a full body search at customs, or having my bags sent into orbit around Saturn to join all the other lost airline luggage that makes up its rings, I have to say that, in my experience, it is not one of the world's best airports. This is because it is a monopoly and is owned and run by a bank. To illustrate, here is my take on the 'Sydney experience'.

You arrive at the departure level and your taxi slows down a bit to let you out. If it stops, a security man of some doubtful foreign origin will move it on while some of your suitcases are still in it. You will have no choice but to arrive in a taxi, however, because parking at the airport is so expensive that if you park for more than a couple of days it would be cheaper to buy a new car on your return than it would be to pay the bill.

If you are lucky enough to get this far you will want a trolley to carry your bags. But these are inconveniently priced to rob you at AU$3, and you won't have the correct change because you will have gratefully used it to tip the taxi driver for not killing you on the way to the airport. So your wife and kids will walk inside, leaving you, the mule, to struggle in underneath five or six bags.

When you get inside the terminal it won't be obvious where to check in and if you can't read English it will be impossible to find out. If you find the check-in counter you should concentrate on enjoying your check-in experience because this is the domain of the airlines, and is something they do quite well.

Once checked in you will want to go through immigration, but you need to understand that this is primarily an expensive shopping mall with an airport attached to it (this is so you can go for a little fly if you get bored with shopping). So, although it will be obvious where to shop, immigration is hard to find. When you find immigration, if it is not 3.23am, or thereabouts, you will usually find yourself in a queue that winds from one end of the hall to the other and then back again about twenty times. So, although you start about 10 m from an immigration officer as the crow flies, you are actually a 5 km walk from getting through immigration. This is a great way to meet people as you shuffle back and forward past the same people who are physically right next to you, but effectively 100 m ahead or behind. Some people make life-long friends at barbecues in Sydney immigration queues.

As your flight time draws ever closer, and sweat is dripping profusely off your brow from the stress and the exercise, you will just get through immigration in time to head to another queue at security. Sydney security are more clever than other security organisations and they turn up the sensitivity on their machines so that no one can get through without first getting naked and balancing on one foot, while touching the toes of the person immediately behind you and singing *Swing Low Sweet Chariot* in harmony with the other queues parallel to yours.

Finally you make it through security, sort through everyone's clothes and get dressed in something you like, possibly taking the opportunity to upgrade your mobile phone at the same time. You then find that to get to your departure gate there is no option other than to take a circuitous tour of the duty free shop, which has been placed there 'for your convenience'. Should your flight be delayed (and it usually is delayed waiting for people like you to get through immigration and security), you may decide to seek sustenance. You will sadly discover that the price of food reflects the bonuses of the bank's executives, so that your credit card will be unable to cope and will be refused by the vendor. You will then spend the rest of your waiting time wandering around with that vacant, slightly startled look on your face which is so typical of international travelers.

You will eventually get airborne and I beg you to rest up because when you return it will be just as hard to get out through the airport. Things to look forward to there are, running the gauntlet of another duty free store, a baggage claim hall with twelve carousels but where only one is being used to service three 747s, and the inbound queues in customs and immigration where good old 'politically correct' Australia makes sure there are more immigration officers looking after the foreigners than the locals, thus ensuring that the foreigners get to quarantine with their deep fired bananas, herbal remedies and pet tarantulas just before you.

The most amazing thing about Sydney airport is that they charge you for all this fine service that they are providing to you. At time of writing, the departure tax at Sydney airport was AU$38, the most expensive in Australia and one of the most expensive in the world.

Enough said. Sydney is definitely not the world's worst airport, but it isn't even fit to be a pimple on the bum of airports like Singapore's Changi Airport. But don't get me started. Actually I started it, didn't I? Sorry. On with the story.

So we had a few more beers and then Rodney and Dee turned up on the ferry. Finally, when all the beer had been drunk, we returned to the Deep Bay Apartments owned by Alan and Lee. The apartments are classy and new, and in a great setting overlooking Deep Bay. Visitors to Stewart Island would be hard pressed to do better than this for accommodation and local hospitality.

Before things got too out of control we checked the weather forecast for the next few days. Tomorrow would be good, but the next day wouldn't be so good. We really needed a day off, but we didn't want to risk getting stuck on Stewart Island. It would be better to get ahead and ride with the good weather up the East Coast of the South Island. Weather systems down south are pretty predictable in that they come through in a regular fashion from the south-west and move north-east up the country. The weather ahead of these fronts is normally bad, and behind the fronts is normally a lot better. What we hoped to do was move up the country at the same pace as the current weather system and stay in between the patches of bad weather. This was something that it was not possible to do when we were heading down the West Coast, and we had had to take on each new system head on.

Our new ground crew, Matt and Pete, were not due to meet us until Monday in Dunedin. Their plan was to arrive in Queenstown on Sunday evening and then drive to Lawrence and stay with my brother Tim's in-laws, Dennis and Marie Kean, at the historic Marama Lodge. Then on Monday they would drive on to Dunedin to meet up with us. I called them both to say that we might end up a day ahead and would make a decision after viewing the weather forecast in the morning. They both generously decided to change their arrangements and head to Queenstown first thing in the morning to be ready for whatever eventuated. With this all organised, we were now able to relax a bit.

We had more beer and some very tasty fresh fish for dinner. Rodney and I caught up some more on the last twenty-five years and everyone had a jolly old time. We retired much later than usual. It had been a big day. We had covered 360 km and were worn out, but euphoria has a way of cancelling out pain.

Burglar crosses Foveaux Strait.

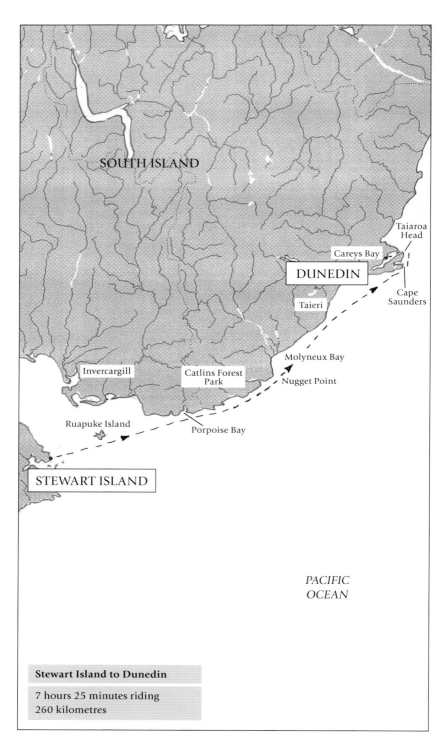

SOUTH ISLAND

Taiaroa
Head

Careys Bay

DUNEDIN

Taieri

Cape
Saunders

Molyneux Bay

Invercargill

Catlins Forest
Park

Nugget Point

Ruapuke Island

Porpoise Bay

STEWART ISLAND

PACIFIC
OCEAN

Stewart Island to Dunedin

7 hours 25 minutes riding
260 kilometres

Chapter 16
The Ride: To Dunedin

Sunday 19th February 2006

Now, I want to ask you something. If you had a rostered day off in a beautiful spot like Stewart Island and you woke to a glorious day, would you lie back and enjoy it, or would you punish yourself and run like hell to stay ahead of threatening weather?

We ran! The weather forecast for the next day was looking worse, so we made the decision to move on. The upside to this was that we would end up nearly a day ahead of schedule.

The downside was that the press and our Cancer Society contacts were not expecting us in Dunedin today. I phoned the long suffering Cath Saunders and let her know of our decision. She would have to reorganise our media and contact schedule yet again but, as always, she did a marvelous job. She understood that it was more important for us to finish the ride than to worry about the odd interview we might miss out on. I also left a message for our ground crew, Matt, informing him of the decision.

It's hard to leave a place like Stewart Island on a nice day. The beauty of the place is astounding. With its fishing charters and fantastic bush walks it's just another example of why New Zealand is the adventure capital of the world. The main island is roughly triangular in shape and has a total land area of about 1740 km². The coastline is very ragged and is deeply penetrated by the branching Paterson Inlet in the north and Port Pegasus in the south. It is fringed by rocky offshore islets. In the north is the complex, rugged highland containing Mt Anglem, at 980 m.

It appears we had turned up on a rare day. Climatic data for Stewart Island is scanty at best, but records from Halfmoon Bay show the average annual rainfall to be 1400 mm, evenly distributed through the year. Summer temperatures seldom rise to 20° C, but winter temperatures seldom drop below freezing. Strong winds are frequent, especially from the west, and calm days are said to be as rare as heavy frosts and prolonged snowfalls.

In the early days European settlements were mostly associated with sealing, whaling, timber, gold and tin. These days the Fiordland-Foveaux-Stewart Island area is New Zealand's chief source of crayfish and blue cod and the fishing industry, directly or indirectly, supports most of the population of Stewart Island.

Stewart Island is known to the Maori as Rakiura; *The Island of the Glowing Sky.*

This is possibly a reference to the sunsets for which the island is famous, or for the *aurora australis*; sometimes called the southern lights; that are a phenomenon of our southern latitudes.

All in all Stewart Island is a dramatic place and we regretted having to leave so quickly.

Our regret was tempered, however, by the fact that we knew we would be back even as we made our preparations to leave. Lee cooked us a fine breakfast. Then we dressed again and Alan drove us over to Oban to refuel the Seadoos with donated fuel from his company, Oban Slippage and Engineering. While there, I made the worrying discovery that my Camelbak was leaking, so if I wanted a drink I would have to stop and open the front compartment to get a drink from the spare drink container. What a hassle!

Once fueling was complete, the Seadoos were towed back over the hill to Paterson Inlet where we launched, had a photo session and said our goodbyes again. Rodney and I promised not to leave it another twenty-five years to catch up again.

After beating into the swells all the way down the West Coast we were looking forward to running with the swells up the East Coast. I had rung Mary Leask from Bluff Fisherman's Radio to check on the sea conditions and she had told me to expect following seas across Foveaux Strait, but then to expect head-on seas up the coast to Dunedin. That didn't sound so good, as we were sick to death of battling into oncoming seas. The wind forecast was for north-westerlies up the coast, which should be okay if we stuck close in to the shore.

We headed out of Paterson Inlet and set our heading northeast in great conditions, zigzagging through all the islands outside the inlet, and aiming to pass just south of Ruapuke Island. Near Ruapuke Island we had a visit and a chat with the Coast Guard, who were doing their Sunday patrol and had spotted us. We spoke with them for about five minutes and then continued on.

From there we aimed for The Brothers Point on the coast of the Catlins. The Catlins is an area of coastline and forest park roughly running from Fortrose in the west to Balclutha in the north-east. It is slowly becoming better known for its natural beauty and rare sea life. There are rare species of dolphin, seal and penguin in the area.

The Hector's Dolphins live at Porpoise Bay near Waikawa all summer and are known to play for hours with bathers, though if they are not in the mood the local rule is that they must not be approached, but left alone to feed and rest. New Zealand Sea Lions; formerly called Hooker's Sea Lions; can be seen at Waipapa Point. A mature bull sea lion can weigh up to 500 kg, and they are not shy of humans. The Fur Seal is another of the family seen around the coast, more often on rocky shores. A very rare visitor to the area is the Elephant Seal, a four tonne giant of the Sub-Antarctic. The Yellow-Eyed Penguin can also be found in the area. These birds pair for life and always return to their favourite nesting sight. They nest amongst the roots of forest trees or flax, within calling range, but not within sight, of the next pair. There is also a large variety of other bird species in the area.

With its natural history and rugged coastline, the Catlins is definitely on my list of places to go back to and explore.

It was off the Catlins where the forecast sea conditions came to pass. In the space of 10 km we went from riding with a nice ½ m following swell, to thumping into 1 m north-easterly bouncers. It became very uncomfortable and slowed us down considerably. We were both extremely grumpy about it, but there was nothing we could do except plough on. I was hurting big time. My infected ankle was sore, my arms were sore and my butt was sore, and we still had 200 km to go. To add to our pain, we kept coming across large deposits of kelp and seaweed which would involve a detour, or a nervous high speed run, while hoping like hell that we didn't block the jet intakes.

When you get into a rhythm, no matter how uncomfortable it is, it is a time for thinking. I can't speak for Burglar on this, but I thought about all sorts of things. On bad days I would always ask myself why we were doing this and would always get the same answers, so I would put that subject to bed and go somewhere else. One of the questions that the press always seemed to ask was how did riding a Seadoo for ten hours a day compare to flying a 747. The answer is, it doesn't. The only thing it has in common is that down here I am riding the queen of the seas and up there I ride the queen of the skies.

Down here I get wet and cold and beaten up and have to argue with myself; most times losing the argument. Up there I am warm, dry, comfortable and well looked after. I always have someone interesting to talk to who doesn't argue too much, because I am the Captain. I consider myself lucky to do what I do. I do a job that is interesting and challenging. I see the world and I work with fantastic people. I am lucky because I get to work with the crème de la crème of Australia's population. That's like saying I work with the finest of the fine, because most Australians are descended from early Australians who were nearly all 'handpicked' by British judges.

There are over two-thousand-three-hundred pilots in mainline Qantas and I meet new people every time I go to work. Almost to a person, they never fail to impress me with their strength of character, commonsense and work ethic. It is a testament to these people that three or four complete strangers can meet at a briefing desk and within minutes form a working team. Within an hour that team is moving four-hundred passengers, on a $200 million aircraft, safely and efficiently from one country to another. It's quite something really, and it's not something the travelling public see. But that teamwork and strict standard operating procedures, backed up by investment in training, are the reasons why some airlines have much better safety records than others. The value of this should not be underestimated.

We pilots are actually *energy management specialists*. Do I hear you asking, "Tell me more"? I was going to tell you anyway, but thanks for asking. We take a 400 tonne aircraft, with a heap of inertia. We use chemical potential energy stored in tanks (fuel), which we set fire to. The resultant heat energy 'works' on the system and is converted to kinetic energy and gravitational potential energy. Once the aircraft is at its cruising level it has a fast reducing store of chemical potential energy, a fairly constant kinetic energy and a truckload of gravitational potential energy. When we approach and land somewhere, we have to manage all the different energies to slow up the aircraft and bring it to a halt, preferably in one piece and in the right place, before the chemical potential energy is totally replaced in the tanks by air. The grand finale of all this is the heat energy created from using the brakes to reduce the kinetic energy of the aircraft to zero (And I can tell you there is enough of this to hold a substantial barbecue).

I will stop now because I can already hear some of you snoring. But to sum it up, apart from jetlag, radiation and being away from family, it's a great job. We go to work, do our job, come home and have a break. The only time this routine is broken is when we are asked to be on standby to operate a flight at short notice in case someone is sick, or there is a disruption of some sort. Pilots and the company have bipolar views on how standby duties should go. The company's view is that you should be sitting in your car with your uniform (including hat)(especially hat) on and the engine running with the garage door open. The pilot's view is that you should be playing golf on a resort island somewhere in Fiji wearing a beeper. The reality tends to end up somewhere in the middle, so it works fairly well.

Getting back to the ride. We plodded on, bouncing from wave to wave and every now and then taking a particularly hard knock that would make us swear in frustration. Our progress was glacial. People were expecting us in Dunedin by three o'clock, but we knew we would be late. We passed across Molyneux Bay and then went by the Taieri River mouth. From there we could see Cape Saunders on the Otago Peninsula, so we cut across directly for that. Around 30 km short of Cape Saunders the wind came up from the northeast at 30 km an hour. To this day I can't believe that happened. The wind should have been north-westerly, if anything, and this headwind was totally unwelcome. It whipped up the sea to about 1½ m; the waves were steep and fast moving. Our pace slowed even further and we were taking a beating. It took us another hour to reach the cape. By then we felt like we had spent the day in a cement mixer. I was cold and sore all over and my arms were numb. There wasn't a single part of me that was happy. As well as this, I was dehydrated, because it was impractical to stop every ten minutes to take a drink.

When your map is wet and unreadable the Otago Peninsula can be tricky to navigate around. It has a series of inlets which all; one by one, and in a particularly devious and purposeful way; pretend to be the entrance to Otago Harbour. When we passed Hoopers

Inlet, Burglar announced that he was again running out of fuel. This was terribly frustrating because, weather-wise, we were up against it and, from what I could tell, we still had about 25 km to go. There was still hope though, as the gauge was pointing to E. There was nothing for it but to go faster so he would get there before his fuel ran out. We were carrying spare fuel in 10 litre drums in our front compartments, but they were installed in such a way that in these conditions it would be impossible to get at them. We slogged our way past Papanui Inlet and across Wickliffe Bay, then past Pipikaretu Point. A little further on we finally made it to Taiaroa Point, and the entrance to Otago Harbour which, to the uninitiated and in complete contrast to the other inlets, doesn't look at all like the entrance to a major harbour.

We made our way in the entrance and enjoyed some respite from the head-on waves. We followed the channel markers in and, when we had made it a kilometre or so into the harbour, my engine started to give me trouble. It was running very rough and would not respond to my request to speed up for the final few kilometres. I was stuck at about 30 km/hr maximum and, every minute or so, the engine would stop altogether.

This was pretty annoying, but we were both thankful that it had waited until we made it into the harbour to start playing up. Any other time in the last eight hours would have been a real pain. Eventually we could see Careys Bay about 4 km away in the distance. This was our final destination for the day and it looked very welcoming.

But, in what can only be described as a complete letdown, as I struggled to cover the last 2 km, Burglar's machine ran out of fuel. So while I limped into Careys Bay, Burglar drifted 2 km out while he refueled from one of his drums. He eventually arrived, much to everyone's relief, as they had all been waiting a while. We had to pose for photos again then Matt and Pete did valet parking of the Seadoos for us while we walked up the beach to meet our greeting party.

There to meet us were Penelope Scott from the local Cancer Society and local residents, Dougal and Carolyn Stevenson. If you are over forty and have lived in New Zealand for the last thirty years you will remember Dougal Stevenson as the premiere television newsreader of his day. I always remember that cheeky, friendly smile and, do you know what, he hasn't changed a bit. He is even more of a character in real life, as he doesn't have to worry about upsetting anyone, or being politically correct. His wife Carolyn is absolutely delightful as well and a real star in her own right. The Stevensons have an association with the Cancer Society because Carolyn unfortunately has cancer, so naturally they volunteered to come down and welcome us. They had organised a sumptuous lunch for us, which we devoured at the Carey Bay Pub.

I'm going to jump back to our ground crew now, because I don't like to ignore them completely while I'm eating and drinking and they are working. Chainsaw and Chinashop had now been replaced by the original Pete and the new Captain Matt Gray of Qantas.

Matt will forthwith be referred to as Mateus because of his vast knowledge of viticulture, and his keenness to partake in the products of same. Pete and Mateus had arrived together in Queenstown early that morning. It had not been difficult for them to identify each other because I had mentioned to Pete that Mateus has a more than passing resemblance to Colonel Klink from Hogan's Heroes. Pete had spotted him straight away. They had picked up the Sorento and driven to Lawrence, where they had *taken tea* with Dennis and Marie Kean at the Marama Lodge. They had then driven to Careys Bay for our imminent, but delayed, arrival. At this very moment they were refueling the Seadoos and generally doing a fine job, as we sat talking with Dougal, Carolyn and Penelope.

By the way I think we may have set a record here, and you are part of it. This has to be the first book outside Scotland that has two characters called Dougal in it and you are reading it. I may approach the Guinness Book of records and see if they are interested. If they are, I'll let you know, because they'll want your names too.

Anyway, we stayed at the Careys Bay pub for sometime and discussed what we would do about dinner. There was some talk about us all attending a local restaurant, but in the end the Stevensons decided it would be more fun to have a barbecue at their place. Dougal organised us some accommodation at Billy Browns backpackers' hostel, so we headed out there to get settled in before the barbecue.

Billy Browns is the nicest backpackers' hostel I have ever seen. It is nestled between Port Chalmers and Aramoana on the western side of Otago Harbour, on a sheep and deer farm opposite the Otago Peninsula. It has excellent views of Otago Harbour. Inside, it is well maintained and has a lot of character. We spent some time there showering and getting organised. Then we headed further east along the coast to the Stevenson's.

They had an awesome place on a twenty acre block and it too had handsome views of Otago Harbour. We had a wonderful time. The food was great, the company was great and the Stevenson's dogs confirmed I haven't lost my touch with dogs. For some reason dogs like to sit on my foot. I was at a triathlon in Sydney once with about a thousand other people and there was one dog there. It managed to find me and sit on my foot twice in the space of an hour. Colin Bowers dog (R.I.P.) was not happy unless it sat on my foot while I watched rugby at Colin's house. Here too, and true to form, one of the Stevenson's dogs sat on my foot, and I'm sure the other one was lining up impatiently for his turn. I don't know what it is. Maybe it's the way I wiggle my toes.

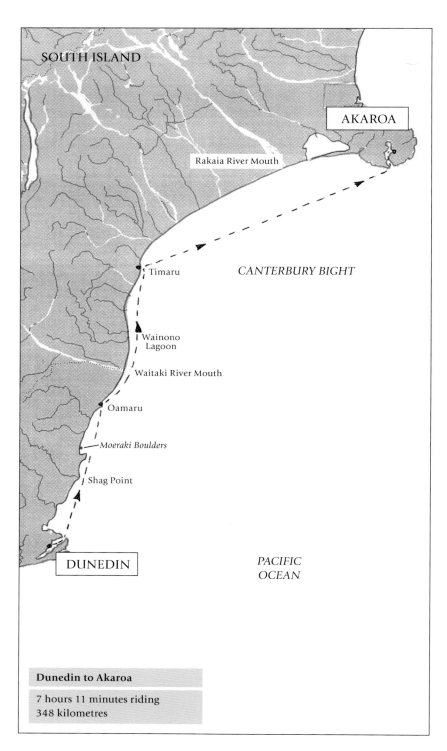

SOUTH ISLAND

AKAROA

Rakaia River Mouth

CANTERBURY BIGHT

Timaru

Wainono
Lagoon

Waitaki River Mouth

Oamaru

Moeraki Boulders

Shag Point

DUNEDIN

PACIFIC
OCEAN

Dunedin to Akaroa

7 hours 11 minutes riding
348 kilometres

Chapter 17

The Ride: To Akaroa

Monday 20th February 2006

Waking at a civilised hour isn't easy when your body is used to getting up early. We woke early out of habit and got up for some breakfast and coffee. The view from Billy Browns was stunning and we could see it was going to be a good day. The sun was shining, there was no wind, and there were thick layers of fog and mist clinging to the hills around Otago Harbour. We would have liked to get an early start, but we had to wait until 9am to take the Seadoos into the Dunedin Seadoo dealer, Read Marine, to get my machine looked at.

The fact that we had a couple of hours to kill was both frustrating and gratifying as we sat and drank extravagant amounts of coffee. I did a radio interview with the local Classic Hits station which went really well and was light hearted and a lot of fun. Then at 8.30am we loaded up the Sorento and headed past Port Chalmers into Dunedin.

The city of Dunedin is situated at the head of Otago Harbour in a setting of great natural beauty. It is surrounded by imposing hills to the west and the harbour to the east. The harbour is a recent creation, formed by the flooding of two river valleys in the last big sea-level rise. Dunedin is famous as a university town and students make a large contribution to the local economy. Young people from all over New Zealand attend Otago University.

One of the attractions of Dunedin is the ski fields of Queenstown, just three hours drive to the west.

The business and industrial portion of the city is concentrated on flat land, most of which has been reclaimed over the years from the harbour. It was to the industrial area we headed now to find Read Marine.

We introduced ourselves to Latham Wardhaugh who is the mechanic at Read Marine. He spent the next two hours working on my Seadoo and calling Brett from Bombardier Recreational Products in Auckland for advice.

While this was happening, Mateus went on a shopping expedition to find a replacement bladder for my Camelbak, which had died the day before, robbing me of the life giving Raro drink (I'll take the house, car, boat, world trip, lifetime supply of Tui beer, *and* a couple of front row tickets for the Burglar Brothers at the finals of the 2006 Swedish women's volleyball tournament).

Latham worked away on my Seadoo while we paced around and fretted about wasting the amazing weather. It was really frustrating that he didn't seem to be able to find anything wrong with it.

One of the other guys there was doing a bit of a cleanup on the machine and suddenly I noticed that the rag he was using looked strangely familiar. This time it was unmistakable. It was the Prime Minister's bikini there for all to see, with it's trademark Labour Party insignia in two tone white and red, albeit a little dirty from the engine filth. I asked him where he had got it and he had no idea. It had just been in the rag bag. How bizarre.

With the twin mysteries of the Seadoo engine problem and the bikini both seemingly unsolvable, we decided to put both Seadoos in the water at a nearby ramp and if my machine went okay we would continue on our journey.

I wasn't entirely happy with the arrangement because there had been a major problem with my Seadoo and we hadn't identified what it was. I hoped it wouldn't manifest itself again somewhere in the middle of nowhere. I suspected that it had something to do with contaminated fuel. The fuel tanks were slowly disintegrating from within. Every day we would find bits of metal and chips of rubber in the fuel filters and we could hear the loose baffles trying to bash their way through the sides of the tanks. We were keeping our fingers crossed that the tanks would hold together until we reached Auckland.

We launched at 11.30am and my machine was working fine, so we zoomed off down the harbour in perfect conditions past Port Chalmers, past Billy Browns and the Stevenson's place, then out through the harbour entrance with Heywood Point on the left, and the massive Taiaroa Head on the right.

Once in the open sea we headed north in almost perfect conditions. The ocean was like glass, with just a small underlying 1 m swell. There was no wind and the sun was beaming down on us. We felt good and were making great progress.

We headed straight for Shag Point near Palmerston. Shag Point is an area of great natural beauty, that boasts seal colonies, Yellow Eyed Penguins and, you guessed it, shags.

There are numerous seal colonies and resting sights along the coast to the north and south of Dunedin just like the one at Shag Point.

Seals and other marine animals are a favoured fodder of great white sharks, which could explain the relatively high rate of attacks on people in this area; when in the water, humans are, in effect, marine mammals too. Great white sharks can swallow quite large prey whole. A 90 kg fur seal was found in just two pieces in the stomach of a 1,520 kg 'juvenile' great white shark in October 2005. Not wanting to become statistics, Burglar and I were taking great care to avoid entering the water and becoming re-categorised as marine mammals. On my advice Burglar had also been practicing walking on water, a skill which I had automatically acquired on becoming a Captain some sixteen years ago.

Fifteen kilometres north of Shag Point is Moeraki Point, and just past there are the famous Moeraki Boulders. The boulders are grey-coloured septarian concretions which have been eroded out by wave action from the cliffs of soft, black mudstone that back the beach. They originally formed on the sea floor when the mudstone was accumulating during the early Tertiary period some sixty million years ago. The largest concretions are traversed by cracks, filled by yellow calcite. In some the upper part is worn away and only a shell remains, looking like discarded segments of orange peel. The concretions weigh several tonnes and are up to 3.5 m in circumference, making them quite magnificent to behold.

From Moeraki Point it is only about twenty minutes to the metropolis of Oamaru. We zoomed into the artificial harbour at Oamaru's Friendly Bay at high speed and made our way towards the beach at the north-west corner. The local newspaper was there to meet us, so we posed for photos and said all the right things. We had just about heard all the possible questions by now and even Burglar was starting to become quite the spokesman.

Our ground crew hadn't turned up yet which showed just what good time we were making. I phoned them to let them know that they were weak and pathetic, and that they could meet us in Timaru instead, but only if they were up to it. We then headed out of Oamaru harbour with three new friends who were going to accompany us halfway to Timaru on their PWCs.

The sea conditions were just as good as before and we had a magnificent ride past the Waitaki River entrance and on to the Wainono Lagoon where, regrettably, our new friends waved us on and turned back towards Oamaru. It's around about Wainono Lagoon that one unknowingly enters the Canterbury region.

Canterbury is well known for its famous Rugby team, the Canterbury Crusaders, who have an enviable record of success, having won over half of the Super 12 and Super 14 titles up for grabs over the last decade.

It could be said that New Zealand is obsessed by rugby.

I suspect that the sharemarket's performance hinges on the results of games and the country is thrown into a red mist of mourning when the national team loses. Just about every New Zealand male has a story about his rugby playing days, and how he just missed out making it to the big time. I believe this religious obsession with rugby is because New Zealand continually punches above its weight at the sport.

The All Blacks are New Zealand's national team. The team is selected from a population of four million people and forty million sheep. A sheep has never actually made the 'run on' national team, but with political correctness gone mad in New Zealand it is only a matter of time before a certain number of sheep will have to be included in each team. That aside, the All Blacks play countries like Australia, South Africa, France and England, all of whom have many times larger populations to choose from. The All Blacks record is outstanding, and they are usually the World's number one ranked team.

Australians and New Zealanders like to wind each other up over sporting results, particularly between the two countries. "Oh really?" I hear you saying, "When did you first discover this?" With all due respect sarcasm is the lowest form of wit and I'll ask you politely not to interrupt and let me get on with the story. Thank you! Australians are also very keen on inferring that New Zealanders do inappropriate things with sheep. My guess is that the reason why they get so up in arms about this is because they didn't think of it first, and we have better looking sheep.

There is a lot of 'friendly and informed' comment flowing both ways across the Tasman Sea about the various deficiencies of our national teams. There have been some notable incidents over the years where sportsmen have embarrassed themselves trying to beat the other country by foul, devious and odious means.

One such event was the infamous underarm bowling incident of February 1, 1981 when Australia was playing New Zealand in a one-day international cricket match. New Zealand required a six from the final ball in order to tie the match. The Australian captain, Greg Chappel, ordered the bowler, his brother Trevor Chappel, to bowl underarm; that is, rolling the ball along the ground to avoid the possibility that the No. 10 New Zealand batsman, Brian McKechnie, would score a six to tie the match.

Australia won the game, but the New Zealand batsmen marched off in disgust and since that day the underarm bowling incident has been a source of discussion, both heated and jocular, between Australians and New Zealanders.

It was described as, "The most disgusting incident I can recall in the history of cricket", by the then Prime Minister of New Zealand, Rob Muldoon, who also observed that, "It was an act of cowardice and I consider it appropriate that the Australian team were wearing yellow".

When the Australian Americas' Cup boat, One Australia, sank off San Diego in 1995, the New Zealand Brewer, Lion Nathan, put a full page advert in Australian papers the next day with a large bottle of Steinlager on it that said, "Never mind Aussies, try sinking a few of these". And New Zealand waste companies that don't plan to pick up rubbish on Christmas day routinely advertise the fact by saying, "Don't leave your rubbish out tonight or Santa will take it over and give it to the Aussies". A more recent report to emerge from New Zealand was that Osama bin Laden had been found in the Australian Wallabies rugby team's trophy cabinet. Apparently he said it was cold, dark and empty, and reminded him of an Afghanistan cave.

You get the picture now I'm sure. All this generally good natured taunting just serves to enhance the fact that contests and matches between the two nations are relished by sports fans in both countries.

Australians are at least as enthusiastic about their sport as New Zealanders are and they have a proud sporting record. I reckon the secret to their success, and one thing I really admire, is their tremendous self belief. Australia has never been famous for their

soccer team and, when the Australian soccer team recently qualified for the World Cup no-one was more surprised than they were.
As sweepstakes were held in workplaces worldwide for picking
the winner of the cup, any one who drew Australia or the US was
immediately entitled to their money back. But the Australian team
played way above themselves and, in an awesome display of skill,
mind over matter and self belief, they made it to the final sixteen.
They then played Italy and lost in the last minute because of a
penalty against them that should not have been awarded. It was a
terrible blow to be swept out of the cup in that way. Subsequently,
in an even greater display of self belief and self flagellation, some
Australian commentators, and even a few of my compatriots at
Qantas, have chosen to assume that had that penalty not been
awarded, then Australia would have eventually beaten Italy.
It then stands to reason that, because Italy eventually won the cup,
Australia would have done so too, if not for the unfortunate turn
of events. Well done, Australian soccer. It was a great effort, but
come down out of the clouds, you are cleared to land.

Australian self belief is one thing, but the thing that they excel
the most at is in their biased commentary of sporting matches.
Most commentators from countries other than Australia will at
least try and look as if they are giving a balanced account of a
match. Australian commentators normally do not. They are
unashamedly and entertainingly Australian and when you listen
to them it sounds like they have bet their house and kids on the
result, and they probably have (Australians are famous for betting
on anything, even the proverbial 'two flies crawling up a wall'). If
Australia is winning, it is because of skill. If they are losing, it is
because of bad luck or poor refereeing. If a foreigner stretches the
rules, he is cheating and should be hung, drawn and quartered.
If an Aussie does, then that is clever play.

All of this makes for a contentious relationship with some
of my Qantas mates. If Australia wins I avoid going to work for
as long as possible and, when I do, I sneak around and keep my

head low, so as not to receive too much of a hard time. When New Zealand wins I rush to work and very subtly pretend not to have seen the game, which then gives me the opportunity to ask the result of the wounded Australians, who are also pretending not to have watched it.

Rugby Union is probably the most important trans-Tasman sport. For those international readers who have never seen the game of rugby, I will now give you a layman's description of it. As you will see, it is a fascinating game. Meanwhile, the rest of you feel free to put out the garbage or empty the dishwasher or do something else as long as it's useful.

Rugby is played on a rectangular grass field 100 m by 69 m. There are two teams of fifteen men each. Each team is divided up into eight *forwards* and seven *backs*. Put simply, the forwards are big and slow and the backs are slightly smaller and fast.

Each of the fifteen men has a named position. There are a couple of *props*, who are normally big and strong, and as ugly as a junkyard dog. There are *tighthead* and *loosehead* props. Loose forwards are sometimes referred to as looseys, but not to their face. There are a couple of *flankers* and, if you plan to get their attention by yelling "hey flanker", make sure you carefully annunciate the 'fl' part of the word, or they will get a little testy. There are also two *locks* who see themselves as the key to the whole team, but they are not.

There is a *hooker*. Until recently, rugby hookers were the only legal hookers in New Zealand. Now hookers are a dime a dozen. The props, hooker and locks are known as the *tight five*. This is not because they are tight with their money, although I have known rugby payers who wouldn't shout if a shark bit them. They are known as the tight five because they are not loose (their mothers are very proud of this), and they stick together running about the field, almost as if roped together by the family jewels.

In the backs there is a *halfback* and a *first five eighth* (don't ask me), a *centre* and an *inside centre* or *second five eighth*. The inside centre, rather than being found with his head up the bum of the centre, is actually found some distance from the centre, and that would be my choice too. There are two *wings*, which is normally where you would expect to find the props, but you would be disappointed if you went looking for them there. There is a *number eight*, who is both big and fast and is normally the last to be potted and there is a *full back*, who is twice the man that the half back is. Confused yet?

Wait!!

The game is played with an oval shaped ball and the general idea is for one team to get the ball down to the far end of the field to the opposing team's goal line and score a *try*. This is a funny name for a score, because each attempt at getting the ball down the field is a good try in my books, even if they don't make it. They try frequently, but frequently fail to score a try. While this is going on the other team that doesn't have the ball is trying to stop the team with the ball from getting a try.

These guys are all warriors and the game is very rough and not for the fainthearted. That is why it is so absurd that a player can be penalised for excessively rough play. This is about as ridiculous as the idea of *touch boxing* as a sport. This is not lawn bowls you know (some of the old girls at bowls are far more vicious).

The officials of the game are the referee, who runs the show, two line umpires who help out from the sidelines, and a video referee who replays contentious events on TV and helps the referee with his decisions. The two line umpires are actually qualified referees who picked the short straw for the particular match. They spend their time interrupting the game to tell the real referee that a player has hit another player with his handbag in back play, or something like that, and that it is nothing serious and that they really only came onto the field to tell the referee so they could get on TV. No one really knows where the video referee lives, but they know it is somewhere near the top of some stairs. Whenever a video decision is required the field referee is said to be *going upstairs*. He then goes nowhere at all and waits for a decision by radio.

Having given you the full briefing so that you are now fully up to date with the game, I will describe a garden-variety passage of play that you can expect to see repeated many times over in a game.

At the start one team kicks the ball to the other team. One of their forwards grabs the ball and falls to the ground. All fifteen remaining forwards from both teams pile on top of the guy with the ball who is, right now, wondering why he grabbed the ball. There is on average about 1,600 kg of players on top of the ball, and this is why it is oval shaped. It would have originally been round, but a couple of good plays will have fixed that for good. With 1,600 kg pushing down on the ball it pops out like a wet bar of soap in one direction, or another. The half back on that side grabs the ball and sees all the forwards looking at him with intent to kill, so he immediately throws it away to the first five eighth who, not wanting to be caught with it either, kicks it into *touch* (i.e., over the sideline).

Hookers are never far from the action and it is now their job to throw the ball back into the field of play, via two lines of opposing forwards called a *lineout*. Hookers like to polish their balls, and on wet days they spend some time wiping them down with a rag to make them less slippery before they throw them in. While they are waiting for the hooker, the lines of forwards run around in circles, change places, lift each other up and do pirouettes and the do-si-do just like a gay line-dance at a county fair hoedown, but without the pleasantries.

Eventually the ball sails in from the sideline and a forward grabs it and tosses it straight to the *blindside* wing. He doesn't see it coming and drops it, but the referee rules that he dropped it backwards so it's *play on*. The wing picks up the ball and runs nervously into a wall of forwards. The opposing prop falls into his rightful place on the wing. The centre comes in in support and the two opposing front rows plow from the outside into the centre, giving him concussion. The other players then pile on, both for good measure and because if they don't they will be accused of lacking enthusiasm.

The ball pops out again, but the halfback *knocks it on* (i.e., drops it forward). "We'll scrum it here" says the referee but play is held up for a minute while a player feigns injury to give his team a rest. Miraculously he recovers from almost certain brain damage or spinal injury and is up hobbling around shortly after his team reorganises itself. The scrum goes down and all sixteen forwards try to out push each other like a reverse tug of war until the ball pops out the back and into play again.

The centre with concussion runs around like a chook with his head cut off, but refuses to be replaced (these boys are tough you know) until he gets the ball and starts to run the wrong way, and is then shot by a team sniper and forcibly replaced by sideline staff. Don't worry, bullet wounds rank low on the scale of rugby injuries. He'll be back next week.

Sometimes as a joke one of the backs will kick the ball over the top of both lots of forwards to one of the other team's backs. That man will then hold onto it for a bit, while both packs of forwards thunder ponderously towards him. When they are almost to him he will kick it back over the forwards heads to where it had originally come from. The forwards will slow up slightly more quickly than an oil supertanker, and slowly head back the other way. In this way the two kickers can have a lot of fun kicking back and forward to each other and the forwards get some much needed exercise. Wise backs don't do this too often, because they still have to go drinking with the forwards after the match and it is good not to get them too offside, so to speak.

Meanwhile, and while nobody has noticed, one team or the other has started to move closer and closer to the other teams try line. Maybe they will score a try, maybe not; no sweat or blood is spared in the attempt. Desperate times call for desperate measures, so the defending team starts to cheat a bit. A player gets penalised and has the look on his face of someone who has been wrongly accused of genocide. Then the kicker from the attacking team kicks the ball through the uprights and gets three points. In spite of the misguided politically correct who say that, "Winning is not important, it's how you play the game that counts", these guys want to know who won and are paid for results, so they keep score. After scoring, everyone on the scoring team cuddles, fondles and proposes marriage to each other for a bit and the other team sulk for a bit, then it's back to halfway for another kick-off, and away we go again.

If a player cheats too much, or tries to kill another player, he is given a *yellow card* and is sent off into the *sin bin* for ten minutes. The sin bin is an imaginary zone on the sideline where you sit and fume while you serve out your ten minute sentence. There is also another imaginary zone called the *blood bin* where you go when you are bleeding too much, so that the team doctor can put some builder's tape on your cut. The blood bin is also good if you need a rest and can find some blood on you somewhere.

At the end of the game the team with the most points wins, which is a victory for commonsense in itself. Then the two team Captains are interviewed for TV. Seldom will you see a bigger contrast in mood between two people. It is a pleasure to watch if your team won.

But enough about rugby already. Since I've digressed we've been stuck in limbo off Wainono Lagoon, politely and patiently waiting for me to finish rambling on about our national sport, so Tally Ho and its back to the ride.

We sped 40 km further north, past Scarborough and into the boat ramp at Caroline Bay in Timaru, to find that Pete and Mateus had finally got their act together and caught us up (Probably due to the amount of time I spent telling you about rugby).

There also to meet us were Gabrielle Hall and Kate McFarlane, both Cancer Society staff from Timaru. While the boys refueled and got food for us we talked to Kate and Gabrielle about the wonderful work that the Cancer Society does and the virtues of Timaru which, it seems, are numerous, if not obvious from the boat ramp. We then did another press interview and photo session and got the skin cancer message out there yet again.

Our original schedule had us overnighting in Oamaru this night and we were already 80 km further on. The next day we were due to ride from Oamaru to Christchurch.

The Seadoos needed a full service, so we would have to allow for some downtime in Christchurch. We calculated that we could still make Akaroa in Banks Peninsula tonight if the sea conditions stayed good. This would put us two hours away from Christchurch the next day. We decided to go for it and stay ahead of schedule as we knew that, at some stage, we would need the extra time.

If you head from Timaru across the Canterbury Bight directly to Akaroa Harbour's entrance, the distance is about 170 km, and you end up around 30 km off the coast for some of the time. But to follow the coast would add probably another 40 km. It was a big call to go direct, given the possibility of fuel contamination problems and an unreliable GPS, but it was still a stunning day and the sea conditions were almost perfect so we were happy that the risk-reward ratio was in our favour.

The boys got back from refueling and we briefed them of our decision, and the entire logistical nightmare that it would entail for them. They would have to cancel and rebook accommodation and advise everyone in Auckland. One of them would have to tell poor old Cath Saunders that our media schedule was changing again, and then they would have to get their unattractive butts to Akaroa before us, which would not be easy given the distance to be driven. The boys took it all on the chin as expected and I congratulated myself once again on selecting such fine team members. Then we ate lunch, said goodbye to Kate and Gabriel, argued for a minute about changing Timaru's name to Kangaru in honour of all our Aussie mates (a decision on this is still pending), and then put our heads down and zoomed directly out to sea in an east-north-east direction.

We made good time into an easterly, 1½ m swell, with only a hint of a ripple on it. The ripple was just enough to define the waves and make them easy to ride. After the beating we took the day before, this was like heaven to us. We felt like we had been released from our chains. We were happy, and even the lingering pains of our previous wear and tear were not enough to dampen our spirits. I could have done without the annoying itch from the rash on my back, but today it seemed like a non-event. We were on the way home and we were going there fast.

As we got further out to sea we could see the coastline getting further and further away and I hoped like hell that we wouldn't have mechanical problems. An hour and a half from Timaru we had already covered 90 km and the sea conditions were holding up. But in the distance I could see what looked like cloud ahead of us. As it drew closer it became obvious that it was sea fog. The tops of it were only about 40 m above the sea, but the fog looked very thick.

Before we knew it, we were in it. It was as thick as pea soup and I checked the GPS to see how far from Akaroa we were. We still had 80 km to run. I hoped that the fog would just be localised and that we would soon be out of it.

Burglar has a bad habit of following from the front. Even though he has no idea where he is going, he zooms around like a dog chasing a butterfly and as we entered the fog he continued to do this. I almost lost sight of him a couple of times as the visibility reduced to about 100 m, so I signaled for him to stop and pointed out to him that if he lost sight of me, he would never find me again, and that it would be wise to stick about 20 m on either side of me. He saw the logic in that and we continued on.

We were becoming seriously spatially disoriented. The combination of low visibility, no horizon and the angle on the easterly swell were making us think that we were heading about 10°

downhill, and that the whole ocean had a 15° lean to the left. This was disconcerting for me, but I knew what was causing it from my instrument flying training. Burglar, on the other hand, had no idea what it was and was suffering from massive disorientation. We had to stop while I explained what it was so that he could tell himself to ignore the false impression which he was getting. Ignoring spatial disorientation is a bit of a learned discipline and I could see he was still frustrated.

We continued on for another 40 km and the fog was as thick as ever. At one stage we startled a flock of large birds and one of them flew straight into my chest. The impact slightly winded me and, no doubt, would have been less than satisfactory for the poor bird as well. I hoped that it didn't have the flu.

We saw what looked like about a 3 m shark on the surface and we gave him some distance as soon as we could. We were now 30 km off the coast and 40 km short of Banks Peninsula in thick fog. Let me tell you that this is about as lonely as it gets. The thick cloak of fog had an eerie feeling to it and an almost overwhelming feeling of claustrophobia. I was almost expecting to come across Jack the Ripper in a rowboat, or a ghost ship heading for King Kong's island.

I had been watching the GPS carefully and looking for signs of trouble. I had also been keeping a mental plot of our position in my head, just in case. At 30 km from the Akaroa Harbour entrance, the thing that I had been dreading most happened. The GPS died again. I invented a couple of new swear words and then worked out what time I thought we would make Akaroa, based on the distance to go at the time of the failure and our present groundspeed. I then concentrated on hitting the swells at the same angle each time, which was difficult given the low visibility we were experiencing. I decided not to tell Burglar about the problem, given that there was nothing he could do about it and he was stretched just coping with his illusions.

As we got to within 10 km of the harbour, I started to become

concerned that the fog would not lift and, with the current visibility at about 100 m, or five seconds riding, that we would run
straight into the rocks below one of Banks Peninsula's many cliffs.
I slowed down considerably to give us more reaction time if this
were to happen. At about 3 km out from my estimated arrival time,
the sea conditions started to get worse, with a steeper and more
uneven wave pattern. This told me that we were getting close, as
we were now seeing the effect of the peninsula on the waves.
Five minutes further on, and with a massive sigh of relief, we
popped out of the fog. We were about 200 m off a cliff which was
situated about 400 m west of the entrance to Akaroa Harbour.

By now the sea conditions were well and truly of *dogs breakfast* standard and the Burglar Brothers stole slowly into Akaroa
Harbour under the cover of patchy fog, and in the troughs of
waves. It was 7pm and only about an hour of daylight remained.

Inside beautiful Akaroa Harbour conditions were magnificent
and we made our way quickly to the township of Akaroa. We felt
good, but weary. We had achieved a lot. We had covered 348 km in
seven hours and eleven minutes. The conditions had been good,
but just the sheer distance involved and the mental stress of the
fog had been enough to wear us out yet again.

We tied up to the main wharf and within a minute Pete appeared
to direct us to the boat ramp. The boys had just arrived. At the
ramp they pulled us out of the water and told us to stay put and
catch up on phone calls while they drove around looking for a bed
for the night. Akaroa is not a big place and we watched as the boys
drove past a few times looking for accommodation. Meanwhile,
I phoned home to see if my family still remembered who I was,
and contacted David Libeau from Qantas and Phil Briars from the
Cancer Society to let them know what was happening.

Just as it was getting dark the boys returned to say that they had
found the last two rooms in Akaroa. We headed down to the hotel
and found that we had indeed lucked out with some very fine
accommodation and a Barbecue put on by our host, who knew all

about us already and had been tracking us on Hereiam.

After a slow start we had had a very good day. And there is no finer way to end a good day than in the company of good people, with a barbecue and cold beer.

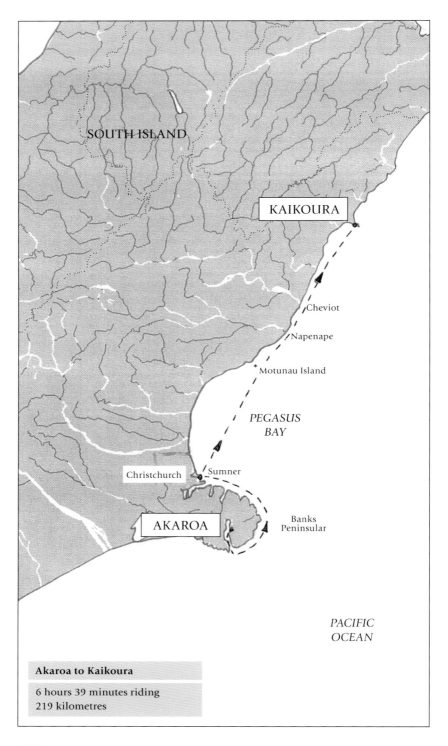

SOUTH ISLAND

KAIKOURA

Cheviot

Napenape

* Motunau Island

PEGASUS BAY

Christchurch   Sumner

AKAROA   Banks
                             Peninsular

*PACIFIC
OCEAN*

Akaroa to Kaikoura

6 hours 39 minutes riding
219 kilometres

Chapter 18
The Ride: To Kaikoura

Tuesday 21ˢᵗ February 2006

Banks Peninsula is situated at approximately the middle of the east coast of the South Island, on the margin of the Canterbury Plains. Its highest point is Mt Herbert at 920 m. It comprises two extinct volcanoes which were active less than half a million years ago. Their craters have subsequently been enlarged to many times their normal size by steam erosion. They were invaded by the sea during the postglacial world-wide rise in sea levels that began about fifteen-thousand years ago. They now form the harbours of Lyttleton and Akaroa. Originally Banks Peninsula was an island, but it became tied to the Canterbury Plains at some late stage in geological history when the growing alluvial plain reached its base. Akaroa was the larger volcano, and it is thought that its height may have originally reached around 1,400 m.

Captain Cook sighted the peninsula on 16ᵗʰ February 1770. On the following day he wrongly concluded that it was an island and named it in honour of Joseph Banks. It was almost as if Cook was just blasting through here on the way to something more important (like a cocktail party in Sydney), as he was to also mis-identify Stewart Island as being part of the South Island. I mean really…it only took us a couple of hours on our Seadoos to work out that Banks Peninsula isn't an island.

Seventy years later, in December 1838, the good old French

were at it again. Jean Francois Langlois de Somewhereorother, commander of the whaling ship Cachalot, embarked on a grandiose scheme for a French Colony at Akaroa. After a dubious land purchase from local Maori he established the Nanto-Bordelaise Company in France to carry out the project. The French representative for the settlement, Captain Charles Francois Lauvaud de Somewheresimilar sailed for New Zealand in April 1840. A month later, the Comte de Paris set off from Rochfort on the west coast of France for Akaroa, carrying fifty-three emigrants.

However, by the time Langlois, Lauvaud and their colonists arrived at Banks Peninsula in August 1840, the Treaty of Waitangi had already been signed and New Zealand's first Governor, Hobson, had declared British sovereignty over the whole of New Zealand. On hearing of the French plan for colonisation, Hobson quickly dispatched the HMS Britomart from the Bay of Islands to Akaroa with police magistrates on board. While the French colonists sheltered from unfavourable winds at Pigeon Bay on the other side of the Peninsula, the British flag was raised at Green Point between Akaroa and Takapuneke and courts of law convened to assert British sovereignty over the South Island.

The French settlers stayed on and, although the colony was not to be French, they left their mark on Akaroa, laying out its charming narrow streets and planting many walnut trees and roses.

It was this beautiful volcanic, French-flavoured setting that we found ourselves in when we woke early on Tuesday 21st. The sun was still hiding below the hills to the east, but we could see it was probably going to be another good day.

Our plan was to ride around to Christchurch and into Moncks Bay in the estuary of the Heathcote and Avon Rivers. There we would pull the Seadoos out of the water and drive them to Mike Phillips' Jet Skis in the centre of Christchurch, where they would get a regular one-hundred hour service and full medical checkup. Once this was completed, we would set off for Kaikoura. This would make our ride to Wellington on the Wednesday much shorter. We had checked the long range weather forecast the night before and the weather around Wellington was due to deteriorate from Wednesday afternoon onwards.

We set out just after first light again and took one last look at beautiful Akaroa. We then headed south down the harbour in good conditions. As we reached the open sea, we were disappointed to find that the sea fog was still there. This was something I hadn't anticipated, so I had only loaded one waypoint on the GPS, and that was at Sumner Head near our destination.

Banks Peninsula is fairly round, albeit with rough edges, so we headed east initially straight into the fog and set up a track about 800 m off the coast. The GPS was choosing to work for once, so I put it to good use. At this point the *To* arrow on the GPS was pointing to Sumner at about our eight o'clock position. As we moved around the Peninsula I slowly altered our track by about four degrees to the left each kilometre and brought the arrow around to the nine o'clock position, then the ten, and so on. In this way we were able to track a circular route around the Peninsula even though we couldn't see it. We did actually see it every now and then, as parts of the Peninsular jut out a little, and they would become visible for a short time through the grey murk.

The sea conditions weren't bad. We had about a 2 m northeasterly swell with a light chop, so we were making reasonable progress.

We were lucky enough to see some more Hector's Dolphins a couple of kilometres east of the Akaroa Harbour entrance. Knowing what we know about these cute little critters, it was hard not to imagine that they were laughing at us as we rode next to them.

I had previously informed Burglar of the fact that the Hector's Dolphin, although only weighing in at about 40 kg, has testes that tip the scales at 1.2 kg. A human male such as Burglar, on the other hand weighs in at 100 kg, yet his testes weigh only about 0.04 kg (Note: This is based on scientific averages. I didn't actually weigh Burglar's nads!). Burglar had replied by saying that, although this may be the case under normal circumstances, he had been away from home for a while and he was confident that, should there be a weigh-off between a Hector's and himself, the dolphin would slink off soundly defeated and with its tail between its legs, so to speak. I mentioned that I might be interested in putting this to the test, but only for the record of course. We decided that should we put it to the test, to be fair to the dolphin, we would use a bath full of cold sea water and we would apply Archimedes Principle and measure the displacement of the bath water to work out the weight (Archimedes Principle states that; 'An object is subject to an upward force when it is immersed in liquid. The force is equal to the weight of the liquid displaced').

As we passed Raupo Bay on the north-eastern side of the Peninsula, the fog bank abruptly cleared and we were able to see Christchurch in the distance. This was good news, and it didn't seem like any time at all until we were riding past Sumner Head and towards the entrance of the Heathcote and Avon Estuary.

The 2 m swell was whipping up some large waves in the Sumner area and the entrance to the estuary looked turbulent and unfor-giving. I wanted to have a closer look before committing to going in, so I rode in towards it between two large waves. I noticed that the wave behind me was catching me, so I tugged on the throttle in order to speed up, but nothing happened.

The engine was playing up again. I couldn't believe it. It would not respond at all. It was only good for one speed and that was about 15 km an hour. The 2 m wave behind me was getting closer and starting to steepen, so I altered heading to the left and headed for a low point in the wave that I could see 50 m further left. By the time I got to it, I was being picked up by the wave and was start-ing to surf, but I just managed to get over it and headed back out to sea. My drama wasn't over yet though as, approaching me head on, was another 2 m monster. Normally this wouldn't be a drama, as I would outrun it or charge over it before it broke, but now I had no power so all I could do was run towards it, almost as if in slow motion, and hope that I cleared it before it broke. As the wave finally reached me it was rearing up, its face almost vertical, and it was all I could do to keep straight and stop from falling over backwards with the Seadoo on top of me. In the end disaster was averted by a split second and I dropped through the air on the other side, hitting the water at a good angle and then continuing to motor out over the next wave to a safe point.

Meanwhile Burglar was faithfully following me around and, as he said later, and these are his words: "I was wondering what you were doing. I asked myself what is the Burglar up to? [He calls me Burglar too] Does he have a plan? I couldn't believe you wanted to have a play in the surf when we were on such a tight schedule. I wondered if I was supposed to follow you".

At the safe point I informed Burglar that I had engine problems again and that I had no intentions of even attempting to get into the estuary, given the turmoil at the entrance. I asked him to ride into the eastern end of Sumner Bay, because it looked like there might be a ramp there. I wanted him to confirm this for me before I attempted to ride in there with my engine problem. He quickly rode in and checked it out while I moved further out to a safer *safe spot* after nearly being wiped out again by the wave of the day. Burglar returned to confirm that there was indeed a ramp there, so I phoned the boys to let them know our predicament and change of plans.

I then edged in closer to Sumner Head and waited for the right time. A break came fairly soon and I rode frustratingly slowly towards the breakwater at the boat ramp just making it in to sheltered waters before another large set of waves came in.

Shortly afterwards the boys and their entourage turned up. Liz Chesterman and Roger Martyn from the Christchurch and West Coast Cancer Society were there and so was Qantas' effervescent manager for the South Island, Milson Thevenard. We had a good chat with everyone and then headed into Christchurch to Mike Phillips' Jet Skis.

Christchurch is the biggest city in the South Island. It sits at the base of the Port Hills, which divide the city and the plains from Lyttleton Harbour and Banks Peninsula. It is a pretty and well organised place with a very English style to it, and I like it a lot. On the way into town I did another radio interview with the guys and gals at Classic Hits. During the interview one of the girls complained that she had never been on a jet ski and so I invited her down for a ride. She thanked me very kindly and said that she would love to but she had a prior engagement cleaning her bathroom with a tooth brush, or something to that effect.

At Mike Phillips' we greeted Brad Clarke again who had fixed my Greymouth stuff up a week earlier. Brad and his boys got started on the Seadoos and we drove into the city centre to do something we had been dreaming about for a while; have a relaxing and civilised morning coffee. We found a nice coffee shop with an outside table and good foot traffic and we sat there drinking coffee and doing what boys do, namely, remark on what nice clothes the women walking past were wearing and discuss fashions and issues and having babies and other small talk like that.

After an hour of that and an announcement by Burglar that the Hector's Dolphin better not even show up for the weigh-off now, we drove back to Mike Phillips' to see if there was any news.

The boys had completed the regular services on the Seadoos, but could still not find anything wrong with mine. It was running perfectly and they could not replicate the problem. I was worried. So far I had had this problem twice; once in Dunedin and once here. Both times I had been lucky in that it had happened in sight of our destination. What if it happened again when we were miles from anywhere or, perhaps, in very rough sea conditions when I needed the power to stay out of trouble?

Again there was really nothing I could do but accept it and hope it didn't happen again.

We thanked everyone, refueled, and then drove out to the yacht club at Moncks Bay. Milson Thevenard from Qantas was there

again to see us off and so was a photographer from the local newspaper, so we posed for photos yet again and answered questions
and talked to a few locals before mounting up and heading off.

We picked our way through the mess of surging water at the
entrance to the Heathcote and Avon Estuary and then zigzagged
out through the surf into open water, setting our heading for
Motunau Island at the top of Pegasus Bay.

Twenty-thousand years ago the shoreline of Pegasus Bay was 50
km further out to sea, and 130 m lower. Now it's half-moon shape,
together with the barrier of Banks Peninsula to the south, make
for some interesting sea conditions. With a north-easterly swell
running into the bay there is a lot of energy coming in and it has
to find a way back out somewhere.

Initially conditions weren't too bad, with the north-easterly
swell and a moderate chop allowing us to make a reasonable pace
towards Kaikoura but, as we reached the northern half of the bay,
we found the area where the waves were heading back out again
and colliding with the primary swell. This was causing an unpre-
dictable and uncomfortable *dogs breakfast* sea condition and our
progress slowed markedly.

By now we had not had a day off since Greymouth. Our bodies
were tired, worn and sore, and I was not enjoying this latest devel-
opment at all. At times like this it is natural to think of places you
would rather be.

I remember in about 2002 I wasn't getting enough judo at home,
so I decided to take my suit away on a trip with me and find some
judo clubs in other countries. I arrived in Bangkok and enquired
as to where I could go to do judo. I was informed that about the
only place was at the national stadium where the Thailand national judo team trains.

Full of enthusiasm, I turned up there to find that the two hour
session was held underneath the grandstand, in a large room without air conditioning, and that it was indeed the national team's

training venue. They were there now, eyeing me up hungrily.

I introduced myself to the coach, a scary looking Japanese man who was much shorter than me, but weighed about 130 kg. I could tell he had taken an instant dislike to me and when the session started he punished me by making me do break falls and other drills continuously for the first hour until I was bruised all over. Then he basically lined me up against the national team one by one and watched smiling while they all beat me up to varying degrees for another hour in 45° heat.

Needless to say I haven't been back, but, in a strange *never say never* twist, right now, in the middle of Pegasus Bay, I would rather have been there getting beaten up than here on the Seadoo.

In conditions like this, mental toughness, persistence and perseverance is everything. and we had to find some as we bashed our way through the *breakfast* to the top of Pegasus Bay and past Motunau Island Nature Reserve, and then on towards Napenape. Thankfully, after Motunau Island the sea conditions improved and we started to make reasonable progress again.

If you're eating or snacking right now I advise you to stop because about 3 km off Napenape Scenic Reserve, another crisis started to develop.

I could feel an urgent need to use a toilet. My insides were bubbling and gurgling, and all the indications were that this was going to be an event of the utmost unpleasantness, such that one of my grandchildren might, many years from now, say, "Grandpa tell us again about the time you had diarrhea off Napenape". "Ok kids gather around, get yourselves comfortable and wipe old grandpa's chin for him and I'll tell ya".

I signaled to Burglar to stop and advised him to stay a safe distance away. By this stage of the ride, I was wearing umpteen layers of clothing and protective gear to protect my worn and beaten body. Under normal circumstances all this gear would normally take about a day to get off, but I believe I managed it in about three minutes on this occasion. It must have been funny to watch as layer upon layer was stripped off and draped over handle bars and seats and in foot wells and on the fins of passing sharks, and then I got into the weird body position that is required to get the wetsuit off without somebody's assistance. Finally I entered the water almost naked except for my helmet and did the business.

If anyone had been watching with binoculars from the scenic reserve, they would have been right to assume something very suspicious was happening and that they should inform the authorities. But we didn't hear anymore about it, so they can't have been. Eventually, I redressed, and after leaving a big, red, unexplainable stationary dot on the Hereiam track that Burglar reckoned should have been brown, we continued further north.

Conditions continued to improve and we passed Cheviot doing around 40 km an hour. We could see the magnificent mountains of the Seaward Kaikoura Range and we knew we were getting close, but at Conway Flat I felt the gurgling and festering start up again and had to go through the whole drill once more. This time was even more desperate than the previous and it was, indeed, a close run thing.

I hoped that this would be the last of it and I was starting to worry about dehydration, so with only 30 km to go, I drained my Camelbak of the life giving Raro (I'll take the townhouse in Queenstown, the Porsche, the boat, the world trip, the life time supply of Tui beer, the volley ball tickets *and a carton of lomitol*).

We continued on and, although I was feeling weaker than normal, the conditions continued to improve and we made good time, so that it wasn't long before we could see the Kaikoura Peninsula and our destination at South Bay Marina.

Before we knew it, we had entered the marina and allowed Mateus and Pete to valet park for us once again while we spoke to the press and Alison Lilley, Viv Butcher and Margaret Hislop from the local Cancer Society. We then made our way to the Kaikoura Top 10 Holiday Park, where we settled in for the night.

I took a shower and was at the basins attending to a few things, like teeth and nose hairs, when an old guy walked in and stood at the basin next to me. I gave him the customary smile that I always reserve for my fellow tourists, and indeed anybody really, and he took that as meaning we should have a deep and meaningful discussion. "New Zealand Dollar down again today" he said. "Really" I said. "What caused that?" "Dunno". "I can't understand the world's fascination with the New Zealand Dollar", I told him. "When I travel around Europe I watch CNBC Europe and there is always some skinny Pom or fat German commentator going on about investors driving the Kiwi Dollar up or down." I said, "Let's put this all into perspective. We are a country of four million people. There are hundreds of cities worldwide that are bigger than that on their own. How does the New Zealand Dollar matter?" "Just does I guess. You travel a lot?" he asked. "Nup. Born and raised in Kaikoura. Went to Blenheim once." I said. And with that he decided I wasn't worth talking to any more and left me to finish my cleanup.

Later as we sat eating a Mateus culinary creation, Burglar's girlfriend Kimmy rang from Australia and asked if I had forgiven them yet. Kimmy is a flight attendant with Qantas. I set her and Burglar up on a blind date and they hit it off straight away, but as a joke they toyed with me for three weeks and pretended that it hadn't worked because, in Kimmy's words, she couldn't stand that I was right again. I had put a lot of work in after the event trying to get them together again, but they had actually been together the whole time and when I found out I had been fooled, I was not impressed.

As I pointed out to Burglar, Mateus and Pete: Revenge is a dish best served up cold.

Kaikoura at the end of another tough day.

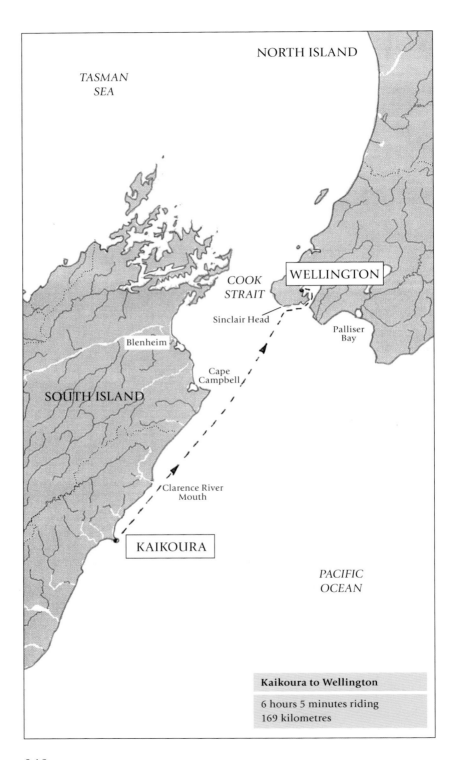

NORTH ISLAND

TASMAN SEA

COOK STRAIT

WELLINGTON

Sinclair Head

Palliser Bay

Blenheim

Cape Campbell

SOUTH ISLAND

Clarence River Mouth

KAIKOURA

PACIFIC OCEAN

Kaikoura to Wellington

6 hours 5 minutes riding
169 kilometres

Chapter 19
The Ride: To Wellington

Wednesday 22nd February

Kaikoura is another one of New Zealand's great tourist spots. With a population of approximately three-thousand-two-hundred residents, the township is located on a rocky peninsula protruding from lush farmland beneath the mountains. In the waters off the peninsula, a complex marine system provides a rich environment for marine mammals and seabirds, making it an ideal place for getting close to nature.

The town is full of tourist operators who provide tourists with opportunities to go whale watching, bird watching and swimming with dolphins, albeit always with the primary emphasis on conservation of marine life. In 1978, the Marine Mammal Protection Act was passed, providing total protection to New Zealand's whales, dolphins and seals. Kaikoura lies within the Southern Hemisphere Whale Sanctuary.

Several different species of whale can be seen off Kaikoura at different times of the year, but one can expect to see the huge sperm whales any time of the year. Orca are often sighted near Kaikoura, and schools of pilot whales are occasional visitors. The fun loving Dusky Dolphin is seen frequently and fur seals, once almost hunted to extinction, are now plentiful there.

Behind Kaikoura the massive mountains of the Seaward Kaikoura Range reach up to 2,610 m at the peak of Mt Manakau and, further inland, the Inland Kaikoura Range peaks at 2,885 m at Mt Tapuaenuku.

The whole combination of sea, peninsula and mountains make Kaikoura a place of breathtaking beauty and a must for anyone who wants to say they've seen New Zealand.

Incidentally, it is not possible in your wildest dreams to mistake, or even imagine, the Kaikoura Peninsula as an island. But someone did in 1770. I won't say who it was because you're going to think I've got something against the guy, but what I will say is that his name started with a C. Enough said.

We rose early again, as Pete and Mateus had a big day ahead of them. They had to drop us in the water and then head up to Picton and catch the Interisland Line Ferry to Wellington to pull us out of the water there. We had also told our contacts in Wellington to expect us at around 2pm and a big reception had been planned at the Loaded Hog.

We had been working on getting the Prime Minister to come down and meet us in Wellington for some months now. My old Air Force mate, Keith Graham, had a contact with the Prime Minister's personal secretary, and both the secretary and the Prime Minister had thought it would be a good thing to do, time permitting. For us it would be a major coop, as the publicity for our cause would be huge. I had passed on that if the Prime Minister allowed me to take her for a ride on my Seadoo, not only would I not tip her into the water, but I would also vote for her in the next election. This would be a major sacrifice on my part, because everyone I had told about the Prime Ministerial ride had offered me money, sometimes significant money, if I did tip her in the water. Some of my Australian mates had almost scared me off by describing how the Prime Minister would turn up in her bikini and climb on the back, throw her arms tightly around my waist like a biker chick, and demand to be taken for the ride of her life, yelling "faster

faster" as we ripped Wellington Harbour to shreds.

Weather-wise it was a nice morning. The sun was shining and there was only a light breeze. The forecast for Cook Strait was for a 2 to 3 m south-easterly swell, with moderate southerly winds strengthening in the afternoon. If we could arrive in Wellington by 2pm, we would avoid the worst weather. It would also be convenient for all the media and our other contacts, and we would still be on schedule for our promised 1.30pm arrival back in Auckland on Monday 27th.

The boys dropped us in the water and set off on their big day, while we headed out of the harbour and around the tip of the peninsula. We spotted some seals on the rocks and a large pod of dolphins that swam with us for a few hundred metres, until we eventually sped up and left them in our wake. From there we headed further north past Hapuku and then past the Clarence River mouth.

Just past the Clarence River we stopped for a snack and a pee. I looked back at the mountains to the south-west and saw a hint of snow on them. It reminded me just how volatile the weather is in New Zealand. In the South Island it is possible to get snow almost any time of the year. Now I'm going to digress here, and at times we will get a long way away from the Clarence River, so bear with me please and try not to lose the plot.

One year on the 7th March (my birthday), I was on a tramp with Mateus, Pete Fleming and my brother Dougal near Lake Wanaka in the far south of the South Island. We had stayed at the Aspiring Hut for the night and the next day we climbed slowly up the side of the very steep Mt Ansted towards the Cascade Saddle. The going was tough and we had remarked how parts of the walk were so steep as to be dangerous if you were coming down them without a rope.

On the way up it started to rain, and by the time we had got within 200 m of the saddle, the rain had turned to snow. The track notes state that this part of the track should be avoided in rain or wind, and particularly in snow, as there have been fatalities there in the past. We reached the saddle at about 5pm and pitched our tents in 10 cm of snow, with snow still falling heavily around us.

We all had very good cold weather gear, as we knew the dangers of being unprepared in the New Zealand mountains. We couldn't light a fire because there was nothing to burn, so we stood around a cooking stove in a circle, drinking Drambuie, cooking and telling stories. One of us was in the middle of another suspect tale, when a lone figure appeared out of the murk. It was a Japanese guy and he was wearing a tracksuit and running shoes and carrying a rucksack. To say that he looked a little out of his comfort zone would be an understatement.

We introduced ourselves to Takehashi San and invited him to pitch his tent and join us for a drink. He gratefully accepted and before long he was back with his cooker and noodles and was enjoying some Drambuie as well. We found out that he was from Fukuoka in southern Japan. His English was okay, and I can speak some Japanese, so we had no problem communicating.

Except for the Thai judo coach, I have pretty much liked all the Japanese I have met. In 1991 I took a leave of absence from Qantas and went to fly for Japan Airlines. I was based in Anchorage, Alaska and I flew 747 freighters across the North Pole to Europe, and passenger aircraft down to Brazil. Frequently I had to fly with Japanese crew members. They were great guys and about the worst thing they ever did was eat the *western meal* loaded specifically for me, leaving me to eat a Japanese meal that consisted of a selection of seaweeds, some sexual organs from fish, a few assorted toenails, various animal parts that normally only end up in McDonalds burgers and, if you were really lucky, a couple of sparrow's eggs.

One of the funniest things about flying with the Japanese was their absolute refusal to lose face, or cause anybody else to lose face. You could be flying along with them and someone would drop an industrial strength fart on the flight deck. As you can imagine, it's a confined space and the atmosphere can get quite lethal. With a western crew this would result in accusations and strenuous denials, or perhaps a proud admission of guilt, but when the Japanese are involved nothing is said. Everyone knows it is there but everyone sits there, silently trying to keep their lunch down and sweating profusely, while gazing out the window.

Having explained that to you, let's return to the circle and Takehashi San. We had all eaten rice risotto the night before, which is known for its great fart inducing properties. There was almost zero danger of the fart police turning up here in this weather, so it wasn't long before a farting contest developed in the circle (Alright already. It's a boy thing! Ok?). To my surprise, Takehashi San seemed to be enjoying it. He wasn't, however, having any success making a contribution.

As a joke I started bashing the side of my butt with my fist and I told him that this can help get things moving, so to speak. We all started doing it, and it wasn't long before Takehashi dropped a prize winning fart; with a noticeable Japanese accent; and worthy of a Ninja. We all cheered and Takehashi responded by bowing. The proud look of triumph and satisfaction on his face was gold and shortly afterwards he said goodbye, bowed once more, and disappeared into the murk towards his tent. Dougal reckoned that he was so happy he was just going to wander off into the snow and lie down and die.

In any event, when we woke the next morning Takehashi and his tent were gone. I don't know if he ever made it down the steep, snow-covered slope, or if he died a cold, lonely, but happy death in one of the many gullies and crevasses. I kept an eye on the papers for the next few months to see if a Japanese tourist had been reported missing, but saw nothing. I hope he is okay, but I won't be totally satisfied until I go back to Fukuoka and walk into a bar to find that all the locals are standing around drinking and bashing their butts with their fists.

We now return to the Clarence River mouth where Burglar was waiting patiently for me to stop gazing at the mountains and laughing to myself. We continued on northwards and moved slowly further out to sea until we were a good 10 km off the coast. Eventually we found ourselves off Cape Campbell at the southern tip of Clifford Bay. It was here that we would leave the coast altogether and head directly across Cook Strait towards the entrance to Wellington Harbour, and it was here that I noticed that, instead of the forecast south-easterly breeze, we were getting hit by a stiff north-westerly.

This 180° wind change is known to happen frequently and suddenly in the Cook Strait area. The strait lies in the westerly wind belt known as the Roaring Forties. As Cook Strait is the only large gap in the chain of mountains extending north-eastwards for 1,400 km from Puysegur Point to East Cape, it is thus a natural channel through which airstreams approaching central New Zealand are diverted and accelerated to pass between the North and South Islands. When the general airflow aloft is roughly parallel to the mountain chain, a slight shift in direction causes a complete reversal of the surface winds in Cook Strait. In today's case, the prevailing wind had started as a southerly hitting the eastern side of the mountains, but it had now swung around about 40° to a south-westerly, which had then put it on the western side of the mountains and funnelled it through the strait as a north-westerly.

We noticed that the wind was freshening to about 30 km an hour and was starting to whip up a steep, fast-moving 2 m wave from the north. We beat into this for a while and, when we were about 40 km short of Wellington, the wind strengthened again to 50 km an hour, with the seas increasing in height up to 3 m. They were fast moving and steep as they collided with the underlying south-easterly swell. We were forced to ride standing up and were frequently concerned at the steepness and speed of the waves, as they threatened to tip us over backwards each time we climbed a wave. Each wave required that we face it straight on and we always dropped off the back of the waves into thin air as they rapidly disappeared from under us.

To add to our woes, the GPS was again not working and I was having trouble figuring out which hole in the hills to head for. From this distance, with part of the land hidden below the horizon, they all looked the same. There were three possibilities. The gap in the hills near Makara, Wellington Harbour, and Palliser Bay. I didn't want to end up in Palliser Bay, so I erred towards the centre and decided I would adjust our track when we got closer, if need be. It later turned out that I had been aiming at the correct place, which was a blessing as we were having a serious battle not getting wiped out completely by the conditions, and any extra distance would have been a disaster. As it was, we were making painfully slow progress and the hills in the distance just never seemed to get any closer.

We had crossed the strait three times before and each time we had been lucky. Now the old girl was getting her revenge, and we knew it. We were only making a forward speed of about 12 km an hour, but eventually we got to a point about 20 km short of Wellington, where I could make out Sinclair Head. The wind had now strengthened to about 60 km an hour and it seemed logical to head for a point just to the east of Sinclair Head and then run eastwards along the coast, sneaking into the harbour inside Barrett's Reef.

This ploy seemed to be working, as the sea conditions started to improve marginally but then, just when we thought we were almost out of it, we stumbled straight into the fury of the eastern end of the Karori Rip. The Karori Rip is one of the tidal rips for which the strait is famous. There are very fast currents through the strait and the rips are caused by a combination of surface current clashes, and the even more deadly effect that the underwater canyons in the strait have. Huge volumes of water travel through these canyons at relatively high speed and, when a canyon abruptly ends or quickly becomes shallow, the water is diverted up to the surface creating a boiling effect at the surface. For these reasons, tidal rips in Cook Strait are best avoided even on good days, because they whip up a washing machine-style sea of steep and breaking 3 m waves that come at you from all directions, usually all at the same time. This is totally frightening stuff and a definite ten on the *pucker factor scale*. It is a testament to the handling qualities of the Seadoos that we are here today to tell this story. They were magnificent.

Eventually we managed to fight our way through the rip and, once clear, we headed towards Owhiro Bay. But instead of becoming more sheltered from the wind the closer in we got, the wind strength actually increased as we hit what we later found out is known as *the wind factory*. When the wind is strong from the north-west a lot of it funnels through the strait, but some is compressed behind the hills to the north-west of Wellington. This creates a high pressure area which then relieves itself by spilling over the top of the hills and accelerating down the valleys on the south-east side, eventually hitting the strait at high speed. Pretty soon we found ourselves riding straight into a 70 km an hour wind. The sea was white with foam and we were continuously blinded by spray as we put our heads down and forged onwards. There was no way we could anticipate each wave as we came to it, and it was like riding with our eyes closed. Finally we could see through the mayhem that we were as close to the land as we needed to get, so we altered heading to the east towards Lyall Bay and Palmer Head.

Now the wind and waves were side on to us and, crossing Island Bay, the wind howled down from the hills and seemed to strengthen yet again. We found ourselves being blown sideways across the tops of the waves. Man and machine would have weighed close to 500 kg, but the wind was picking us up and throwing us sideways across the waves like skipping stones. To make good our desired track we had to head about 20° upwind and lean into the wind with all our body weight. We were overawed by the sheer power of the conditions.

Crossing Lyall Bay the wind dropped a little and I discovered that my Seadoo was again not responding well to throttle movements. It was able to maintain about 30 km an hour, but that was all and there was very little acceleration available. Burglar was ahead of me, so I couldn't catch him to let him know, and I was worried that my machine would give up altogether and I would end up drifting at high speed back out into the strait.

I gingerly battled across Lyall Bay towards Barrett's Reef. This was the reef that the ill-fated *Wahine* hit in New Zealand's answer to a perfect storm in 1968, eventually sinking with the loss of fifty-one lives. I had been fascinated with the whole event when it had happened and I found it quite ironic now that I should be approaching Barrett's Reef, just as the *Wahine* had and with control problems, as she had had.

Burglar had finally slowed down and I was able to communicate over the noise of the tempest around us to let him know that progress into the harbour would be slow. We rode inside Barrett's Reef and slowly made our way into the harbour entrance, past Point Dorset and across Worser Bay to Point Gordon, and then Point Halswell. At Point Halswell the harbour opened up before us and the funnelling effect of the wind reduced, so that we were riding with an uncomfortable chop, but in only about 40 km of wind.

We could see the city ahead of us, and it was then that I realised that I didn't really know exactly where everyone would be waiting for us. I knew it was somewhere near Te Papa Museum and I knew where that was, so we headed into Lambton Harbour and straight for Te Papa. Near Te Papa, at the Taranaki Street Wharf, there is a small manmade harbour which looked like a good bet, so we rode in there to find............ absolutely nothing at all.

We drifted around for a minute or two, enjoying being out of the wind, but knowing that we needed to be elsewhere, and knowing that we had no idea where elsewhere was. Are you with me?

The only option was to swallow our pride and ask directions, so we motored over to a couple of guys who were fishing and told them we were thirsty and asked them if they would kindly direct us to the Loaded Hog. They were very obliging; "You go past McDonalds and…..."; and soon we were under way again as we headed out of the tiny harbour and around the top of Queens Wharf, into the wharf at the front of the Loaded Hog.

It was obvious now that we were in the right place, as there were Qantas and Cancer Society signs everywhere and a crowd of people all clapping and cheering and, with a huge sigh of relief; and in need of a beer and a change of underwear; we tied up and stepped gingerly and unsteadily onto the wharf. It had been a tough, and at times frightening, ride and we were relieved it was over. We were totally saturated from head to foot and we must have looked like drowned rats, but we had learned that there is no time for licking your wounds under these circumstances. You just have to put on a brave face and a wide brimmed hat and walk up the steps to face the media. We did this now.

There were a couple of television crews and various people from Qantas. Katherine Monks and Herini Coffin were there from the Cancer Society and Carl Lampe and his mate Shaun from Boyz Toyz in Porirua were there to welcome us. But the nicest surprise of all was that, waiting at the top of the stairs were Ron and Dorothy Terry from Wainuiomata. I had been friends with their daughter Janette when I was a teenager. They had been very good to me then and I was touched that they had made the effort to come down and welcome us.

We spoke to the Terrys for a little while, while the TV cameras rolled and then we met everyone else who was there. We followed this up with formal TV interviews. When asked in one TV interview what Cook Strait had been like, I responded "It was nasty out there!" And I meant it!

Once all the excitement had died down, we sat down outside the Hog with Carl and Shaun and some of the Qantas staff for a few beers. Eventually they all had to go back to work, so we were left on our own to enjoy even more beer and make a few calls. I rang my brother Tim from the Interisland Line and jokingly asked if the ferries were still running given the conditions in the strait. Then I rang Pete and Mateus who right at that moment would be on a ferry in the middle of the strait. They didn't answer, so I left a message asking them to call back when they had stopped being seasick.

I then rang the Prime Minister's secretary and he told me that she was still hoping to make it, but that the Foreign Minister, Winston Peters, was upsetting the Americans again so Helen was currently running around with an extinguisher and a smothering cloth putting out bush fires. We realised that we had to stay around the Hog in case she did turn up, and anyway there was no where else to go until the boys turned up, so we got some food and coffee and settled in for a long siege.

We waited around until about five o'clock and then, within five minutes of each other, first the Prime Minister's secretary rang apologising that she wouldn't be able to make it after all (something about a missing or burnt bikini) and then the boys rang to say that they were in Wellington and there was nowhere to pull the Seadoos out, so we would have to kit up again and ride around into Evans Bay to a ramp there.

For the second time in a day we got into wet gear and then rode around to the Evans Bay ramp where we were retrieved and driven to our accommodation just 200 m down the road.

The first thing I did there was check the next day's weather forecast for Wellington to Napier. It was ugly, with strong southerlies and huge swells from the south. We decided that there was no way we would be riding the next day, and besides, my Seadoo needed looking at again, so we let everyone know that tomorrow would be a rest day in Wellington.

Later my brother Tim turned up for a few beers and we sat and chatted for a while, and discussed the fact that Cook Strait was sniggering to itself and waiting for a chance to have one last crack at us.

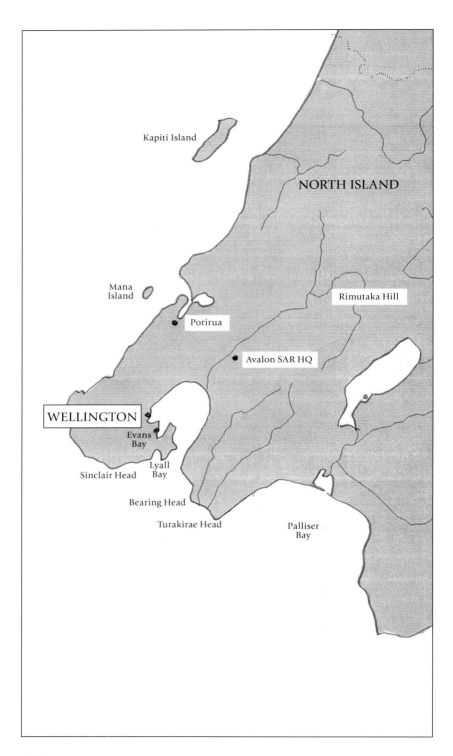

Kapiti Island

NORTH ISLAND

Mana
Island

Rimutaka Hill

Porirua

Avalon SAR HQ

WELLINGTON

Evans
Bay

Lyall
Bay

Sinclair Head

Bearing Head

Turakirae Head

Palliser
Bay

Chapter 19
Wellington

Windy Wellington is situated at the south-western extremity of the North Island. It reaps the benefits of the previously mentioned wind effects in the Cook Strait area. The weather can be consistently nasty, but when it does fine up it is a stunning place because the air is crystal clear and you can see for miles. It is also a friendly city. I grew up in Paraparaumu, 50 km to the north, and spent a great deal of time in the city as a teenager for sport and social reasons.

While Mateus made breakfast and coffee, Pete fussed around getting ready to take the Seadoos to Boyz Toyz in Porirua so that 'Dr Carl' could give my machine the full medical it badly needed. I was not prepared to start the next leg without knowing what was causing the engine problem. The leg from Wellington to Napier is far too remote to take any risks with. It is 360 km of almost deserted coastline, with only one real chance of rescue at Castle Point, halfway to Napier.

This was an enforced day off and it would mean that we would have to miss the planned day off in Napier. This was disappointing because we had been booked in to visit some of the local schools to talk to the kids about being sun smart and we had been quite looking forward to it, given the interest that my son Douglas' school had shown in the event.

In spite of the disappointment, Burglar and I were determined to relax as much as possible and get as organised as possible.

While drinking coffee we checked the weather for the following day and found that it was forecast to be even worse than today. The forecast was for strong southerlies in Cook Strait. These were predicted to whip up a southerly swell in the strait of around 5 m. We thought we could handle that, but the problem was that the winds were supposed to be even stronger along the East Coast up to Napier, with gusts up to 60 km an hour and swells of up to 8 m. We didn't relish the idea of going anywhere near that sort of weather and we found ourselves quite depressed again at the prospect of being stuck in Wellington for a couple of days or more. This would mean that we would be unable to make Auckland on schedule. I was also worried, because I was due to go back to work a few days after our scheduled arrival in Auckland and I thought that doing so would be a good idea to deter the company from inviting me to find alternative employment.

Mateus was grumpy! He had phoned his wife Lorraine the night before and had been grumpy ever since. I asked him what was bugging him and he told us with a serious and angry look on his face that his cow had got loose and gone into the neighbour's paddock and was reaping havoc. Mateus lives on a farm two hours south of Sydney and they have a menagerie of animals, not unlike Old MacDonald.

He went on to tell us that the cow was an ornery, mean spirited animal that went out of its way to annoy him. Both Burglar and I found it very amusing that Mateus would think that a cow would conspire to do something like that on purpose, or as an act of revenge against its long suffering owner, and we told him so. But he was convinced that the brainless beast had it in for him and announced that the unfortunate animal would be hamburgers when he got home. Burglar, who has never met an animal he didn't want to shoot, kindly offered to help out by inserting a lead pill at high speed between its eyes, but Mateus was adamant that the pleasure would all be his. I pointed out that he sounded like a father complaining about a wayward teenage son and, as he has no children, perhaps this was his way of compensating himself for the joy that he was missing out on. The upshot of it all was that Mateus went to Porirua grumpy, and Burglar and I spent the rest of the day with sore stomach muscles from laughing.

After the boys had left, Burglar and I decided to go into the city to see what was going on there, and search for some padded underwear and more electrolyte solution. We crossed the road to the bus stop and after five minutes of waiting we decided that we would walk because the weather was still fine.

It's a pretty nice walk along Evans Bay Parade into the city. The road winds north along the western side of Evans Bay past numerous smaller bays. At Point Jerningham it turns sharply to the south-west and becomes Oriental Parade. Once you get to Oriental Parade you get stunning views of the city as you walk towards it. The sun was still shining and people were out walking, and some were even sunbathing on the beach at Oriental Bay making the most of the weather before the predicted southerly change around midday.

We really enjoyed the walk. It was nice to be doing something other than bouncing across the top of waves. We made our way right into the centre of the city, onto Lambton Quay where we found a coffee shop with a good viewing platform, and spent the next hour watching people. It's amazing how enjoyable the simple things become when they are no longer available to you for a period of time, and we made the most of it now.

We then went shopping for all the things we needed, which took another hour, and at the end of that we found ourselves in another coffee shop further down the street. Being in Wellington, it was not surprising that the conversation eventually turned to politics, so I filled Burglar in on how it worked here.

Wellington is the capital of New Zealand. Politicians are based in a building near the end of Lambton Quay called *the Beehive*. It is called the Beehive mainly because it looks a little bit like one, and definitely not because of the amount of work that is done there.

New Zealand's politicians are much like their overseas counterparts, in that they range from supremely intelligent and well intentioned at one end of the scale to complete self serving idiots at the other. There are only a few who are so well intentioned that they say what they think, rather than what will get them elected, and naturally these people find it hard to get elected. Some politicians are known for getting into power by making bold and popular promises, knowing that they will never be in a powerful enough position to have to carry them through.

The problem I have with politicians is that, rather than doing what is right, they do what it takes to stay in power and the country suffers as a result. But, in spite of what all my Australian mates say, I reckon Prime Minister Helen Clark is a good, strong and well meaning leader. Helen and I differ on philosophical grounds, though. I believe that there are aspects of socialism that are indispensable, but I also believe that people need to be responsible for themselves as much as possible and the government should encourage them to be that way.

Recently the New Zealand government used millions of taxpayers dollars to advertise on television to remind people that there may be more handouts available to them, and giving them a number to call to find out. How ridiculous. But at least most of this money goes straight back into the economy through consumption.

Before the last election, the Labour Party did a huge makeover of the Prime Minister, probably using both conventional and nuclear techniques that made her look quite the glamour. They plonked this image all over billboards and most people, at first, were wondering who this *hot babe* was. I don't quite know what Labour was trying to achieve but, personally, I prefer the *robber's dog* look. It makes me more able to sleep easy at night and feel safe, knowing that the country is in good, tough hands.

One of the things that Helen's government has done over the

last few years is rationalise the defense forces using the 'ostrich' approach. The air force has been run down to the extent that it has almost become a true kiwi; that is, a flightless bird. It has been run down so far that last year Helen found herself in Rotorua wanting to get to Wellington and with no VIP plane to do it. She ended up chartering a small twin engine Twin Comanche aircraft. Twenty-five years ago when I was learning to fly I refused to fly Twin Comanches because they were so old and decrepit then. Now our fearless leader was flying in one. The aircraft was so crapped out that, as it neared Wellington, a door flew open and Helen was in danger of permanently losing her grip on power. Fortunately, order was restored and the aircraft landed safely. Please Boss, next time you fly, fly with the airlines. The thought of Michael Cullen running the show is too much to bear.

A few years ago a referendum was held on a new proportional representation voting system called MMP (Mickey Mouse Politics). It was voted in and has been a complete failure; if you ask anyone on either side of the political spectrum, you won't find anyone who will admit to having voted for it.

The system allows for a certain number of politicians to be elected normally in their electorates and then each party gets more seats dependant on how many people voted for that particular party. The party then gets to nominate who will be their representatives in Parliament. In this way, people can become politicians even though they would have come dead last in their electorate vote. This means that some fairly interesting people end up in Parliament making decisions on how to spend our tax dollars.

Our current foreign minister was unable to get elected in his own electorate but, because of MMP, he is now the spokesperson of our country and holds the balance of power in Parliament. Another Member of Parliament, when asked, couldn't remember whether he had been charged with drunk driving four times or five times before he entered Parliament. My personal favourite, however, is a Green Party politician called Nandor Tanczos. For most of his life Nandor has been a professional demonstrator. He hates any sort of authority and believes that people should have the right to do anything they want, even at the expense of other people's rights. No where does he mention the responsibilities that go hand in hand with rights. He wants to legalise marijuana. I believe he thinks that he is the reincarnation of Bob Marley, and I doubt that this would sit well with Bob. On the front page of his website he greets the unfortunate visitor with: "Greetings in the name of the Creator, the most High JaH Ras Tafari".

So as you can see it is definitely not boring times in New Zealand politics and, if you don't take it too seriously, there are laughs a plenty for all. Australians though, will rightfully claim the gold medal for entertaining sessions of parliament. Former Prime Minister Paul Keating was the standard setter for a parliament that prides itself on the sort of name calling and abuse that you would not even find in a schoolyard. By Australian standards, New Zealand's Parliament is like afternoon tea with the vicar. New Zealand has, however, had some memorable moments in the past, such as when former Prime Minister, the late Sir Robert Muldoon, said that the exodus of unskilled labour from New Zealand to Australia was raising the average IQ of both countries.

You can only talk about politics for so long, and you can only drink so much coffee in a day. The last cup of coffee had made my eyes bulge out like Marty Feldman's and my hair frizz up a little bit like Nandor's and so it was that we decided to jump on a train and go and visit the Marine Rescue Coordination Centre at Avalon in Lower Hutt. We and the boys had been talking to the guys at the centre over the past two weeks, letting them know when we left somewhere and when we safely made our next destination. The guys at the centre had said that if we had time while we were in Wellington, that we should come and visit them so that they could give us a smacked bottom for being so stupid as to attempt the ride, but also as a social and informative visit.

Burglar and I walked down to Wellington Railway Station. By now the weather had turned to custard, as predicted, with strong southerly winds, rain and hail. We bought tickets to Wingate Station and then boarded the train. Now I don't want to appear too critical here, but from a tourist's point of view, these trains are old. Thirty years earlier I had used the Wellington train system to get around and I don't think the carriages have been upgraded since. I told Burglar if he looked around he would probably find my name carved into the wood somewhere in the carriage. We sat in the first carriage and were amazed to see that there was a crew of three. There was a driver, a ticket clipper and another old guy who oversaw the whole operation and sat next to the driver, watching the track ahead for things like recalcitrant cows that may have been tied to the tracks by their owners.

There is a case here for a full apology to the French for my general attitude towards them in this book. Perhaps we should have let a few of them colonise New Zealand because in Paris there are now trains that are driverless, fast and efficient. When it comes to trains, Viva la France!!

We rode the train out to Wingate station in Lower Hutt and disembarked in cold and windy conditions. From the station we walked south-west towards the only building that looked anything like what we imagined we were looking for. Amazingly, it turned out to be the right place and we were shown in by security.

The Rescue Coordination Centre is responsible for coordinating major aviation and maritime Search and Rescue Operations in New Zealand's SAR Region, which stretches from the mid-Tasman Sea to halfway to Chile, and from Antarctica almost to the equator, including Niue, Samoa, Tokelau and the Cook Islands.

The centre is staffed by a team of Search and Rescue Officers who provide coverage 24 hours a day, 365 days a year. It coordinates searches involving missing aircraft or vessels, the activation of an emergency beacon, and searches that require greater resources than can be provided by the New Zealand Police. Search and

Rescue Officers determine the area to be searched and then plan the search strategy alongside, and in consultation with, specialist aviation, defense force, marine, police, and land SAR advisers.

We had phoned Mateus and Pete to let them know we were at the centre, and that they should join us when my Seadoo was well again. Eventually they turned up and the four of us were given the grand tour. After the tour we were standing around talking and one of the Rescue Coordination Center guys, a bloke's bloke called Neville, asked me what I did for a living. Now bear in mind here that these guys had been following our exploits for a couple of weeks already. Anyway I told him that I was a Qantas pilot. He said, "Oh really? I have a good mate who is a Qantas pilot". "Do tell", I said, "What's his name?" "Jeremy Burfoot", he said. When someone is being a complete Bonehead, Mateus always gets a big wide grin on his face and he had it now as he looked at me as if to say, "What are you going to say to that?" Over the next half a second my brain processed all the options for a reply that would not be offensive, or too embarrassing, and then I gave up and said, "That's me!!"

If I had just made a name dropping clanger of these proportions I would have been seriously embarrassed, but Neville was just fine and, in his defense, we had been to the same school for a year and we had known each other for a while in the New Zealand Air Force, although I only recognised him after he told me his name. We chatted at length about old times and it was a good catch up, but eventually it was time to jump back in the Sorento and head back into the city.

On the way back the boys briefed us on the sick Seadoo. Apparently the disintegration of the long range tanks had finally taken its toll. Somehow chips of metal and rubber had made it right through the extra fuel filter and through the fuel pump, destroying that on the way. They had snuck past the primary fuel filter and into the fuel injectors. The injectors had been almost completely blocked. Carl and the boys had completely cleaned the system and replaced the ailing fuel pump, so the Seadoo was as good as new. They had also added an extra filter to the system to stop it happening again.

It was a relief to know that we could trust the Seadoo not to fail us on the next few legs, so we were a lot more confident to continue now, provided the weather was right.

The camera that TV3 had lent us had been taking a bit of a battering and we had organised to visit the TV3 studio in Wellington to get a technician to look at it. The boys dropped Burglar and I off there and went back to our hotel to cook dinner. An hour or so later, the camera was fixed and we went downstairs to get a taxi back to the hotel.

Getting in a taxi in Wellington reminded me of the famous taxi bill of the former Speaker of Parliament, Jonathon Hunt. He had managed to run up taxi bills in one year of $30,000. When the news first broke of the $30,000 taxi bill, his name wasn't mentioned, and three other politicians, wanting to be prepared for damage control, had rung the auditor's office to ask if it was theirs. At a dollar a kilometre he could almost have had the taxi take him on a world trip for that amount and, if he merely hired the cab and asked the driver to, "Wait here, I'll just be a minute", he could have come out nearly six months later before the waiting time exceeded the $30,000. Extraordinary, don't you think?

We arrived back at the hotel to find Mateus in a buoyant mood again. Lorraine had reported that her father had retrieved the wayward cow from the neighbour's property and, even though Old Betsy was still officially on death row, there was still a possibility of a full pardon for good behaviour over the next couple of months. To celebrate the good news, Mateus cooked another sumptuous dinner and then we checked the weather again. The forecast hadn't really changed, but we decided to have a go the next day because there comes a time in a man's life when he asks himself and his mate, "Are we men or are we mice?" And there can only really be two answers to that can't there. "Men" or "Pass the cheese!"

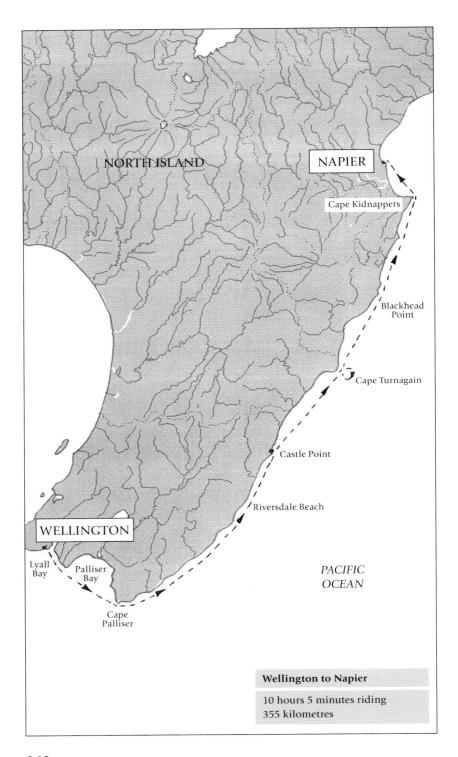

NORTH ISLAND

NAPIER

Cape Kidnappers

Blackhead
Point

Cape Turnagain

Castle Point

Riversdale Beach

WELLINGTON

Lyall
Bay

Palliser
Bay

Cape
Palliser

PACIFIC
OCEAN

Wellington to Napier

10 hours 5 minutes riding
355 kilometres

Chapter 21
The Ride: To Napier

Friday 24th February 2006

There was an atmosphere of intense anticipation as we ate breakfast and readied ourselves for what we could only imagine would
be a very big day. We left the hotel in the dark and Pete drove us
to a small launch ramp on the western side of Lyall Bay. The wind
was a light southerly, but we had noticed that the wind was always
light around this time of the day and we expected it to strengthen
shortly after sunrise.

We launched and boarded the Seadoos, and started to head
south-east towards Baring Head. As the light slowly increased
we could see that we had a 3 to 4 m southerly swell and a heavy
overcast, that made the whole scene appear totally colourless and
eerily ominous.

As we approached the entrance to Wellington Harbour, one of
the Cook Strait ferries was coming out and we noticed it pitch-
ing quite a bit as it hit the swells. We gave the ferry a wide berth
and continued on. I can only imagine what the crew of the ferry
would have been thinking when they saw us in those conditions,
at that time of day, and heading towards nowhere. Whatever it
was, I guess they were probably right.

From Baring Head we rode on past the seal colony at
Turakirae Head and into Palliser Bay. Palliser Bay is about 30
km across and, as we rode, we were joined once again by those ever

friendly dolphins.

From Palliser Bay, on a good day, you can see the Rimutaka Range and the Wairarapa extending northwards, but this morning all we could see was cloud and low scud. As we crossed the bay, we could just see Cape Palliser in the distance.

Cape Palliser (Matakitakiakupe) is the southern most point of the North Island. It is a rugged and spectacular place. It was named by Captain Cook after one of his old drinking buddies, Captain Sir Hugh Palliser.

Dad and Mum took my brothers and I to Cape Palliser camping as a family on summer holidays a couple of times when we were young. Dad would load up the trailer to about four times its legal carrying capacity, with gear stacked so high that we would have to watch out for low over-bridges. He would then hitch it up to the old Ford Cortina. The Cortina was affectionately known as Gertrude and I can't remember what year she was, but I'm guessing about 1966. She had tail lights that looked like a pie cut into three equal segments, so that might give some of the older folk a clue. Gertrude was small by today's standards and I can't believe we used to fit seven people in her. She had a 1500 cc engine, which is the same size as the engines in our Seadoos.

Anyway, Dad would hitch up the trailer and then feed the last of my four brothers through the window, because to open the door would have been a backward step. Then off we would go much like a Chevy Chase vacation movie.

On the last family camp to Cape Palliser all was going well until our *rig* hit the Rimutaka Hill that stands between Upper Hutt and the Wairarapa. The hill is long, winding and steep and, in what proved to be a defining moment for me which helped make up my mind this was my last family camp, Gertrude overheated halfway up. Old Gerty just wasn't up to it anymore and she belched steam out of her radiator. Dad pulled over to a rest area and did his normal trick of burning himself on the scalding water. "I'm going to take the radiator cap off with my bare hands kids, just to see if pressurized boiling water still scalds you to the point where you get third degree burns...........Why yes it does!!"

A few minutes later a sheep truck pulled into the rest area. The driver had pulled in for his lunch break. Dad went to ask him for some water and came back, not only with water, but with the very good news that the truck was going to tow us up the hill. This was too much for me as a fifteen year old and I decided to run to the top of the hill rather than suffer such a humiliation.

I made it to the top of the hill well before the circus, and when it turned up I was pleased to see that my decision to run had been a sound one. In order to tow Gertrude effectively up the steep hill, her bonnet had to sit under the end of the truck. When she arrived at the top there was a pile of sheep shit on the bonnet about 5 cm deep. I refused ownership of my family for quite a while after that.

Cape Palliser is pretty rugged and bare, but with Dad running the show we managed to have a great holiday. We went hunting in the hills behind the cape and fishing off the rocks on calm days. We would frequently climb the two-hundred-and-fifty steps up to the lighthouse, and we found an excellent swimming hole in a canyon about 2 km to the east of the lighthouse.

The cape has the North Island's largest breeding area of fur seals and the fishing village of Ngawi is just down the road. Most of the beaches around Palliser Bay are shingle, so the fishermen at Ngawi launch their boats using bulldozers. At any one time there is always an impressive lineup of bulldozers on the beach. A little bit further down the road are the famous Putangirua Pinnacles. I remember those camps fondly.

To this point we had been riding side-on to the waves and they had increased in size to around 5 m. This was a bit like riding an elevator up and down, as the waves lifted us 5 m when they passed under us, and then we quickly dropped 5 m into the trough behind. Because the waves were relatively steep, we had to keep our wits about us in case they started to break, which they occasionally did. We would have to then do a quick maneuver to avoid the breaking peak, and realign with our eastward track when clear. This slowed progress down a bit and it took us a good hour and a half to finally reach the cape.

I guess it's human nature to get used to almost anything, but before this event started, a 2 m wave would have been enough to get my attention. Now here we were, routinely and almost nonchalantly, riding 5 m monsters.

I had anticipated that things would improve for us once we rounded the cape and headed north-east because the waves would be on our tail. In spite of their huge size I thought that at least we would be riding with the waves, and that would raise our average speed somewhat.

I was, however, quite nervous at the prospect of the waves getting up to around 7 or 8 m further up the coast, with the stronger winds which were forecast for further to the north-east.

Once we rounded the cape, the waves did end up right behind us and we started surfing them at high speed. When you are sitting at the peak of a fast moving 5 m wave, the trough in front of you appears steep and long. Because the wave surfaces were also chopped up a bit, riding down their faces was not smooth, so we found ourselves speeding almost out of control down them. As we surfed down the faces we would accelerate to speeds approaching 80 km an hour, and the chopped up surfaces required us to work continuously and hard with the steering to maintain directional control. There was also a lot of bouncing and rapid dropping going on. The whole experience was mentally and physically demanding to the extreme, and we were initially quite tense because it always felt like we were a whisker away from losing control at high speed.

As we were moving faster than the waves, we found ourselves having to make the long climb up the back of the next wave in front of us each time before we would eventually go over the top and reach the point of no return again. It was as if we were on a perpetual roller coaster.

After about thirty minutes of this, we started to get used to what we were doing and, even though it was demanding, it actually started to become fun. The fact that the coastline seemed to be disappearing behind us at a great rate also made us feel better.

The south-east coast of the North Island is one of the most rugged, wind-battered and desolate areas I have ever seen. From Cape Palliser, as you head north-east up the coast there is nothing for 90 km until you pass Riversdale Beach. Then it's another 25 km further on to the first real safe haven at Castle Point.

Castle Point is really the only significant break in the 300 km coastline from Cape Palliser in the south, to Cape Kidnappers in Hawke Bay. It was named in 1770 by Cook, who was struck by the similarities of the magnificent 162 m high Castle Rock to the battlements of a castle. There are long stretches of beach on the northern side of the lighthouse and, to the south, there is an impressive lagoon, which is frequently used for water sports.

As we rode past Riversdale, we could see the Castle Point lighthouse in the distance. We were ecstatic that the forecast strengthening of the wind and increase in wave size had not eventuated. If anything, the swells had died down somewhat to between 3 and 4m and, at the same time, they had smoothed out so that the roller coaster ride was getting easier all the time.

While we were in Wellington, I had talked to a Castlepoint fisherman by phone about getting ashore at Castlepoint. He had told me that if the weather was coming from the north then we should enter the lagoon, but if it was coming from the south we should ride around the lighthouse and come in at the beach.

We rode around the lighthouse and into the shore and were pleased to see Pete and Mateus there waiting for us. As it was a sandy beach, we decided to refuel the Seadoos in the water and Pete got straight onto it. Meanwhile, Mateus gave us lunch and briefed us about the three young ladies who were the newest members of our fan club. As he briefed us, they turned up wearing some of our sponsored gear that the boys had given them while waiting for us to arrive.

The girls were taking part in a local fishing contest and had got bored and come across to see what was happening. We spoke to the girls while we ate lunch, and suddenly it struck me that it was a school day and they all looked very young, so I asked them why they weren't in school.

One of the girls, Danielle, a particularly pretty girl, looked indignant and said, "Well, I am actually twenty you know". This impressed Burglar noticeably and it allowed an increase in the scope of the conversation somewhat. Danielle was quite an intelligent girl and she asked some good questions. She asked us what we thought about while we were out there on the Seadoos. While she was distracted with something else Burglar leaned over and whispered in my ear, "I know what I'm going to be thinking about for the next few hours anyway".

Shortly afterwards, in a fine example of how a good conversation can bounce from one extreme to another, Burglar noted that a particularly persistent fly (must have been Australian) had been trying to land on his sandwich. This led me to tell the story about the game of chance I had witnessed while flying in Papua New Guinea. I had to spend an hour on the ground one time out at Suki in the Western Province and I decided to go for a walk around to take in some of the culture. I found a group of men sitting in the shade of a large tree playing a card game, so I stopped to watch and try and work out what the game was.

They would each lay a card in the circle face up and then sit back and wait with looks of great anticipation on their faces. Eventually, after some random amount of time, they would all erupt into cheering and clapping and then the process would start again. Try as I might, I could not work out the rules, so eventually I asked one of the other spectators.

The rules turned out to be very simple really. The first card that a fly landed on was the winner. Each player had his favourite card that he used for many tournaments, and it is particularly interesting to try and imagine the things that they would rub on the cards, or the places they would put them, to help attract flies. The mind boggles, and the thought of this was almost enough to put Burglar off his sandwich.

All good things must come to an end and, all too soon our lunch break was over, so we said goodbye, hit the water again and headed out past the lighthouse and north-eastward towards Napier.

We got back out onto the roller coaster to find that conditions had improved even more and the swell had dropped to about 3 m. We enjoyed a good run direct to Cape Turnagain, covering the 60 km in about an hour.

Cape Turnagain is another place named by old Cookie. When he arrived in New Zealand from Tahiti on his first voyage in 1769, he made landfall at Poverty Bay, south of Gisborne. From there he headed south to as far as Cape Turnagain, before returning north and going anti-clockwise around the North Island to Cape Turnagain, thus confirming that the North Island was in fact an island. Then he turned again (get it?) and headed south on a mission to misidentify Banks Peninsula as an island, and Stewart Island as a Peninsula, which he successfully accomplished (And I know I have previously mentioned this, but I find it particularly amusing so humour me).

Because we were much more focused than Cook, we didn't even deviate one degree at the cape; much less turn again; and we continued on past it at a great rate of knots to avoid the temptation of doing so.

Soon the following swell had dropped to first 2½ m, then 2 m, and then down to 1 ½ m, until the waves were hardly assisting us at all. We continued to make good progress, however, and it wasn't long before we found ourselves off the well known fishing spot of Blackhead Point (Don't ask). From there we continued on and eventually we could see Cape Kidnappers way in the distance.

An hour later we rounded the thriving gannet sanctuary at Cape Kidnappers, at the southern most point of Hawke Bay. The name Kidnappers refers to an incident during Cook's first voyage when an attempt was made to trade with the occupants of an armed canoe. Tiata, the Tahitian servant of Tupia, Cook's interpreter, was seized by the Maori and escaped by jumping into the sea when the canoe was fired on.

Once we rounded the cape we could see Napier in the distance about 25 km away but, as luck would have it, the sea became very shallow and chopped up. We were reduced to battling untidy chop again and making much slower progress than we would have liked at the end of such a marathon session.

There was nothing for it but to dig deep and put our heads down again and eventually we reached the breakwater at Napier's Port Ahuriri, then headed around the corner towards Westshore and the marina which was our destination.

As we slowly entered the marina, we spotted the Sorento, the boys, and Debbie Sheard and her son Josh and daughter Casey. The Sheard family lives in Napier and have been friends for a few years now. We regularly camp at the same time each year in Whananaki, north of Whangarei. David Libeau from Qantas was also there to meet us. He had come down from Auckland for the weekend to attend the annual Mission Estate Winery concert which has become a feature of New Zealand's summer entertainment. Gavin Scoble of the local Cancer Society was also there.

After such a huge day we were expecting a hero's welcome, but everyone had their backs to us and no one saw us come in. We motored up to the ramp and sat reading *War and Peace*, while waiting for someone to look. Eventually Josh saw us and everyone hurried down to the ramp.

David greeted us and waited just out of the water with his hand extended to shake Burglar's hand. Burglar stood his ground in 40 cm of water and held his hand out. David, being the good sport that he is, took off his shoes and walked in.

TV3 had sent another freelance cameraman to film us and he had missed our arrival due to some immaculate bad timing, so we rode in and out of the marina a few more times to allow him to film us. After 360 km we needed this extra time on the Seadoos like a hole in the head, but we were so pleased to have cracked the longest leg that it didn't matter.

With filming and interviews complete, David again showed that he is a marketing man who knows his target audience, by pulling a case of cold Crown Lagers out of the back of his car. We stood around for some time downing Crownies; for medicinal purposes, of course; and telling the day's war stories.

We were pretty happy because this day had looked to be the biggest day on the map and, with the weather forecast, we had expected to be lucky to make Castlepoint, much less Napier. If we didn't take our day off in Napier we could consider ourselves back on schedule for our 1.30pm arrival in Auckland on Monday 27th, but everything would have to go perfectly from here.

Eventually, when all the beer was gone, we packed up and headed back to the Sheard residence where we settled in for a barbecue and overnight stay.

Just as everyone was starting to get into the swing of things, I suddenly decided that I was exhausted, made some weak excuse and went to bed. I was in survival mode and I knew that the only way I would make it was by listening to what my body was trying to tell me. We had ridden for over ten hours again today and my body wasn't happy.

It's been said to me a thousand times over the years that you only live once and that sleeping is cheating. All I can say to that is that on this night I was 'guilty as charged, Your Honour'; just a great big cheat!

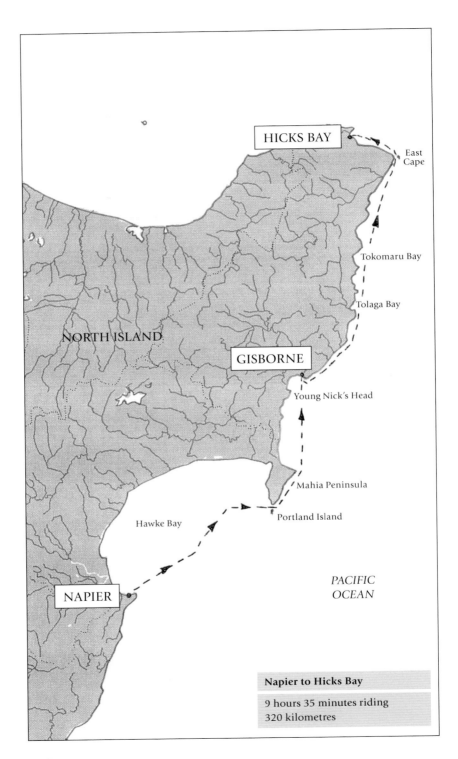

HICKS BAY

East
Cape

Tokomaru Bay

Tolaga Bay

NORTH ISLAND

GISBORNE

Young Nick's Head

Mahia Peninsula

Hawke Bay

Portland Island

NAPIER

PACIFIC
OCEAN

Napier to Hicks Bay

9 hours 35 minutes riding
320 kilometres

Chapter 22
The Ride: To Hicks Bay

Saturday 25th February 2006

Napier is a friendly city on the western shore of Hawke Bay. It is named after General Sir Charles Napier, the hero of Sind and the leader of the expedition to Magdala in Abyssinia (You will have to look this up yourself under Nineteenth Century British Imperialism if you want more info!).

The city is a very popular tourist destination and is famous for its wineries. We had hoped to have a day off there to partake of some wine tasting, but we had wasted a day sorting out problems in Wellington, so it wasn't to be.

Historically, Napier is interesting as well. It is probably most famous for the great earthquake of February 3rd 1931. This was New Zealand's deadliest recorded earthquake and it devastated the cities of Napier and Hastings. At least 256 people died in the magnitude 7.8 quake. Many thousands more required medical treatment.

Within minutes of the earthquake itself, fire began in three chemist shops in the business district. Firefighters were almost helpless as water pressure faded to a trickle, due to broken pipes. Fanned by a sea breeze that sprang up at midday, the flames spread rapidly. By mid-afternoon Napier's business area was ablaze. Some thirty-six hours later the fires smoldered out, having gutted almost eleven blocks of central Napier.

One of the remarkable consequences of the earthquake was the raising of the harbour bed and the consequent disappearance of much of the inner harbour. In its place were 7,500 acres of new land, which is now part of the city.

Through the curtains it looked like Napier had managed to conjure up a good day for us. I looked across at Burglar and noticed that he was looking at me with one eye open and one eye closed, making it patently obvious to me that he was still half asleep. I walked over to him and shook the still sleeping side of him causing the other eye to open. It was obvious that he had had a few the night before and was feeling a little sorry for himself, but he neither demanded, nor got, any sympathy from me.

Five minutes later we were drinking coffee and checking the weather on Debbie's computer. The weather forecast was pretty good for most of our route. The only part of much concern was the bit from East Cape to Hicks Bay, where strong north-westerly winds were forecast.

Today would be another big day, almost as big as the previous one, as we planned to ride to Gisborne, then around East Cape and north-westwards to Hicks Bay, a distance of around 320 km. With this in mind we stuffed as much food in as we could bear and then got, once again, into our damp gear.

We thanked Debbie for her hospitality then we drove down to the marina, launched the Seadoos at first light and made our way out into Hawke Bay, heading east.

We were taking a fairly big risk by heading directly east. Our initial track would take us directly from Napier across Hawke Bay to Portland Island at the southern tip of the Mahia Peninsula. This would mean that at some stages we would be more than 50 km away from the nearest land. At the midpoint of this leg we expected that we wouldn't be able to see either Napier behind us or Portland Island in front of us. The only thing we expected to see were the tops of the hills near Wairoa in northern Hawke Bay.

David Libeau had brought us down another GPS, our third of the trip, and I was hoping that this one would work better than the other two, but I wasn't confident.

As we headed east the sea conditions were moderately annoying, as there was both a primary and a secondary swell, which were at odds with each other, so that we had waves coming at us from two different directions. This took a fair bit of effort to negotiate and our pace was not as good as expected.

There was worse to come though, because soon the sun peeped up from below the horizon and it was shining straight off the sea in front of us so that we were effectively blinded. I liken riding blind in rough conditions, or any conditions for that matter, to being in a boxing match wearing a blindfold. You just don't want to be there. The light was so painful on our eyes that, in spite of our tinted goggles, it wasn't long before we were forced to start tacking, in much the same manner as a yacht sailing into the wind. For five minutes at a time we would ride a heading just to the left of the reflected light and then we would alter heading to ride just to the right of the reflected light. We continued on in this way right out into the middle of Hawke Bay.

At about the exact point where we would have been as far from any land as we could possibly get, the GPS decided that it didn't like the water; or the bumping and thumping; and failed.

I pulled out the map and surveyed our situation. On the horizon to the east I could see what looked like an island and then, further to the north there were more substantial lumps of land, so I assumed that the island was Portland Island and the more substantial land was Mahia Peninsula.

I pointed to the gap and Burglar nodded. Off we went, liking the visual aim point, and liking even more the fact that the sun was no longer in our eyes. The only problem was that when the GPS had failed and we had been heading in the right direction, the sun had been in our eyes. This bothered me, and I kept running it through the thought processes trying to work out the anomaly.

We kept riding towards the gap. When we were about 20 km away, and a lot more land had appeared above the horizon, I realised what we had done. The land that we thought was Portland Island was actually Te Kapu, the high point of Mahia Peninsula. The gap we were heading for was actually low-lying land, and the lumps of land to the north were part of the mainland.

A long way to the south east we could now see Portland Island coming up from below the horizon. There was no way through in the direction we were heading, so there was nothing for it but to alter heading to the south-east and ride the extra 20 km we had created for ourselves.

I waved Burglar down to give him the 'good news' that we had an extra 20 km to ride. The poor bloke knew 3/5ths of stuff-all about navigation, and had been forced to follow me around on the whole ride, always guessing where our destination was and how far it was to go. It must have been tough at times, but he handled it well. Until now I hadn't made any navigational stuff ups and so I decided to come clean and admit it straight up.

I was reminded at this point of the black American civil rights leader the Reverend Jesse Jackson who blew his whole credibility, and any chance of doing any more good, when he was sprung for getting his secretary pregnant. When he was interviewed on CNN he said, "This is not a time for denial. This is a time for reconciliation and prayer". In English this means, "I've been caught red-handed. I hope Mrs Jackson doesn't help my sorry butt out the door with her boot and take all my money, and I'll be praying for that".

Having learnt from the good reverend's experience, I admitted to my mistake, said I owed Burglar a beer, and suggested we pray for some track shortening, but Burglar was okay and admitted he had been suckered by the same wrong conclusion. So we headed off towards Portland Island with our relationship intact and some extra track miles to work on improving it further.

We rode between Portland Island and the Mahia Peninsula and

headed north-east up the coast of the peninsula. It's a very pretty area and we enjoyed the scenery, with the deep blue of the sea contrasting against the olive green of the hills on our left. It's no wonder the peninsula and its beaches are a favourite summer resort for people from all over the North Island.

We rounded Table Cape and headed for Gisborne some 50 km directly to the north. At this point the wind became calm and the sea like glass, but there was an underlying chop and, so it was, that in perfect weather conditions, we found ourselves getting beaten up again by *bastard glass*.

I found myself going through a particularly bad time as I struggled to keep up with Burglar. My injuries were all still there. My back rash was painful and the lack of feeling in my arms had gotten worse. I was now having to use both my middle and index fingers to operate the throttle, as one finger wasn't enough. My right wrist was sore and swollen, and the wear on my butt was widespread and painful. The hole in my ankle from boot wear was wide and deep and an ugly grey colour. The only thing that had improved was that my bruised kidney had recovered. Right at the moment, with all the wet gear, I probably weighed about 110 kg, but whenever I tried to stand up I felt like I weighed 300 kg. The whole of my body felt heavy and sore. Mentally I knew I could make it to Auckland, but I was fairly sure that physically, I would probably just crawl over the line at the finish.

Looking back on the physical aspects of the ride, a lot of my problems could be traced back to the spinal compressions experienced on day two while riding around Cape Reinga. They resulted in the loss of feeling in my arms that affected the way I rode for the rest of the trip. That certainly made it harder for me but I believe that nutrition and hydration were my biggest downfall. I was so busy organising and planning that I didn't concentrate enough on ensuring that I ate enough good food on land and while at sea. I probably wasn't drinking enough either. Burglar was frequently finishing his drink while I would arrive with mine still half full and he never got sick of our 'at sea' snacks whereas I couldn't stomach them from about day four onwards.

I suppose you could say that I was suffering from *jet ski lag*. You heard it here first. It's the feeling you get when you've spent too much time on a jet ski. The media have a very poor understanding of real jetlag. Most of them write about it as if it's something you get from time spent on an airplane. This is not true, of course. It's caused by time zone changes. You might fly from Sydney to London and arrive early in the morning, but it will be night time where you came from and you will want to go to bed. That's jetlag.

If, however, you took a nine hour flight from Tokyo to Sydney, you would remain within an hour of the same time zone, so although you may feel like you have been run over by a truck when you get there, this is not jetlag. It is, no doubt, a combination of dehydration from the dry aircraft cabin environment and a hangover from drinking the free grog and that, my friends, is your own fault.

While I'm on the subject of misinformation, there is also no such thing as an air pocket. Air pockets are supposedly holes in the sky where air has 'forgotten' to go, or has fallen out of, or perhaps has intentionally avoided in a mean spirited way. The media love to say that aircraft fall into air pockets, and unfortunate passengers, who have been ignoring the advice to keep their seat belts fastened, end up inspecting the contents of the overhead lockers from the inside, with their heads stuck fast and the rest of their bodies dangling below them. These supposed air pockets are nothing more than updrafts or downdrafts of air. But I digress, yet again!

I knew that I had been holding Burglar up for some days now, as he was always waiting for me. He was like a dog out for a walk with its owner. The owner marking out the route and going the same pace all the way, and the dog out in front exploring and running first this way, then that, tail wagging, sniffing lamp posts and other dog's butts, and once in a while looking back and saying, "Come on Boss. Hurry up". All his zigzagging was becoming a bit annoying at times too, because every time his track would cut across in front of me it would cause the sea to become more chopped up for me from his wake.

There is a reason why professional sports people retire and make way for younger people. There is a reason why there are veterans sporting events. No matter how hard you fight it and how much work you do, you can't stop yourself getting old and suffering the reduction in physical performance that goes with it. Sure you can slow it down and delay it, but it is still inevitable. I could see this now. Even though I could out-lift Burglar in the gym and out-ride him on a push bike, his fifteen year younger body was handling the beating better and bouncing back better, and there was nothing I could do about it except bow in his direction and tip my hat.

With all this in mind and the clank clank of the fuel tank baffles beating away at the inside of the tanks, I rode on, silently willing Gisborne to get closer, willing the weather to stay good, and knowing that 1.30pm on Monday couldn't come soon enough.

We forged on towards Gisborne and passed Young Nicks Head on our left. On Cook's first voyage he offered a reward of rum to the man who first sighted land, and promised that, "part of the coast of the said land should be named after him". The sighting was made by the surgeon's boy, twelve year old Nicholas Young on 6th October 1769.

As we entered Poverty Bay, the underlying chop on the glassy sea disappeared and we were riding on totally smooth seas. We could see Gisborne 10 km away, so we rode at full speed towards it. It was an exhilarating ride and raised my spirits somewhat for the arrival into Gisborne.

Gisborne's main claim to fame is that it is the first city in the world to see the sun each day. The Maori name for the district is Tairawhiti which means, *The coast upon which the sun shines across the water.* Kaiti Beach, near the city, was where the Maori immigrational waka, Horouta, landed. Gisborne was also the first European landing place in New Zealand. Captain Cook sailed into Poverty Bay on 8th October 1769 and came ashore near the mouth of the Turanganui River.

We entered the Port of Gisborne and rode up past a large bulk cargo ship, and then as far as we could go until we found a marina and launching ramp. The boys were nowhere in sight, so I turned the engine off and drifted around while I extracted the mobile phone from its protective covering. I then phoned the boys. There was no reply, so I left a message to say that we were here and when they were out of the massage parlour, if it wasn't *too* much trouble, could they come down and service us as well. By that I meant food and fuel of course!

While we waited for the boys we drifted around some more and spoke to some of the locals up on the wharf about the ride and the sun smart message.

After ten minutes of this Pete turned up in the Sorento to tell us we were in the wrong place. I agreed and said that I would much rather be lying in a hammock suspended between two trees, adjacent to the cocktail bar, at a Fijian resort.

Pete then informed us that there was another ramp up the Turanganui River, where the Mayor and many other people were all waiting for us, so we fired up the Seadoos and headed back out to the open water, around another breakwater and into the Turanganui River.

We rode slowly up the river until we found everyone at a stunning spot where the Taruheru and Waimata Rivers join to form the Turanganui. The Turanganui exits to the sea only 1,200 m away, making it the shortest river in New Zealand.

We rode the Seadoos straight onto the trailer, climbed down, and met everyone. Dr John Rouse, Kevin Tims, Jacqui Thomas and

Janice Hobbs were all there representing the Cancer Society. We had a good chat with them and also met Mayor Meng Foon. Say what you like, but I was surprised to find an Asian Mayor in a place like Gisborne. But he seemed like a really good bloke and he apparently speaks Maori, so both Burglar and I were quite impressed.

Mateus had bought us some lunch, so we tucked into that. We then did a photo shoot for the local newspaper. Finally we were ready to head off again, so we boarded the Seadoos and made ready to leave. Mayor Foon had asked for a photo of him leaning over the edge of the nearby dock shaking our hands and wishing us well, and we had agreed.

While we were motoring around waiting for the photographer to get organised, Burglar suggested that we both pull him off the dock and into the water. Appealing as the idea was, I suggested that we don't because Meng might not find it as funny as we would and it may well be that, being Asian, he might know karate or jujitsu or some other Japanese words, and we might just hear a blood curdling scream and then suddenly find ourselves floating around in the water with him standing on the dock rubbing his hands together and doing a formal martial arts bow.

We survived the photo session without incident and slowly motored out of the river into the open sea. From there we set our heading in perfect conditions south-east towards Tuaheni Point. We rounded the point and suddenly lost all the shelter that we had had from the wind and the swells. A sea breeze was now blowing and the sea began to become chopped up. This made the going reasonably slow again, as we plodded on towards the north-east and East Cape.

From time to time conditions would improve for a few kilometres, but mostly it was just hard slog again. We discovered that this is a coastline with many reefs and we spent a lot of time off track, or riding extra track miles around them.

We continued on past Tolaga Bay with its famous 660 m long

wharf jutting out into the bay. The coast line is quite pretty in this area and it made us feel better that we were able to see it while we rode. Another 30 km further on, we passed Tokomaru Bay, with about 50 km to run to East Cape.

The East Cape region is probably the most isolated, and one of the least known regions of the North Island. As we approached East Cape I decided that this would be quite a milestone for us, so I told Burglar that we would stop and take some video of the occasion once we got there. But when we got to within about 10 km the wind started to come up. It was coming at us head-on from between East Cape and East Island. East Island sits about 2 km off the cape. By the time we reached the cape, we were battling steep 1½ m waves and 35 km an hour winds, so we decided shooting video would be impossible.

As we rounded the cape we got a nasty surprise. The forecast strong north-westerly winds were there as promised, and conditions were foul. We were straight into 3 m breaking waves and a wind of about 50 km an hour. We forged on into the waves, jumping each one and falling into the narrow trough behind, before almost immediately tackling the next wave. We were doubly nervous because we could see that, in the current conditions, the height of the waves could have only been caused by the sea being very shallow at this point. We were quite worried that while dropping off the back of the waves we might hit the bottom at some stage and do damage to the Seadoos.

We slogged on over the next hour and finally made it to Horoera point. The GPS had failed again and we had no idea exactly where Hicks Bay was. I knew it would be about another 20 km or so, but there are a lot of small bays and inlets in this area. I had studied a photo of Hicks Bay before leaving on the ride, so we resolved to just keep running up the coast until we saw something that looked like it.

At this point it occurred to us that we only had about 20 km to go and we had plenty of time and fuel, so we started to have some fun. The waves were perfect for jumping and we would ride up the front of a wave at full throttle and then get airborne a good metre above the top of the wave. We would then drop at least 3 m through the air, before thumping tail-down into the following trough. By now we were totally confident on the Seadoos, and in our ability to put them where we wanted to, as well as at the angle we wanted to. It was exhilarating stuff and we took turns watching each other jump as we continued towards the north-west.

I was having so much fun that I suddenly felt young again and was back on my feet and throwing my machine around and feeling fantastic. A bit of adrenaline can do that for you, and we were getting our share. On some of the less steep waves we were getting airborne at speed and sailing though the air a good 10 m, clearing the following wave before gently alighting into its trough. It was probably the best riding of the whole trip and it was tempting to try and get some photos or video, but the conditions would not allow it.

After about forty-five minutes of hooning, we saw a bay that looked like it could be Hicks Bay, so we headed into it. Thankfully it was and it wasn't long before we had found Pete and Mateus and had been 'retrieved'. We then drove up to the Hicks Bay Lodge and went through the ritual of cleaning up and getting organised.

I rang home and reminded my family who I was, and then I rang my old mate Colin Bower in Te Puke to confirm that we would be arriving in Tauranga the next day. We would be staying with Colin and I wanted to make sure the spa was hot and the beer was cold. I then spoke to Matt Kneesh from Makz Gear in Tauranga. Matt and his boys had installed our long range tanks and Matt was organising a group of riders to ride out from Tauranga and meet us the next day.

While unpacking and reorganising the gear we made an unwelcome discovery. TV3's camera, which we had been carrying around for the last three weeks, had finally succumbed to the serious thrashing we had given it. It had ripped itself clear of the mounts in its waterproof container and bashed around loose inside the container all day. There were bits of broken casing and screws rattling around in the container and, although the camera still turned on, the picture on the screen was split, with one half of the picture looking like it was viewing the world through the eyes of someone who is blind drunk. Don't ask me how I know what the world looks like when you are blind drunk, however, if you must know, it's because I've seen pictures. I wondered how TV3 would take the news and decided to deal with it after we got back. In the event they were actually fantastic about it.

With everything organised and under control we ate another culinary delight de'Mateus and enjoyed a few beers and a chat. The sad state of the TV3 camera was mentioned again. I made a comment that Campbell Live would have to do without any footage from the last few days. Mateus, having very little experience of New Zealand television, wanted to know what Campbell Live was all about, as he had heard us mention it more than a few times. It became obvious that he was under the impression that Campbell Live was a show named after its host, a Mr. C. Live. We informed him that he was indeed a bonehead of the highest order and that it was John Campbell 'Live'. We then laughed as he made fun of himself by saying "Hello Mr. Live, Matthew Gray, I'm very pleased to meet you".

The subject of Mateus's cow came up again and Burglar asked Mateus if he had heard of the 'sport' of cow tipping. Apparently cows sleep standing up and it is quite easy to sneak up to them in the dark and stick your shoulder in their side and tip them over. The unsuspecting beast doesn't wake up until it's at a 45° angle and by then it's way too late.

On hearing this, Mateus suddenly got that look on his face that a person gets when he has just come up with the perfect revenge and we could all see that sometime soon he would be sneaking out of bed, with his pajamas and a long night cap on, donning some gum boots, black face paint and night vision goggles, and disappearing quietly into the night towards his renegade cow.

I wondered if there was any way to stop this impending das-
tardly deed, but what could be done short of warning the cow
and betraying a friend. And, in the end, even if it knew its fate,
what could it do? You can't stay awake forever. With that thought
foremost in my mind I quietly slipped away to bed to dream about
paddocks full of upturned cows.

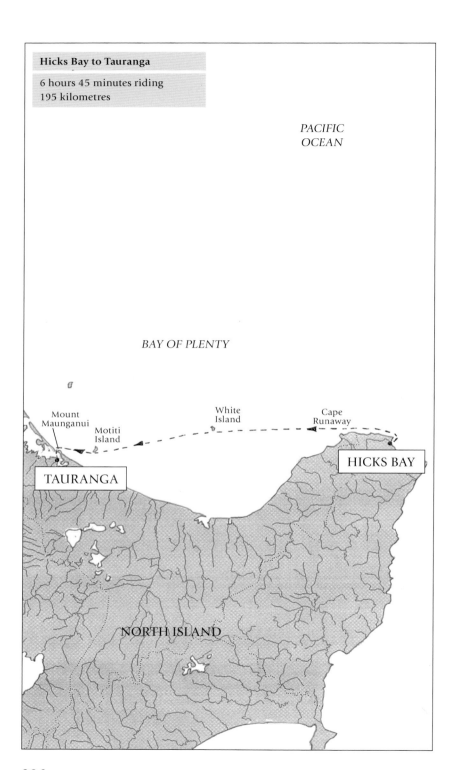

Hicks Bay to Tauranga

6 hours 45 minutes riding
195 kilometres

PACIFIC
OCEAN

BAY OF PLENTY

Mount
Maunganui

Motiti
Island

White
Island

Cape
Runaway

HICKS BAY

TAURANGA

NORTH ISLAND

Chapter 23
The Ride: To Tauranga

Sunday 26th February 2006

The Hicks Bay Lodge sits high on a hill overlooking Hicks Bay. Hicks Bay is not so named because of the type of people who live there. It was named after Lt Zachary Hicks, one of Cook's crew. The scenery in the area is magnificent, and the area is well worth a visit.

We woke early again and enjoyed a good breakfast while we took in the excellent scenery starting to become visible as darkness turned into dawn. Today would be a short day of around 200 km, so we felt good at the prospect of an early finish and a relaxing afternoon in the Bower spa.

I could see that the strong north-westerly was still whipping up the sea outside the bay, but it certainly seemed like it had reduced in intensity.

We suited up again for the second-to-last time and then headed down to the bay. When we got there we prepared to launch. Doing the same were a couple of commercial fishermen. One of them came over with his phone and said, "You're those guys who are riding jet skis around New Zealand aren't you. You's guys are famous. Can I take a photo with my phone?" We were only too happy to oblige. We were appreciative that we were becoming well known around the country to this extent, because it meant that we must be getting our sun smart message out there. We talked to the guys for a little bit longer then boarded the Seadoos and headed out to sea.

We rode around Matakaoa Point and headed just north of west. Conditions were quite good. There was about a one metre westerly swell, with reasonably smooth seas. It was still annoying though, because, with the weight in our long range tanks, this style of wave meant that we basically bounced along, getting airborne off each wave and thumping down onto the next one. We settled into a rhythm, tried to ignore the thumping and, instead, enjoyed the amazing scenery along the coast to our left. The hills were steep and towering, and a stunning emerald green. It was a different type of scenery yet again compared to all those we had already seen on the ride. New Zealand is, without question, a magnificent country.

After about an hour of riding we reached Cape Runaway. This is where we would stop following the coastline and 'runaway' direct-ly towards White Island.

Cape Runaway was named by Cook after he scared off five canoes full of angry Maori by firing warning shots over their heads. The cape is the easternmost promontory of the Bay of Plenty. Here the coast curves towards the south-west and then curves fur-ther in a large circle until it is heading north-west at Tauranga and Mount Maunganui. By cutting straight across via White Island we would save ourselves a huge amount of distance, and also get the chance to see New Zealand's only active marine volcano.

While on the subject of running away or getting away, it probably doesn't need to be pointed out that this is something that some burglars do particularly well (notably the ones who are still free). It's one of the skills of the trade and can be quite useful at other times as well, such as with our encounter with the shark.

One time a few years ago Burglar and I had gone into the Sydney CBD to do a few things. We were walking down Pitt St Mall when we noticed a large crowd gathered at the bottom of Centre Point

Tower. We wandered over to the edge of the crowd to see what was going on. It turns out that we had stumbled on the annual Police race to the top of Centre Point Tower. The tower is about 300 m high and there are stairs all the way to the top. Each year the Police have a race to the top.

As we watched, about one-hundred very fit looking police stood around in their uniforms and running shoes listening to a commentator prattling on to the gathered crowd. He was interviewing a famous rugby league player. First he asked him where he grew up and the rugby player said New Zealand. The commentator asked if there were any Kiwis in the crowd and a loud cheer went up. The two of them waffled on some more and then the rugby player said, "Jeez those police look fit. I wouldn't want to be a burglar with them chasing me". Then, unbelievably, the commentator asked if there were any burglars in the crowd. This was too much for Burglar and I and we proudly raised our hands. This caused great laughter from the crowd as they first looked at us then back at all the police who were looking at us with looks of utter disbelief and contempt. We were both wondering if the run to the top of the tower was about to be postponed as one-hundred police chased two burglars through Pitt St Mall, but the police didn't move and we wandered off for a coffee, laughing until our sides hurt.

We left Cape Runaway, heading west towards where White Island was. We couldn't see the island yet and the GPS wasn't working, so it was a bit risky to go so far away from the coast, but I figured that, if for some reason we didn't find the island then it would only be a matter of turning left towards the coast and following it to our destination.

I had discovered the night before that the GPS didn't like the jarring from the waves. By trial and error and a bit of fiddling I had eliminated battery as the problem and also eliminated moisture. The only thing left was bumping or jarring. I turned the GPS on and waited for it to fire up. Then I gave it a gentle tap on the side and, sure enough, it turned off. This was an interesting discovery, as all three GPSs had had the same problem. They were basically useless except on a good day and, generally, they would only work when we least needed them to. When the going got tough and visibility was low they always failed when we really needed them.

We bounced further away from the coast in the general direction of White Island. There was nothing to see and nothing to do but bounce and crash, and bounce and crash, and then, for a change, crash and bounce. It was all about as exciting as the planning, implementation, and then debriefing, of a reorganisation of your sock drawer.

I kept looking into the distance for any signs of White Island, and then suddenly I realised that the cloud I had been looking at on the horizon was actually the island. It didn't look white though. From where we were, it looked sort of off-white with a pink bias.

We rode on and on towards the island and it never seemed to get any closer, but after what seemed like about a week, we arrived.

White Island (Whakaari) is a rhyolite volcano which forms an island in the Bay of Plenty, 50 km north of Whakatane. Scientists say that it appears to have been built up by fairly quiet volcanic activity and is the seat of considerable hydrothermal activity with hot springs, geysers and fumaroles widely distributed inside the crater. The island lies at the northern end of the Taupo-Rotorua Volcanic Zone, within which occurs the bulk of New Zealand's modern hydrothermal and volcanic activity.

White Island is one of the most fascinating and accessible volcanoes on earth, carrying with it an A-grade level of scientific importance. As New Zealand's only live marine volcano, volcanologists and other scientists worldwide are attracted by its unique features.

The volcano is estimated to be between one-hundred-thousand and two-hundred-thousand years old. However, the small portion of the island visible above sea level has only been in its present form for an estimated sixteen-thousand years.

Cook was the first European to discover and name White Island in 1769. He noted in the *Endeavour's* log book, "We called it White for as such it always appear'd to us".

Incidentally, and surprise surprise, he never did come close enough to the island to realise it was a volcano.

There have been attempts over the years to mine sulphur and other minerals from the island, but they have proved uneconomical. The island is now owned by the Buttle Family Trust. It was declared a private scenic reserve in 1953. In 1997 the owners of White Island Tours were appointed official guardians of the island by the Buttles. Now access is further restricted, and the only way in which anyone is permitted to visit the island is with one of the four designated tourist operators, or by Seadoo with long range tanks.

Actually, we assumed it was okay to ride in the water near the island and we didn't go ashore, so I'm guessing we didn't break any rules.

We hung around the south side of the island for about half an hour and ate a snack while looking straight into the crater. The south side is where the wall of the crater has collapsed, and it is possible to ride right up to the edge of the crater and look in. It is a very spectacular sight and we got some great photos. We were also amazed at the deep blue of the sea surrounding the island. The area is said to be a diver's paradise.

We had a visit from a guy in a runabout who had heard about us and was amazed to see us out here so far from the coast. We chatted for a while about the ride and then got ready to leave. It was turning into quite a hot day, so we both took an extra large slurp of our life giving Raro and electrolyte solution (The town-house in Queenstown, the Porsche, the boat, the world trip, the life time supply of Tui beer, the volleyball tickets, the carton of Lomitol and two real 'Get out of jail free' cards please!).

With a tick in the box next to *White Island Visit*, we headed west again towards our rendezvous off Motiti Island with all the Tauranga riders. We had arranged to meet them at 1pm at Taumataika Point on the southern tip of Motiti Island. From there we would all ride in together to Tauranga.

The sea conditions had smoothed out quite a bit, so I turned on the GPS to see if it was interested in making a contribution to the success of our operation and, surprisingly, it was. This was quite helpful because, at this point, all we could see on the horizon in front of us was the edge of the earth and there was no way either of us wanted to fall off that.

I followed the GPS track towards Motiti and Burglar rode around in circles like an escapee from an institution, with his head down and his tongue hanging out the side of his mouth. He would ride off in one wrong direction for a while and then cross over in front of me and head 45° to the other side of our desired track. Finally it got too much for me, so I waved him down and asked him if he knew where he was going. This was a stupid question really, because I knew the answer had to be no, but I thought I would give him the benefit of the doubt in case he knew something about navigation that I had missed. He admitted he didn't know where he was going at all, but said that where ever he *was* going, he was going there *fast* and he was taking the scenic route. He also mentioned that he had heard something about a great circle route. I told him that a little knowledge can be dangerous, to forget about the great circle, and to go straight.

We continued on for a while more in much the same fashion. Eventually Motiti Island came into view and we both became focused on a visual aiming point at the southern tip of the island. We got there early, at 12.30pm, beached the Seadoos and ate lunch.

Just as we finished lunch we saw the group of Tauranga riders arrive a few hundred metres off the point, so we cleaned up and rode out to meet them. It was a great reunion. Good old Colin

Bower was there and so was his daughter Tasha. Matt Kneesh from Makz Gear was there, and so were Colin and Bevan, who had installed our long range tanks. Pete's wife and daughter were there too, as were a few other local riders. We drifted around talking for a while in about 6 m of crystal clear water and brilliant weather conditions, and it was all a lot of fun.

We had to wait until 1.30pm before heading in, because Tauranga's Mayor was coming to meet us at our arrival point at 2pm, so we had to time it right. At 1.30pm we all headed in towards the extinct volcano, Mount Maunganui, in perfect conditions and at high speed. It was a great feeling to be part of the group and we really enjoyed it. Once we reached the Mount we zoomed around the north side and through the Tauranga Harbour entrance, directly into the reception at the Tauranga Yacht Club.

It was quite a welcome, with the Mayor, representatives from the local Cancer Society, some old family friends, Rae Bower, and a heap of people who I didn't know, but got to know soon enough.

There had been a PWC event the day before in the area and they had taken up a collection for our cause. They made a most welcome presentation in front of everyone there. It was a great occasion generally, and we were glad to be there with only one day's riding left.

Eventually we pulled the Seadoos out of the water for the second to last time and Pete took Mateus home to his place to stay, while we headed out to the Bower's at Te Puke.

We drove into the Bower hacienda and saw the spa bath sitting waiting in the garden at the side of the house. Needless to say, the spa was where we were to be found thirty seconds after our arrival, with beer in hand.

Colin, Burglar and I sat in the spa telling war stories. We ordered Devonshire teas to be made and delivered to the spa by Rae and, in a manner to which I have become accustomed, she 'politely' told us where the ingredients were and that we could get it ourselves. We then laid down the law to Rae and stated that our absolute no compromise position was that she should bring us fresh cold beer in the spa every fifteen minutes or so. The three of us ended up taking turns to get the beer after that. Everyone was happy and the status quo was intact, and as long as the status quo is intact no one can really complain, can they. And no one did!

A Tasha Bower 'bad hair day' off Motiti Island, Tauranga.

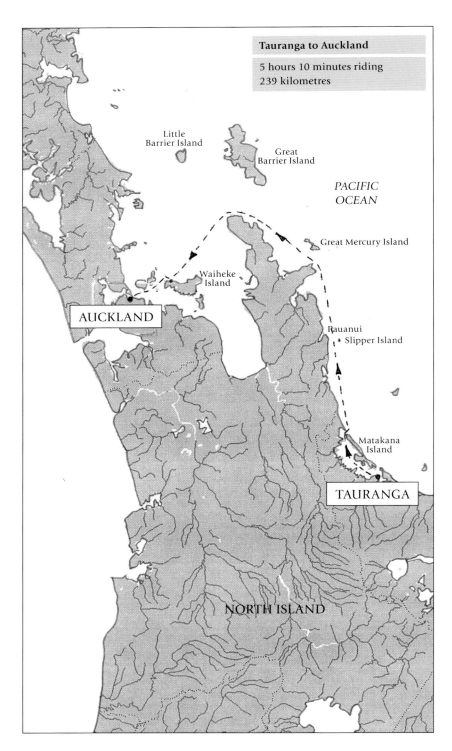

Tauranga to Auckland

5 hours 10 minutes riding
239 kilometres

Little
Barrier Island

Great
Barrier Island

PACIFIC
OCEAN

Great Mercury Island

Waiheke
Island

AUCKLAND

Rauanui
Slipper Island

Matakana
Island

TAURANGA

NORTH ISLAND

Chapter 24
The Ride: Home

Monday 27th February 2006

For the last time that bastard, heartless alarm woke us in the dark. We stumbled out of bed and into the kitchen, where Colin was already eating breakfast. We joined him and talked about the day ahead.

We had to leave as early as possible, and go as hard as possible, because it was imperative that we arrive on schedule at the Viaduct Basin in Auckland at 1.30pm. This had become a matter of serious pride to us. We wanted to show everyone who said it couldn't be done, that it could be done.

For both of us, completing the ride would be only half the victory. Doing it on schedule was a must. This would not be as easy a proposition as it sounded, though. We had found over the last twenty-three days that the weather can change at any time and riding conditions can go from good to bad very quickly. We still had 240 km to go to get to Auckland, but we only had until 1.30pm to achieve it, not the usual 5 to 6pm.

To add to our stress, Phil Briars from the Cancer Society had confirmed that there would be a lot of people waiting for us at the Viaduct at 1.30pm, so we had better not be late.

The night before, I had sat down with Burglar and plotted a time and distance chart working backwards from Auckland to

Tauranga. I had based it on a speed of 30 km an hour, which is the speed that we knew we could make in marginal conditions. We ended up with a list of places, and times that we needed to pass those places to be on schedule, based on the speed of 30 km an hour. The problem was that we were starting behind schedule even before we had left. Two-hundred-and-forty kilometres at 30 km an hour would mean that we would have to leave at 5.30am from Tauranga, and that wasn't happening as we were still having breakfast at that time. At some stage during the ride we would need to be doing a lot better than 30 km an hour to get there on schedule.

With breakfast completed we jumped in the car and drove down to the launch ramp near the Tauranga Yacht Club and met up with Pete and Mateus. Matt from Makz Gear was there too. He was going to ride up the inner harbour with us to the Katikati entrance. He was going to carry Louise from the local Classic Hits radio station on the back of his Seadoo.

We climbed into our wet gear for the last time and, because it was the last time, it was only half as disgusting as it normally was, and we seemed to manage it more easily too. Louise organised an interview with Brian Kelly back at Classic Hits and Brian asked how Louise looked, because she had never been on a PWC before. I mentioned that she had probably taken about an hour to do her hair and all the hard work was about to be blown away in the first minute, but apart from that she looked fine.

Soon we were ready to go and I looked at my watch to see how we were doing versus our schedule. It was already 7am, so we were an hour and a half behind. We were effectively chasing an imaginary moving 'on schedule' point that was already 45 km north of us up the coast. With that in mind we took off up the inner Tauranga Harbour at a blistering pace. It was a beautiful, clear morning and the ride up the harbour was stunning. We enjoyed the great scenery and the birdlife, and we enjoyed the high speed company of Matt and Louise right next to us.

At 7.30am we made the Katikati Entrance and waved goodbye to Matt and Louise, before zooming out through the entrance into the open sea. We found out later that we were supposed to have done another live interview with Louise at the entrance, but we had no idea and, in any event, we just wanted to get going.

The sea conditions were almost as good outside the entrance as inside, and we charged towards the north for all we were worth. Thirty kilometres up the coast, and just off Whangamata, the sea chopped up a little to *bone shaker* status. We were both thinking, "Here we go again. It's about to turn to custard". But instead of getting worse it improved again and we had a good run past Slipper Island and Pauanui. The view of the hills behind Tairua was magnificent as we sped further up the coast past Hot Water Beach, Cathedral Cove, and then Opito Bay, before heading north-west towards Cape Colville.

Great Mercury Island looked impressive off to our right, as we continued on at high speed. The sea conditions had now improved to flat glass and we were making great time.

We could have gone even faster, but we didn't want to push our luck and run the risk of an engine problem on the last leg. The chances of this happening were slim, but we wanted to nurse the machines home as best we could anyway.

This thinking was just a little bit of last leg paranoia, because throughout the ride the Seadoos had been absolutely awesome. The only problems we had had were due to the extra equipment which we had attached for the ride.

Because the sea was so smooth we were both sitting on our seats for long periods at a time without moving. I started to notice that I could feel heat coming through the seat, which I had never noticed before. I changed the engine instrument indications so that I could monitor engine temperature and continued on. It soon became obvious that there was nothing wrong at all, except that we weren't used to feeling the heat because we were usually moving around or standing.

We rode on past Waikawau Bay and Port Charles, and it wasn't long before we found ourselves off Port Jackson at the tip of the Coromandel Peninsula. I was astounded to see that it was only 9.45am. We had covered 190 km in two hours and forty-five minutes.

We were nearly two hours ahead of schedule, and we had been holding back.

We fiddled around a bit in the area, took some photos and had a snack. I tried to ring my old mate, Wing Commander Keith Graham from the New Zealand Air Force. He had mentioned that an Air Force Orion would be in the area to photograph us, but he had no idea we were going to be so early, so the aircraft wasn't even airborne yet.

After about fifteen minutes of dithering and enjoying our good fortune, I mentioned to Burglar that we should keep going and go on to Oneroa on Waiheke Island, to 'hide out' for a while. I suggested we could find a coffee shop to spend some time in until it was time to head into Auckland. He thought this was a fine idea, so we headed off around Cape Colville and set heading towards the south-west.

Even though the weather had been fantastic on the east side of the Coromandel Peninsula, it wasn't the best on the west side. There was a light to moderate south-westerly wind blowing and a grey overcast that made the whole scene quite gloomy. The weather didn't worry us, however, because we were in fine spirits and we bashed our way over *bone shaker* seas yet again, enroute to Waiheke.

I had bet Burglar $50 at the start of the day that he could not ride the whole leg without cutting across in front of me, so I was delighted when he finally did, and I pointed it out to him. We continued on in towards Oneroa as hard as we could, knowing that we didn't need to conserve energy or fuel. Approaching Waiheke we both transferred fuel for the last time from the long range tanks to our main tanks. With full main tanks, and only an hour to go, we were both consciously relieved that the long range tanks had made it to the end. Now they could collapse, or even fall off the back, for all we cared. They had served their purpose.

At 10.45am we rode into Oneroa Bay at the western end, and northern side, of Waiheke Island. We pulled out our sand anchors, filled them with sand and then pulled the Seadoos out to a safe depth. We took all of our loose gear with us because, as Burglar said, 'We wouldn't want to be liberated of our possessions 20 km short of our destination, and there is nothing more humiliating for a burglar than to be burgled".

We walked up the beach, and then up the track to Oneroa township, where we sat down in a coffee shop with a view of the ocean and the Seadoos. We ordered coffee and pies and, when we finished that, we ordered pies and coffee. We enjoyed ourselves to the max. We took some photos. We got some locals to take photos of us. We were going to make it and *it felt good*. I rang Phil Briars to say that we were in Oneroa and then I rang Colin Bower and left the same message for him. I rang my wife, Manola. She was due to pick up the boys from school to bring them in to the Viaduct for our arrival and we were so early that she hadn't even left home yet.

Burglar rang his girlfriend Kimmy who had come over the night before. She told him that she had a surprise for him and that he would have to wait to see what it was. After he hung up it took the two of us about ten seconds to guess that Burglar's parents had secretly come over for the arrival. We were later proven to be correct.

At 12.30pm, with stomachs bulging from pies and our hair standing on end from the coffees, we made our way down to the waiting Seadoos. We jumped on, fired them up and headed off slowly towards Auckland. We had just over 20 km to go, and just under an hour to do it in. I had again made a plan as to where we should be, and at what times, so that we would end up outside the Viaduct Basin at 1.27pm.

We rode a zigzag course all the way at a leisurely and extremely enjoyable pace, first over towards Motutapu Island, and then between Browns Island and Rangitoto. From there we zigged across towards Mission Bay, before zagging back across to Devonport. Then we rode a big, slow curve across the harbour and arrived outside the Viaduct at exactly 1.27pm.

We rode in through the entrance of the Viaduct and around past the Alinghi Base, until we were in sight of the Loaded Hog and all the waiting people. This time there was no wandering in at 10 km an hour, as we both did a huge burnout; or at least the marine equivalent; and then rode in at a good pace to the wharf below the Loaded Hog.

The *Burglar Brothers* had been on the run now for twenty-two days and three hours and we finally gave ourselves up to the authorities at exactly 1.30pm on Monday 27th February 2006.

The welcome we received was exceptional. As we rode in, a conch shell was being blown at the end of the wharf. A haka was performed for us on the wharf and everyone was clapping and cheering. Much to our delight we got countless kisses and many handshakes. My family was all there and pleased to see me. Jamie even gave me a hug. It's pretty cool to get a hug from a thirteen year old son in public! We were interviewed numerous times by the media, and photographed until we were all photographed out. It was all very special.

At the top of the ramp was my mother Pauline and stepfather Don. Mum has successfully used the ostrich approach to raising five sons. She didn't want to know when we all tried sky diving and she didn't want to know when I went to fly in Papua New Guinea. Apparently with sons, you are "sometimes better off not knowing", and this approach had worked well for her on this event too.

Burglar's parents, Rob and Beryl Burton, had indeed turned up and were standing there with Kimmy, as proud as I have ever seen them. I suspected that Kimmy and Mrs. Burglar were fighting over the custody of Burglar, which didn't bother me as long as one of them was prepared to sign for him being returned in good working order and almost undamaged.

We had done it. It had taken us twenty-two days and three hours. We had ridden for one-hundred-and-forty-seven hrs over nineteen days, and had covered 4,970 km. We were a little bit worse for wear, but the euphoria of finishing was negating that. We felt on top of the world.

We made our way up to the Loaded Hog with everyone for drinks, food and some final speeches. Dame Cath Tizard spoke and confirmed that we were now officially members of the *Nutters Club*. Phil Briars and John Loof from the Cancer Society, and David Libeau from Qantas all made speeches. Then I made one and, to underline how he had grown in confidence over the past month, even Burglar got up there and spoke.

It was all a fantastic ending to an extraordinary event. When we had finished celebrating we went back down to the wharf and got ready to ride the Seadoos one more time around to the ramp at the Westhaven Marina. As we rode out I took one more look back at the Hog and was about to turn away when something odd caught my eye. Now I knew someone was playing games with me. If I asked you to guess what it was you would never get it in a thousand years, but flying from the top of one of the flag poles outside the Hog was an astonishing sight. Flapping proudly in the breeze, in all it's glory and for all the world to see was, unless my eyes were seriously deceiving me, the Prime Minister's Bikini!

Chapter 25
What Next?

A lot of people have asked Brad and I what we plan to do now it's done.

My initial reaction is to say catching up with family, gardening and the real world.And right now I honestly feel that way.

We've been asked if we would do it again, and my answer to that is why would you bother? I suppose we could cut a couple of days off the time by taking short cuts, but it really wouldn't achieve anything, so it's not an option.

But I know better than to think that I won't be craving some adventure sometime soon.

I want to go back and explore some of the magic places we saw, like the West Coast of the South Island, Doubtful Sound, Stewart Island, Akaroa and the East Coast from Gisborne to Tauranga.

There's a few other ideas being put forward by Brad, like the jet ski around Sweden (he obviously hasn't looked at a map of Sweden) and a four-wheel farm bike ride somewhere exotic. I'm expecting a call from Ferrari sometime soon to ask me to take a formula one test drive, and why not? I'll just have to lose 30 kg and a few inches, but it's do-able. I might run for Mayor of Invercargill, and I might not, too.

......and I guess there's always bowls...yes that's it....bowls. Where do I sign up?

Something is bound to come up soon. Someone will make the mistake of saying something can't be done, and I'll take Brad and sit him down with a few beers and we'll work out a way to make it happen.

And what about my melanoma? Supposedly it hasn't gone anywhere bad, but I still have to get quarterly checks. It's not something I dwell on though. I just have to get on with life. I have to keep a good look out for other melanomas forming on my body too, so it's an on-going thing. All in all, it's a right pain in the proverbial and the saddest thing of all is.......

Skin Cancer is Preventable.